George Washington

Engraving by R. Staudenbaur, circa 1889, based on a painting by Charles Willson Peale

George Washington

AN ILLUSTRATED BIOGRAPHY

BY DAVID A. ADLER

HOLIDAY HOUSE / *New York*

Title page art is from *Catchpenny Prints: 163 Popular Engravings from the Eighteenth Century*, Dover Publications, Inc. New York

Text type is Foundry Caslon, an eighteenth-century English typeface.
Chapter opening ornament is from Briquet's *Épreuve des Caractères*, Paris, 1757

Illustration credits appear on page 265–266.
Maps by Heather Saunders

Library of Congress Cataloging-in-Publication Data

Adler, David A.
George Washington : an illustrated biography / by David A. Adler.—1st ed.
p. cm.
Includes bibliographical references and index.
ISBN 0-8234-1838-3 (hardcover)
1. Washington, George, 1732–1799—Juvenile literature.
2. Presidents—United States—Biography—Juvenile literature.
[1. Washington, George, 1732–1799. 2. Presidents] I. Title.
E312.66.A39 2004
973.4'1'092—dc22
2003067606

For Renée,
of course

Contents

Genealogy   ix

Maps   x–xi

Preface   xiii

1. A Time of "Tearful Ecstacy"   1

2. A Clap of Thunder, A Bolt of Lightning   13

3. A Quiet Year   19

4. "Being in the Spring of Life"   27

5. "Young Men Have Ever More a Special Care"   36

6. Washington's Journal, *My Journey to the French*   41

7. "I Have Heard the Bullets Whistle"   46

8. "Such Deadly Sorrow"   57

9. Martha Dandridge Custis Washington   61

10. Sell Him "for Whatever He Will Fetch"   67

11. "If This Be Treason, Make the Most of It!"   76

12. "I Do Not Think Myself Equal to the Command"   89

13. "The Ragged Fellows Are the Boys for Fighting"   102

14. "I Think the Game Will Be Pretty Well Up"   110

15. The "Old Fox"   119

16. "Stand Fast, My Boys!" 127

17. "Whom Can We Trust Now?" 135

18. "Posterity Will Huzza for Us" 142

19. "I Here Offer My Commission" 153

20. "No Longer a Public Man" 161

21. "Untrodden Ground" 173

22. Mrs. Washington's Dearest Wish 185

23. "I Am Just Going" 192

Epilogue: "Our Washington Is No More!" 204

Washington's Words 209

Washington's Generals 211

Washington's Cabinet 216

George Washington Time Line 222

Important Battles of the American Revolution 225

Source Notes 228

Selected Bibliography 262

Illustration Credits 265

Recommended Websites 266

Index 267

Genealogy

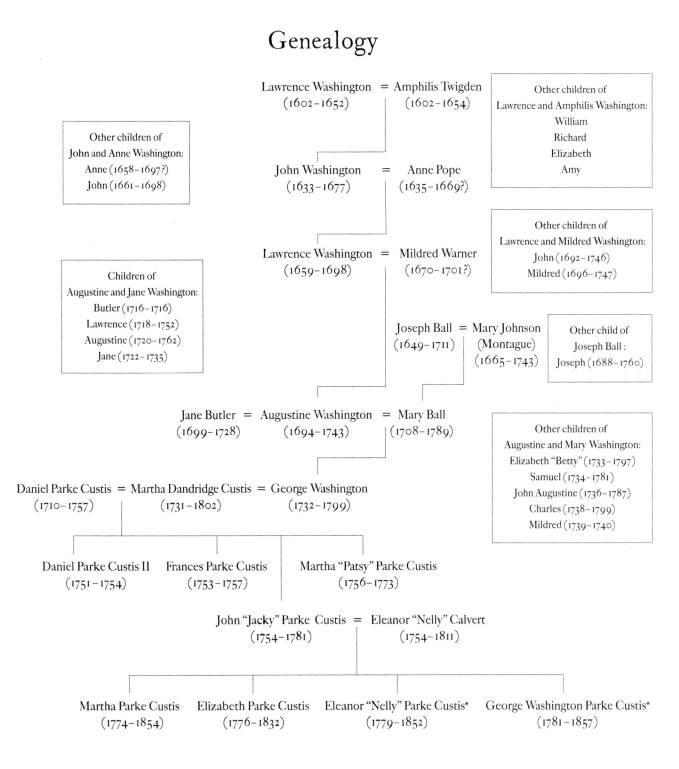

Lawrence Washington = Amphilis Twigden
(1602–1652)   (1602–1654)

Other children of
Lawrence and Amphilis Washington:
William
Richard
Elizabeth
Amy

Other children of
John and Anne Washington:
Anne (1658–1697?)
John (1661–1698)

John Washington = Anne Pope
(1633–1677)   (1635–1669?)

Lawrence Washington = Mildred Warner
(1659–1698)   (1670–1701?)

Other children of
Lawrence and Mildred Washington:
John (1692–1746)
Mildred (1696–1747)

Children of
Augustine and Jane Washington:
Butler (1716–1716)
Lawrence (1718–1752)
Augustine (1720–1762)
Jane (1722–1735)

Joseph Ball = Mary Johnson
(1649–1711)   (Montague)
(1665–1743)

Other child of
Joseph Ball:
Joseph (1688–1760)

Jane Butler = Augustine Washington = Mary Ball
(1699–1728)   (1694–1743)   (1708–1789)

Other children of
Augustine and Mary Washington:
Elizabeth "Betty" (1733–1797)
Samuel (1734–1781)
John Augustine (1736–1787)
Charles (1738–1799)
Mildred (1739–1740)

Daniel Parke Custis = Martha Dandridge Custis = George Washington
(1710–1757)   (1731–1802)   (1732–1799)

Daniel Parke Custis II   Frances Parke Custis   Martha "Patsy" Parke Custis
(1751–1754)   (1753–1757)   (1756–1773)

John "Jacky" Parke Custis = Eleanor "Nelly" Calvert
(1754–1781)   (1754–1811)

Martha Parke Custis   Elizabeth Parke Custis   Eleanor "Nelly" Parke Custis*   George Washington Parke Custis*
(1774–1854)   (1776–1832)   (1779–1852)   (1781–1857)

* Adopted by George Washington

The Washingtons' Residences

Potomac River

BELHAVEN
(*now* ALEXANDRIA)
Mount Vernon

Rappahannock River

Ferry Farm
FREDERICKSBURG

Wakefield

Pamunkey River

James River
White House
RICHMOND

York River

WILLIAMSBURG
YORKTOWN

Chesapeake Bay

Atlantic Ocean

V I R G I N I A

● Towns
■ Homes of the Washingtons

The United States During the Revolutionary War (1775–1783)

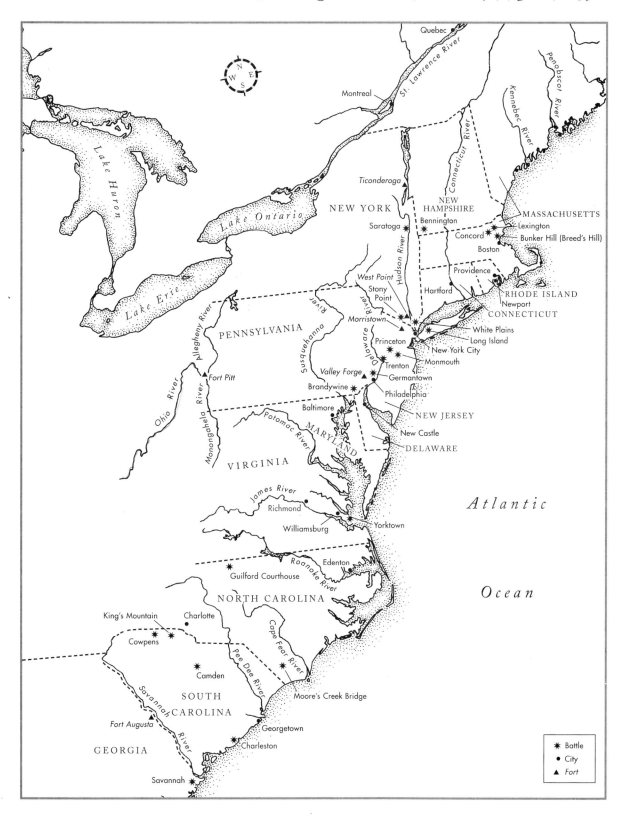

Preface

Soon after the American triumph in the Revolutionary War, Benjamin Franklin was at a dinner in the French palace of Versailles. In a toast, the British minister compared his king, George III, to the sun. The French minister followed and compared his king, Louis XVI, to the moon. Then Franklin toasted George Washington, who, he said, "like Joshua of old, commanded the sun and the moon to stand still, and they obeyed him." Surely, to the legions of Americans who revered Washington, he seemed that powerful.

According to John Adams, normally a harsh critic of his fellow man, George Washington was "the most illustrious and beloved personage which this country ever produced." Washington's sound leadership guided the Continental army to victory in the Revolution. The people's trust in him led them to accept the Constitution and the new government. His disdain for monarchy and his view of the presidency shaped America's democracy.

America's great hero had fairly modest beginnings. As a young child looking east from his simple birthplace on the Atlantic seacoast, he could see ships arrive from across the water. But he never crossed that ocean. His character was shaped by what lay to the west—the American frontier. His first work was as a surveyor in the wilderness, and his first battles were not with Europeans, but with American Indians.

The young soldier was well-known by his early twenties, and his fame continued to grow, culminating in the great triumphal march of 1789, when he left his Virginia home for New York City to be sworn in as the first president of the new nation. The American people were confident they had chosen the right man, but Washington was not. When he took the oath of office, he rested his hand on an open Bible. The page he chose to place his hand, and entries he made in his personal diary, show him to have been filled with doubt.

Mount Vernon, the Virginia estate along the Potomac River that Washington inherited from his half brother Lawrence, from a circa 1870 engraving by Lossing and Barritt, based on a drawing by Benson J. Lossing

I. A Time of "Tearful Ecstacy"

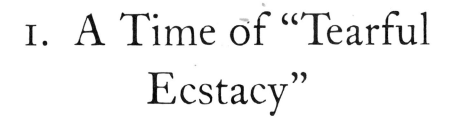

On February 4, 1789, the members of the first Electoral College cast their ballots for president of the United States. Then, for more than two months, their votes remained sealed, waiting to be counted in the presence of the Senate and House of Representatives. But roads were poor and rivers hard to cross. A trip that would take just several hours today could take several days in 1789; so the members of the first Congress were slow in gathering. It wasn't until April 6 that a majority of both houses was present and the ballots were opened. When they were counted it was found that each of the sixty-nine members of the Electoral College had voted for one man—George Washington. John Langdon, president of the Senate, wrote to tell him the news.

Langdon's letter would be no surprise for Washington. A couple of months earlier, he had written and asked his friend Henry Knox to buy enough "superfine American broadcloth" on

Henry Knox of Massachusetts, Washington's friend, chief of artillery during the Revolutionary War, and the nation's first secretary of war, from a circa 1875 engraving by Benson J. Lossing

Secretary of Congress Charles Thomson, a classical scholar and step-uncle of President William Henry Harrison; he delivered official notice to Washington that he was elected president, from a circa 1870 engraving by Lossing and Barritt, based on a drawing by Benson J. Lossing.

sale in New York to make a suit for him and a riding habit for his wife, Martha. In mid-February Knox had written back, "The cloths have not yet arrived. . . . The moment they come to hand I will forward those for you and Mrs. Washington." Then came the real, but unofficial, news he had for Washington. "It appears by the returns of elections hitherto obtained, which is as far as Maryland southward, that your Excellency has every vote for President."

Soon after that, Washington began packing for the trip to New York City, at that time the nation's capital. For weeks, he stared down the long drive that led from his home, paced, and waited for official notice of his election. Finally, on Tuesday, April 14, 1789, Charles Thomson, secretary of Congress, arrived at Mount Vernon, Washington's Virginia home, and delivered Langdon's message.

"Sir," Washington wrote back that afternoon. "I had the honor to receive your official communication, by the hand of Mr. Secretary Thomson, about one o'clock this day. Having concluded to obey the important and flattering call of my country, and having been impressed with the expediency of my being with Congress at as early a period as possible, I propose to commence my journey on Thursday morning, which is the day after to-morrow."

That night George Washington made a hasty ride to Fredericksburg to visit his ailing mother.

"You will see me no more," Mary Washington

Washington at his mother's side in her Fredericksburg, Virginia, home, their last meeting, from a circa 1910 engraving by Gerlach-Barklow, based on the painting by J. L. G. Ferris

told her son. "My great age, and the disease that is rapidly approaching my vitals, warn me that I shall not be long in this world. . . . May that Heaven's and your mother's blessing be with you always."

She was right. Mary Washington died four months later.

On Thursday, April 16, George Washington set out for New York City.

"About ten o'clock," he wrote in his diary, "I bade adieu to Mount Vernon, to private life, and to domestic felicity." He modestly added that he went "with the best disposition to render service to my country, in obedience to its call, but with less hope of answering its expectations."

His trip turned into a weeklong triumphal march.

About one mile from Mount Vernon, he was met by friends and neighbors who invited him to a public dinner at Wise's Tavern. At the end of the meal, Colonel Dennis Ramsay, the mayor of Alexandria, spoke. "George Washington, President of the United States," he said. It was the first time in public that Washington heard himself addressed as president. "The first and best of our citizens must leave us. . . . Farewell! Go and make a grateful people happy."

Washington stood before his neighbors. At about six feet two inches, he was much taller than the average American of the time, but he was thin. "His frame would seem to want filling up," Senator William Maclay of Pennsylvania wrote about him in 1789. "His motions rather slow than lively. . . . His complexion pale, nay, almost cadaverous. His voice hollow and indistinct, owing, as I believe, to artificial teeth before his upper jaw."

"Words, my fellow citizens, fail me," Washington said. "From an aching heart I bid all my affectionate friends and kind neighbors—farewell."

He traveled north to Baltimore where he was given a multi-gun salute and a large public supper. When he left the next morning, he was saluted again, this time with cannon fire, and escorted for seven miles by an honor guard of the city's leading citizens.

Early Sunday morning, April 19, George Washington entered Pennsylvania. There his carriage was met by an honor escort of the governor and two troops of cavalry. They all rode north toward Philadelphia. When they were near the city, Washington mounted a beautiful, white horse. He rode slowly and waved to the crowds of cheering people standing along the way. At every step, people called to him, "Long live George Washington!"

At the outskirts of Philadelphia, Washington passed under an arch entwined with laurel branches. There had been a plan for a boy to hide in the branches, then reach down and set a crown of laurel on Washington's head, but the plan was abandoned—people were afraid the tribute would startle their hero. Washington continued into the city and rode down Market and Second streets to a dinner prepared for him at the City Tavern.

President-elect Washington passes through an arch on his triumphal entrance to Philadelphia, April 19, 1789, from a circa 1900 engraving, artist unknown.

The next morning, a unit of soldiers assembled by his carriage, ready to escort him to Trenton, New Jersey, but it was raining hard and Washington wouldn't let them go. He told the soldiers to go indoors. By the afternoon, the clouds had lifted. When Washington crossed the Delaware River and approached Trenton, the sun was shining.

More than twelve years earlier, on December 26, 1776, George Washington had entered that same city under very different circumstances. The American Revolution had seemed lost then as he led twenty-four hundred near-frozen soldiers across the Delaware River. "The Quantity of Ice," Washington wrote in his journal, "impeded the passage of the Boats." On reaching the other side, he led his exhausted troops on a nine-mile march through a bitter sleet storm. In Trenton they met the enemy. After some confused fighting, the British and Hessian soldiers, some still groggy from Christmas celebrations, surrendered. It was an important victory for the American side.

Now the people of Trenton were prepared to welcome Washington back. They built a twenty-foot-high arch supported by thirteen columns decorated with greens and flowers. On the arch, in large, gold letters, was the message, "The defender of the mothers will be the protector of the daughters." Schoolgirls and their mothers, dressed in white, stood beside the arch. Thirteen of the girls, each wearing a floral crown, scattered flowers before Washington.

"Welcome, mighty chief, once more," they sang.
"Welcome to this grateful shore;
Now no mercenary foe,
Aims again the fatal blow,
Aims at thee the fatal blow.

"Virgins fair, and mothers grave,
Those thy conquering arm did save,
Build for thee triumphal bowers.
Strew, ye fair, his way with flowers!
Strew your hero's way with flowers."

The celebrations continued as Washington traveled through New Jersey to Elizabethtown Point, where he arrived Thursday morning, April 23. There he was met by a joint committee of Congress. They all boarded a barge powered by thirteen oarsmen, each wearing a white smock and black fringed cap. On their way into New York Bay, small boats, with flags flying, followed them, forming a sort of naval parade.

"No king of kings' divinity could have looked for so heartfelt a welcome

Washington arrives in New York City, April 23, 1789, from a circa 1895 engraving, artist unknown.

to his throne," Woodrow Wilson, the twenty-eighth president, later wrote, "as this modest gentleman got to the office he feared to take."

While the people of the United States were confident in their new president, Washington himself was filled with self-doubt. A soldier with little experience in politics, he had no past president to look to for guidance. "The decorations of the ships," Washington wrote in his diary, "the roar of the cannon, and the loud acclamations of the people which rent the skies as I walked along the streets filled my mind with sensations as painful (considering the reverse of this scene which may be the case after all my labors to do good) as they are pleasing."

Federal Hall in New York City, where Washington stood on the center balcony, rested his right hand on an open Bible, and took the oath of office as the first president of the United States, from a circa 1895 engraving, artist unknown

The inauguration took place on Thursday, April 30, 1789.

Beginning at 9 A.M., church bells throughout the city tolled, and prayers were said for God's blessing on the new government. At noon, soldiers marched to Washington's door. Members of Congress and other government officials arrived. Then out stepped George Washington, with his hair tied back and powdered beneath a three-cornered beaver-fur hat. He wore a dark brown suit with tiny embossed eagles on its buttons, white silk stockings, silver shoe buckles, and his dress sword, all made in America.

The honor guard of troops led the parade to Federal Hall, followed by government officials in carriages, Washington in the presidential carriage, and a long line of citizens. About two hundred yards away from the entrance, they stopped. The troops lined up on either side of the road and Washington and the officials walked between them and into the hall. There they were greeted by Vice President John Adams, who had already been sworn in. Adams announced that all was ready for Washington to take the oath of office.

General Washington walked out on the balcony of the Senate chamber. The crowd outside, an estimated ten thousand, in the street, on rooftops, and by open windows, cheered wildly. He placed his hand on his heart, bowed several times, and then sat by the table in the center of the balcony. The people outside were suddenly silent. They seemed to understand. Their hero was overcome with emotion.

A few moments later, George Washington stood again. Robert R. Livingston, chancellor of the State of New York, who would administer the oath of office, was at his left, and Vice President John Adams at his right. Samuel Otis, secretary of the Senate, held a red velvet pillow, and on it was a Bible open to a page Washington, an exacting man, surely had selected.

The Bible was open to the fiftieth chapter of Genesis, which tells of the death of the patriarch Jacob. After his death, Jacob's sons were afraid of their brother Joseph, whom they had sold into slavery years before. Perhaps now, with their father gone, Joseph would take his revenge. They bowed to Joseph, ready to be his slaves. But Joseph told his brothers, "Do not be afraid. Am I a substitute for God?"

The Bible used in 1789 at Washington's first inauguration,
from a circa 1870 engraving by Lossing and Barritt,
based on a drawing by Benson J. Lossing

Like Joseph, Washington knew he was no substitute for God. And he would not substitute for King George III of England, either, whose forces he had fought in the Revolution. He was not swayed by all the fanfare and praise. He would not rule this new nation; he would lead it.

"Do you solemnly swear," Livingston asked, "that you will faithfully execute the office of President of the United States and will, to the best of your ability, preserve, protect, and defend the Constitution of the United States?"

"I solemnly swear," Washington said, and repeated the oath. He bent forward, kissed the Bible, then closed his eyes and added his own brief prayer, "So help me God."

"It is done!" Livingston called to the crowd. "Long live George Washington, President of the United States!" The people outside took up the chant. "Long live George Washington! God bless our president."

The cheers from the crowd were so loud, they seemed to shake the canopy above the balcony. It was a time, a witness later wrote, of "tearful ecstacy."

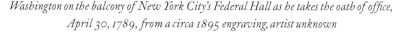

Washington on the balcony of New York City's Federal Hall as he takes the oath of office, April 30, 1789, from a circa 1895 engraving, artist unknown

The Daily Advertiser

(Vol.) New–York, Friday May 1, 1789 (No 1309)

PRINTED BY FRANCIS CHILDS, No. 190, WATER STREET, CORNER OF KING STREET

New-York, May 1

Yesterday took place, according to the resolution of the two houses of Congress, the ceremony of the introduction of his Excellency GEORGE WASHINGTON, to the Presidency of the United States.

The scene was extremely solemn and impressive; we imagine the public cannot be more satisfactorily informed than by an unembellished recital of the events, and a simple picture of the figures which composed it.

At nine o'clock A.M. the clergy of different denominations assembled their congregations in their respective places of worship, and offered up prayers for the safety of the President.

About twelve o'clock the procession moved from the house of the President in Cherry Street, through Dock Street, and Broad Street, to Federal Hall; in the following order:

Col. Lewis, supported
by two officers,
Capt. Stakes, with the
troops of Horse, Artillery,
Major Van Horne,
Grenadiers, under
Capt. Harsiu,
German Grenadiers, under
Capt. Scriba,
Major Bicker,
The Infantry of the
Brigade,
Major Chrystie, Sheriff,
The Committee of the
Senate,

The PRESIDENT and
suite,

The Committee of the
Representatives,
The Hon. Mr. Jay,
General Knox,
Chancellor Livingston,
and several
other gentlemen of
distinction.

Then followed a multitude of citizens. When they came within a short distance of the Hall, the troop formed a line on both sides of the way, and his Excellency passing through the ranks, was conducted into the building, and in the Senate Chamber introduced to both houses of Congress—immediately afterwards, accompanied by the two houses, he went into the gallery fronting Broad Street, where, in the presence of an immense concourse of citizens, he took the oath prescribed by the constitution, which was administered by the Hon. R. R. Livingston, Esq; Chancellor of the state of New-York.

Immediately after he had taken the oath, the Chancellor proclaimed him President of the United States. — Was answered by the discharge of 13 guns, and by loud repeated shouts; on this the President bowed to the people, and the air again rang with their acclamations. His Excellency with the two Houses, then retired to the Senate Chamber where he made the following SPEECH.

Fellow Citizens of the Senate, and of the House of Representatives.

Among the vicissitudes incident to Life, no event could have filled me with greater anxieties than that, of which the notification was transmitted by your order and received on the fourteenth day of the present month.

On the one hand, I was summon'd by my Country, whose voice I can never hear but with veneration and love, from a retreat which I had chosen with the fondest predilection, and in my flattering hopes, with an immutable decision, as the asylum of my declining years, a retreat which was rendered every day more necessary as well as more dear to me, by the addition of habit to inclination and of frequent interruptions in my health to the gradual waste committed on it by time. On the other hand, the magnitude and difficulty of the Trust to which

the voice of country called me, being sufficient to awaken in the wisest and most experienced of her Citizens, a distrustful scrut-iny into his qualifications, could not but overwhelm with despondence, one, who (inheriting inferior endowments from Nature and unpracticed in the duties of civil administration) ought to be peculiarly conscious of his own deficiencies. In this conflict of emotions, all I dare aver, is, that it has been my faithful study to collect my duty from a just appreciation of every circumstance by which it might be affected. All I dare hope, is, that if in executing this Task, I have been too much swayed by a grateful remembrance of former instances or by an affectionate sensibility to this transcendent proof of the confidence of my fellow Citizens; and have thence too little consulted my incapacity as well as disinclination for the weighty and untried cares before me; my error will be palliated by the

motives which misled me, and its consequences be judged by my Country with some share of the partiality in which they originated.

Such being the impressions under which I have in obedience to the public summons repaired to the present station; it would be peculiarly improper to omit in this first official act my fervent supplications to that Almighty Being who rules over the Universe, who presides in the Council of Nations and whose providential aids can supply every human defect, that his benediction may consecrate, to the Liberties and happiness of the people of the United States, a Government instituted by themselves for these essential purposes: and may enable every instrument employed in its administration, to execute with success the functions allotted to his charge. In rendering the homage to the great author of every public and private good, I assure myself that expresses your sentiments not less than my own; nor those of my fellow citizens at large, less than either. . . . Having thus imparted to you my sentiments, as they have awakened by the occasion which brings us together—I shall take my present leave; but not without resorting once more to the benign parent of the human race, in humble supplication, that since He has been pleased to favor the American people with opportunities for deliberating in perfect tranquility, and dispositions for deciding with unparalleled unanimity on a form of government, for the security of their union, and the advancement of their happiness; so His divine blessing may be equally *conspicuous* in the enlarged views, the temperate consultations, and the wise measures on which the success of this government must depend.

George Washington.

His Excellency, accompanied by the Vice President, the Speaker of the House of Representatives, and both Houses of Congress then went to Paul's Chapel, where divine service was performed by the Right Revd. Dr. Proyost, Bishop of the Episcopal Church in this State, and Chaplain to Congress.

The religious solemnity being ended, the President was escorted to his house, and the citizens returned to their homes.

Cherry Plank for Stairs

Sold by Daniel Hitch cock, corner of Gold and Georges-streets. Also WHITE WOOD, suitable for Bedsteads.

April 22

The Managers in behalf of the subscribers of the Dancing Assembly, give notice, the Ball will be next Thursday evening, the seventh instant at the City Tavern May 1.

Charles Gilmore

Boot & Shoemaker

At the sign of the BOOT and SHOE, No. 161, Queen-street, opposite where the Bank formerly was kept,

Takes this method of returning his sincere thanks to the public in general and customers in particular, for their generous encouragement, and hopes a continuance of their favors, as he shall make it his study to merit their approbation. He makes and has for sale, a genteel assortment of gentlemen's boots and shoes at moderate prices; likewise, ladies silk and stuff shoes of the best kind—children's shoes of all sorts.

April 15

2. A Clap of Thunder, A Bolt of Lightning

A dispute between an English king and Parliament, the English congress, brought George Washington's great-grandfather to America.

The Washington family lived in Northamptonshire, England, a place of gentle hills, winding roads, ivy-covered walls, rose gardens, and farms. The Washingtons were mostly farmers, but could also claim a few sailors, merchants, lawyers, and ministers. One of these ministers was Lawrence Washington, the great-great-grandfather of George.

Lawrence Washington was born about 1602, graduated Oxford University, and in 1632 became the rector of a wealthy parish. That same year he married Amphilis Twigden. For eleven years the Reverend Lawrence Washington pros-

The Northamptonshire, England, home of Washington's ancestors, from a circa 1895 engraving, artist unknown

pered, but his loyalties to his church and king were his undoing. He remained steadfast to the king during the English Civil War, a dispute Charles I lost to the Puritan members of Parliament, who were led by Oliver Cromwell.

Charles I had been crowned king of England, Scotland, and Ireland in 1625, and from the very start had trouble with members of Parliament. He disagreed with them on finances and foreign affairs, but the core of the discord was over religion. The king, who was the leader of the established church, the Church of England, and his courts demanded strict adherence to the beliefs of that sect. He prosecuted and restricted the rights of those who disagreed, including the Puritans. This led to civil war. In 1645, in the midst of the fighting, the king fled London. The next year the Puritans, who were now in control of Parliament, took revenge on many of the king's supporters, including the Reverend Lawrence Washington. They declared him to be a drunkard, "a common frequenter of ale-houses . . . encouraging others in that beastly vice," and dismissed him from his parish, one of twenty-eight hundred ministers that Oliver Cromwell and members of Parliament discharged from their posts.

In 1649 King Charles was put on trial and charged with high treason, but he refused to cooperate. He expressed his contempt for the court: "A king cannot be tried," he said. "I do stand more for the liberty of my people than any here that come to be my pretend judges."

The court demonstrated its contempt for the king by declaring him to be a tyrant, traitor, murderer, and public enemy, and sentenced him to death. Three days later, on January 30, 1649, he was led to a scaffold and beheaded, the only sitting English monarch ever to be executed.

After the death of the king, the Reverend Lawrence Washington had no hope of returning to his original parish. He was forced to move to a terribly poor one and preach there. Only the charity of wealthy relatives helped the family survive. Washington died in 1652, a broken man. His wife, Amphilis, died two years later.

The family's poverty prevented their eldest son, John, the great-grandfather of George, from pursuing a university education and the ministry. Instead he found work on the London waterfront. At first he acted as a bookkeeper, then, in 1656, he invested with Captain Edward Prescott in the *Sea Horse,* a merchant ship. In 1657 they sailed to America, where they planned to buy tobacco, bring it back to England, and sell it at a profit. Washington was the ship's first mate.

In February the ship was anchored in the Potomac River, loaded and ready to sail home. A storm hit, the tobacco was ruined, and John's dreams were dashed. Rather than work his way back to England, he decided to remain in America to seek his fortune and soon found it in the hand of a wealthy bride. In 1658 John Washington married Anne, the daughter of Nathaniel Pope, a rich tobacco planter. Among her father's gifts to the young couple was seven hundred acres of riverfront land.

Despite the *Sea Horse* disaster, Washington felt he was due wages, but Edward Prescott refused to pay him and sailed back to England. The next year the captain returned. Washington, considered by some to be a rogue himself, was told that on this latest journey, Prescott had accused a woman passenger of witchery and hanged her. Washington, with possibly both justice and revenge in mind, had him arrested and charged with murder.

The trial date was set but Washington, called as a witness, was unable to attend. "I am sorry," he wrote. "An extraordinary occasion will not permit me to be at the next provincial court . . . then I intend my young son baptized. All ye company and Gossips being already invited." Captain Prescott was set free for lack of evidence. The young son whose baptism prevented John Washington from testifying was Lawrence, George's grandfather.

Lawrence Washington was born in September 1659 by Bridges Creek in Westmoreland County, Virginia. He made his living mostly as a public official—a justice of the peace, sheriff, and representative in Virginia's legislature, the House of Burgesses. He married Mildred Warner, the daughter of the Speaker of the House of Burgesses, and they had three children, John, Augustine, and Mildred. In 1698, when Lawrence Washington died at the age of thirty-nine, his middle child, Augustine, the father of George, was only three.

Mildred Washington remarried, but soon after she moved with her new husband, George Gale, and three children to Cumberland, England, she died. After some schooling in England, nine-year-old Augustine was brought back to Virginia. There the young boy, Gus to his friends, lived in the home of his uncle, John Washington.

Augustine grew tall, strong, and by all reports handsome. In 1715 he married Jane Butler, the daughter of a local lawyer and planter. They bought land where Popes Creek meets the Potomac River, built a four-room house, and named it Wakefield.

During his lifetime, Augustine bought more land, including twenty-five hundred acres along the Potomac River that one day would be called Mount Vernon. Like his father, he became a justice of the peace and sheriff. He and Jane had four children: Butler (who died in his infancy), Lawrence, Augustine, and Jane. Mrs. Jane Washington died in 1728.

On March 6, 1730, the elder Augustine married again, this time to Mary Ball. They had six children together. Mary's first pregnancy, the one that produced George, was marked by a traumatic event.

One summer afternoon in the first year of her marriage, Mary was at home, having dinner with some friends. Outside, there was a storm, a clap of thunder, and a bolt of lightning. The lightning struck the Washington house, traveled through the chimney, and struck a young girl who was sit-

George Washington's mother, young Mary Ball Washington, in perhaps an idealized portrait, from a circa 1900 engraving, artist unknown, based on an earlier print

ting next to Mary. The girl was killed instantly. The knife and fork she held melted. At the time, Mary Washington mourned her friend and worried what the shock of her horrible death would do to the baby she carried. Luckily the following February she gave birth to a strong, healthy son.

Augustine and Mary Washington were members of the Popes Creek Congregation, an Episcopal church and part of the Church of England. It was probably there, on April 5, that they baptized their son and named him George. Some time later the boy's birth was recorded in the family Bible. "George Washington, Son to Augustine & Mary his Wife was Born, on 11th Day of February 1731/2 about 10 in the Morning."

Today people know the date of Washington's birth as February 22, 1732. But young Washington didn't.

Washington's birth as noted in the family Bible, a circa 1870 facsimile by Benson J. Lossing

George Washington Son to Augustine & Mary his Wife was Born ye 11th Day of February 173 1/2 about 10 in the Morning & was Bapti^zd the 3: of April following Mr Beverley Whiting & Capt Christopher Brooks Godfathers and Mrs Mildred Gregory Godmother(s)

At the time of his birth, England and its colonies were still using the "old-style" Julian calendar. This calendar was based strictly on the earth's rotation about the sun and had a built-in error of one day every one hundred sixty years. In 1582 Pope Gregory XIII had authorized a new calendar, now called the Gregorian calendar after him, to correct this error. Anti-Catholic England refused to accept the revised calendar until 1752. By that time, the original discrepancy of ten days had grown to eleven days. With the new calendar the old February 11 became the new February 22. The date of the New Year changed, too, from March 25, the Day of the Annunciation, to January 1. The ambiguous 1731/2 became, simply, 1732.

In 1799, shortly before he died, Washington wrote in his diary, "Went up to Alexandria to the celebration of my birth day." The date of the entry was February 11. Throughout his life, it seems, he celebrated the date written in his family Bible as his birthday.

3. A Quiet Year

The year of George Washington's birth was a relatively quiet one in the American colonies, with the struggles of the first settlements past, and the French and Indian War, also called the Seven Years' War, more than twenty years in the future.

Each region of the English colonies had its own character. New England was a place of Puritan English farmers, traders, trappers, sailors, and clergymen, a place of towns closed in by thick forests. The settlers in the middle colonies—New York, New Jersey, and Pennsylvania—were a mix of many nationalities, including English, German, Dutch, Scottish, Irish, French, Spanish, and Portuguese, with various trades, customs, and languages.

New York City in the 1680s, soon after it passed from Dutch to English control, from a circa 1900 engraving, artist unknown

Colonial Williamsburg, capital of the royal colony of Virginia, from a circa 1895 engraving, artist unknown

The Southern colonies, including Washington's Virginia, were largely agricultural, with the greatest concentration of African-American slaves.

The Virginia of Washington's boyhood was populated mostly on the coast and along rivers until the Blue Ridge Mountains. Beyond that was the mysterious wilderness. The only two real population centers of the colony were the seaport town of Norfolk and the capital, Williamsburg. Other places, called towns on maps, were each no more than a few houses, tobacco warehouses, and a tavern, all clustered near a church or courthouse.

In 1732, the roads in Virginia were little more than woodland paths. There were still no stagecoaches or other public means of transportation, so

travel was by foot, horseback, or riverboat. Mail was delivered once every two weeks. Virginia still didn't have its own newspaper. Occasionally Virginians saw a peddler from the north or a trapper who returned from the mountains. The real excitement was the

A scene in eighteenth-century Virginia, from a circa 1900 engraving, artist unknown

Mail delivery in the Ohio territory in Washington's time, when people were much more isolated than they are today, from a circa 1895 engraving, artist unknown

arrival of English ships, which dropped off goods and brought news from the old country.

The English ships came for tobacco. "In Virginia and Maryland," one planter wrote in 1729, "Tobacco is our staple, is our All, and indeed leaves no room for anything Else; It requires the Attendance of all our hands, and Exacts their utmost labour." The "hands" he spoke of weren't his. Slaves and indentured servants performed most of the labor on tobacco plantations.

Vast differences could be found among the plantations. While some had thousands of acres, hundreds of slaves, and mansion-like homes, others were much smaller. George's birthplace was mostly woods with some cleared, planted sections on a mile-wide plot, about one thousand acres between Popes and Bridges creeks. The house, Wakefield, faced the Potomac River; behind it was forest.

Wakefield featured four rooms on the ground floor, an attic, and a huge outdoor chimney at each end. Inside, in the hall that served as the family dining room, was a wide

Facing the Potomac River, the four-room Virginia house that was Washington's birthplace, from a circa 1870 engraving by Lossing and Barritt, based on a drawing by Benson J. Lossing

brick or tile fireplace, two tables, some chairs with leather seats, and a mirror. The other rooms held several beds. At the time, few people in Virginia owned rugs, so the wood floors were probably bare.

When George Washington was one year old, his sister Betty was born, followed soon by Samuel, John Augustine, Charles, and Mildred. His two elder half brothers from his father's first marriage, Lawrence and Augustine, and his half sister, Jane, completed the family circle.

There was tragedy in young George Washington's life. When he was a toddler, his half sister, Jane, died. A few years later, his sister Mildred died in her infancy. And, one windy morning, shortly after his third birthday, he lost his home when sparks from some burning trash landed on the roof and set the house on fire.

The family moved to a plantation along the Rappahannock River, close to Fredericksburg. They called the house Pine Grove, but others called it Ferry Farm. Here, George developed a deep love of horses and the outdoors, and he took an interest in his father's tools, including an ax, a tripod, and a box of survey instruments.

Two 1741 letters give a glimpse of young George Washington.

Young Washington's second home, this one near the Rappahannock River close to Fredericksburg, Virginia, from a circa 1900 engraving, artist unknown

"Pa bought me two pretty books full of pictures," his friend Richard Henry Lee wrote. "If I learn my tasks good he will let uncle jo bring me to see you. Will you ask your ma to let you come see me." Along with the letter, Richard sent George one of the books.

"Dear Dickey," nine-year-old George wrote back. "I thank you very much for the pretty picture-book you gave me. . . . I can read three or four pages sometimes without missing a word. Ma says I may go see you, and stay all day with you next week if it not be rainy."

At about that same age, George received a copy of *The Young Man's Companion,* a popular English book that claimed it could teach a young man to read, write, and figure "without a Tutor." Nonetheless, Washington probably studied it with an instructor at a school in Fredericksburg, perhaps with Mr. Hobby, a sexton at a nearby church.

Washington copied a list of one hundred ten *Rules of Civility and Decent Behaviour,* probably to practice good ciphering—penmanship. Among the rules he copied were "When in Company, put not your Hands to any Part of the Body, not usually Discovered." "TAKE no Salt or cut Bread with your Knife Greasy." "In visiting the Sick, do not Presently play the Physician if you be not Knowing therein." And, "When a man does all he can though it Suc-

"Rules of Civility" in Washington's handwriting, a circa 1870 facsimile by Benson J. Lossing

Mason Locke Weems, an early biographer of Washington and inventor of the "I cannot tell a lie" cherry tree story, from a circa 1870 engraving by Lossing and Barritt, based on a drawing by Benson J. Lossing

ceeds not well blame not him that did it." His practice at penmanship paid off—Washington always wrote with a clear, easy, flowing style.

There are few other known facts about Washington's first years, but there are many myths, the most popular being the invention of the Reverend Mason Locke Weems, a one-time minister and later a writer and seller of pamphlets and books.

After Washington completed his second term as president, Weems began work on his biography. In 1799 he wrote to a publisher that his book, *The Beauties of Washington,* was ready and that it would "sell like flax seed at a quarter of a dollar." Yet the publisher didn't respond. Just after Washington's death, Weems wrote to the publisher again. "I've something to whisper in your lug. Washington, you know is gone! Millions are gaping to read something about him."

Weems was right—Americans were eager to read about George Washington. The first edition of the Weems biography was published in 1800. By 1806 it was in its fifth edition, and for the first time Weems included the now well-known cherry tree story. He claimed it was told to him "by an aged lady, who was a distant relative, and when a girl spent much of her time in the family."

According to the story, six-year-old George Washington was given a hatchet. "One day, in the garden, where he often amused himself hacking his mother's pea-sticks, he unluckily tried the edge of his hatchet on the body of a beautiful young English cherry-tree, which he barked so terribly, that I don't believe the tree ever got the better of it. The next morning the old gentleman finding out what had befallen his tree, which, by the by, was a great favourite, came into the house. . . . 'George,' said his father, 'do you know who killed that beautiful little cherry-tree yonder in the garden?' This was a tough question; and George staggered under it for a moment; but quickly recovered himself: and looking at his father, with the sweet face of youth brightened with the inexpressible charm of all-conquering truth, he bravely cried out, 'I can't tell a lie, Pa; you know I can't tell a lie. I did cut it with my hatchet.'"

With his response, Weems gave Augustine Washington the noble nature he surely felt fitting for the father of Washington. "Run to my arms, you dearest boy. . . . Such an act of heroism in my son, is worth more than a thousand trees." And Weems added how "Mr. Washington conducted George with great ease and pleasure along the happy paths of virtue."

In another famous Weems story, young George strolled along a gooseberry walk and found cabbages growing, "in all the freshness of newly sprung plants, the full name of GEORGE WASHINGTON." George showed it to his father, who admitted he had planted the cabbages to spell out his name, "not to scare you," he said, "but to learn you a great thing which I wish you to understand. I want, my son, to introduce you to your *true* Father." Just as George had not seen his father plant the cabbage seeds "yet you know I was here." So, too, he must know that God "put together all those millions and millions of things that are now so exactly fitted."

With these bits of invention, Weems filled out the early history of George Washington and gave Augustine Washington a major role in the upbringing of his son, probably more than he had. Augustine, who owned land along the Potomac River and more in Westmoreland County, as well as iron mines, traveled often from one property to the next and was away for weeks at a time.

However great or small Augustine's true role was, it ended shortly after George's eleventh birthday.

One cold April morning in 1743, Augustine rode for several hours in the rain and came home soaked. By midnight, he was in terrible pain; by morning, he had a high fever. He grew steadily worse and, on April 12, 1743, at the age of forty-eight, Augustine Washington died.

In his will, Augustine left most of his almost ten thousand acres, mill, slaves, and cattle to Lawrence and Augustine, his sons from his first marriage. Lawrence inherited the land along the Potomac and a share in his iron mines, and Augustine the land in Westmoreland County. George, when he came of age at twenty-one, was to have Pine Grove, a few small lots in Fredericksburg, and ten slaves. Until then his mother would have it all. It wasn't a big inheritance, but Mary Washington wouldn't give it up, and George never received any of it until her death in 1789.

4. "Being in the Spring of Life"

Mary Ball Washington was just thirty-seven years old in April 1743, with five fatherless young children to raise. She became a strict disciplinarian, her word law. "I was often here [at Pine Grove] with George," a cousin later wrote. "Of the mother I was more afraid than of my own parents."

Mary was described in her youth as being beautiful, with flaxen hair and cheeks "like May blossoms." If this was so, she didn't age well. When Augustine died in 1743, she became absorbed with her own needs. In later years she was, according to many reports, a hard-looking, self-centered woman.

In 1755, while her son George was fighting in his first big military battle, she wrote to him that she needed butter. Later, in the midst of the Revolution, she complained that George had left her with almost nothing. "No corn in the woodshed," she wrote another of her children. "I never lived so poor in my life." In 1781 she petitioned the Virginia Assembly for money.

"Before I left Virginia," an embarrassed Washington wrote the speaker of the Assembly, "I answered all her calls for money; and since that period have directed my Steward to do the same." He didn't want the Assembly to give her money. "I request, in pointed terms, if the matter is now in agitation in your assembly, that all proceedings on it may be stopped." And they were.

There's a story about young George Washington and his mother that makes a point of the boy's honesty, and though it's not as widely known as Weems's cherry tree tale, the source of the story is George Washington Parke Custis, the grandson of Washington's wife, Martha, so it is of particular interest. Custis wrote that one morning young George rode a wild horse, his mother's favorite, that "reared, and plunged with tremendous violence," and died in the effort to throw him off. At the breakfast table he told her what happened. "I rode him," he said. "He fell under me and died on the spot." Mary Washington's supposed answer was, "I rejoice in my son who always speaks the truth."

Soon after the death of his father, George was sent to a school run by Mr. Williams, a teacher and mathematician. Perhaps it was Mr. Williams who encouraged his lifelong passion for measuring and numbers, as evidenced by his early career as a surveyor, his later precise calculations, such as the number of red clover seeds in a pound (71,000), and his careful records of his expenses as commander of the Continental army. The school, where George studied arithmetic and continued to practice penmanship, was some thirty miles away, so to be closer to it, George moved to the home of his half brother Augustine.

George also visited his other half brother, Lawrence Washington. Lawrence had served as an officer in the British navy during the War of Jenkins's Ear, so called because of a tale of an English sailor who returned to London with his left ear in his pocket. He said Spanish sailors had boarded his ship, tied him down, cut off his ear, and told him to take it to his king. (It's not known how he really lost his ear, just that it wasn't by the

Lawrence Washington, the first master of Mount Vernon, who introduced his half brother George to the glory of battle, from a circa 1870 engraving by Lossing and Barritt, based on a drawing by Benson J. Lossing

sword of a Spanish sailor.) When the people of London heard Jenkins's story, they were outraged. An attack on Cartagena, a Spanish seaport in the Caribbean, was planned. The American colonies were asked to send men to fight and Lawrence volunteered.

The battle took place in 1739 and the English were soundly beaten. Of the more than three thousand Americans who went, only eleven hundred returned, Lawrence among them. But he'd caught tuberculosis there, the disease that would eventually kill him.

Lawrence returned to his Virginia home with stories of gunfire and heroism. He named his estate Mount Vernon after his commanding officer, Admiral Edward Vernon.

George went there often, finding in his older half brother the father figure he missed. Men who had served with Lawrence in the British navy joined the

Admiral Edward Vernon, Lawrence Washington's commanding officer in the War of Jenkins's Ear, from a circa 1870 engraving by Lossing and Barritt, based on a drawing by Benson J. Lossing

The interior of the house at Mount Vernon during Lawrence Washington's time, from a circa 1893 drawing by Allegra Eggleston

many other visitors to Mount Vernon, and they would talk of great battles and strategies. All these stories excited young George, and he decided to be a navy man, too. To fulfill his brother's ambition, Lawrence got him an appointment as a midshipman. His future seemed set, but in December 1746 Mary Washington wrote to her brother Joseph Ball, a London lawyer, and asked his opinion about her fourteen-year-old son's plans.

Uncle Joseph was against it.

"I understand," Joseph Ball replied in May 1747, "that you are advised and have some thoughts of putting your son George to sea. . . . A planter that has three or four hundred acres of land and three or four slaves, if he be industrious, may live more comfortably, and leave better bread, than such a master of a ship can." He counseled that George "must not be too hasty to be rich, but most go on gently and with patience, as things will naturally go. This method, without aiming at being a fine gentleman before his time, will carry a man more comfortably and surely through the world, than going to sea."

According to some reports, by the time Mary Washington received the letter, George was ready to leave. He already had his uniform, and his luggage was on board a British warship anchored in the Potomac; it was to set sail the next day. On the advice of her brother, Mary Washington refused to let her son go.

With his navy career dashed, George Washington returned to his studies and concentrated on mathematics and surveying. By the fall, he was finished with school. Washington had about the least formal education of any president. An intelligent man, he nevertheless felt insecure about his intellectual capabilities due to his lack of schooling. Years later, believing someone else could do it better, he asked an aide, David Humphreys, to write his memoirs for him. Humphreys began the work but never finished it.

Fifteen-year-old Washington in his uniform, ready to join the British navy, from a circa 1895 engraving, artist unknown

*Washington the surveyor, perhaps on the March 1748 trip through
Lord Thomas Fairfax's land, from a circa 1884 engraving
by Whitney Jocelyn Annin*

With his studies behind him, George Washington lived at Mount Vernon with Lawrence and his wife, Anne Fairfax Washington. There George met Virginia's leading families: the Carys, Masons, Lees, and Fauntleroys. He also met Anne's father, William Fairfax, and her father's cousin, Lord Thomas Fairfax.

Lord Thomas was an English baron who left his homeland in the 1740s and came to Virginia to live at Belvoir, his estate built on a section of his family's land grant of some six million acres. Lord Thomas Fairfax loved to hunt and George excelled at that, so much so that he became a favorite of Lord Fairfax's. Their friendship led to quite an adventure. In 1748, when Lord Fairfax decided it was time to have his land surveyed, he hired an experienced surveyor named James Genn, Anne's brother George William Fairfax, and sixteen-year-old George Washington to do it.

The survey team left on March 11, 1748.

"Went in to the Bed," Washington wrote in his diary at the beginning of the journey, "when to my Surprize I found it to be nothing but a Little Straw—Matted together without Sheets or any thing else but only one Thread Bear blanket with double its Weight of Vermin such as Lice Fleas &c. I was glad to get up."

A few days later he wrote, "Last Night was a blowing & Rainy night. Our Straw catch'd a Fire that we were laying upon & was luckily Preserv'd by one of our Mens awaking." He also wrote of shooting wild game, meeting American Indians "coming from War," and of "doing our Intended Business of Laying of Lots." On Wednesday, April 13, Washington returned home, "safe to my Brothers," he wrote, "which concludes my Journal."

His friendship with Lord Fairfax enabled young George to educate himself. Fairfax lived at Belvoir in a home he called Greenway Court, where he kept a library and allowed Washington to borrow his books. Still, George's mother worried about him and wondered if she should send him to school in England. Lord Fairfax was against this plan and wrote to Mary Washington, "It is a country for which I myself have no inclination."

Lord Thomas Fairfax, sixth Baron Fairfax of Cameron, who settled in Virginia in the 1740s and befriended young Washington, from a circa 1900 engraving, artist unknown

Greenway Court, the home on Lord Thomas Fairfax's Virginia estate, from a circa 1900 engraving, artist unknown

Washington and Lord Fairfax on a fox hunt, from a circa 1860 engraving by H. B. Hall

But he did have some ideas about young George.

"He is strong and hardy, and as good a master of a horse as any could desire," Fairfax wrote. "His education might have been bettered, but what he has is accurate and inclines him to much life out of doors. He is very grave for one of his age . . . not a great talker at any time. His mind appears to me to act slowly, but, on the whole, to reach just conclusions, and he has the ardent wish to see the right of questions. . . . I presume him to be truthful because he is exact. I wish I could say he governs his temper. He is subject to attacks of anger on provocation, and sometimes without just cause; but he is a reasonable person."

Lord Fairfax also wrote, "He is, I suspect, beginning to feel the sap rising, being in the spring of life." He warned Mary Washington that her son would soon be interested in women.

Lord Fairfax was right.

Excerpts from
Washington's 1748 Surveying Journal

Friday, March 11th
Began my Journey in Company with George Fairfax, Esqr. We traveled this day 40 miles to Mr. George Neavels in Prince William County.

Sunday March 13th
Rode to his Lordships Quarter about 4 miles higher up y. River we went through most beautiful Groves of Sugar Trees and spent ye. Best part of y. Day in admiring ye. Trees and richness of ye Land.

Thursday March 31st
Early this Morning one of our Men went out with ye. Gun and soon Returned with two Wild Turkies we then went to our Business run of three Lots and returned to our Camping place at Stumps.

Wednesday April 13th
Mr. Fairfax got safe home and I myself to my Brothers which concludes my Journal.

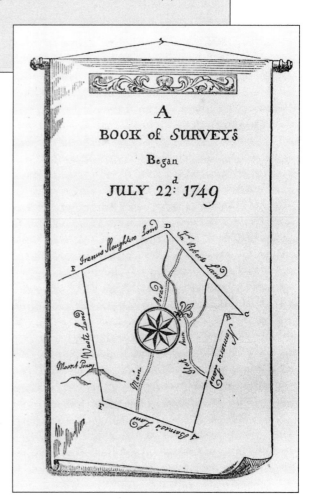

Title page of Washington's surveying book, from a circa 1858 copy

5. "Young Men Have Ever More a Special Care"

Washington's *The Young Man's Companion* offers the advice, "Young men have ever more a special care, that Womanish Allurements prove not a snare." Young George Washington didn't heed that warning.

In his surveying journal is a draft of a letter sixteen-year-old George Washington wrote to a friend about a "Low Land Beauty" who had rejected him and his great sorrow at losing her. Whatever sorrow he felt must have been short-lived. In the same letter he wrote, "There's a very agreeable Young Lady Lives in the same house." The young lady living at Greenway Court was fourteen-year-old Mary Cary.

Washington's flirtation with Mary ended when he asked for her hand in marriage. "If that is your business here," her father, Colonel Wilson Cary, is said to have replied, "I wish you to leave the house."

If young Washington ever really loved Mary Cary, he was soon over that, too. But he had lifelong feelings for Mary's sister Sally.

"You have drawn me, my dear Madam, or rather I have drawn myself, into an honest confession of a simple fact," Washington wrote to Sally ten years later. "The world has no business to know the object of my love, declared in this manner to you when I want to conceal it." He had good reason to conceal his love for Sally—she was married to George William Fairfax, the same friend who had accompanied him on the suveying adventure. Many years later, after Washington led the ragtag Continental army to victory over the British, he wrote to Sally that he still remembered "those happy moments, the happiest of my life, which I have enjoyed in your company."

In 1751 he had a flirtatious adventure of another sort. He was swimming nude in the Rappahannock River when mischievous Ann Carrol and Mary McDaniel stole his clothes. Washington, who was never known for his sense of humor, had the young women arrested, and after Ann testified against Mary, Mary was punished with fifteen lashes on her bare back.

The next year Washington pursued the beautiful sixteen-year-old Betsy Fauntleroy. Twice she dealt him, in his words, a "cruel sentence." After her second rejection, Washington moved on.

In 1756, Washington met Mary Philipse, the pretty daughter of one of New York's richest men. She was said to be stubborn and bossy, which may explain why, at twenty-six, she was still not married, already a spinster by the standards of the 1750s. According to some reports, she "engaged his heart" and then refused him. According to others, bossy

Mary Philipse of Yonkers, New York, whom Washington briefly courted in 1756, from a circa 1870 engraving by Lossing and Barritt, based on a drawing by Benson J. Lossing

Washington's first meeting with Mary Philipse, from a circa 1910 wood engraving based on an earlier painting by Edward Percy Moran

Mary Philipse was too much like his mother, and it was Washington who ended the flirtation.

Young Washington went to country dances with pretty young women, their skirts flying high. He went to kissing dances, too, with pauses, sometimes a minute or more, for kissing your partner. The balls he attended in later life were more sedate, featuring minuets, in which men and women would dance with their hands raised and only their fingertips touching. At one time Washington compared this and other forms of dancing to war, just a "gentler conflict."

Washington never lost his interest in women and often commented on them in his diary, even after he married Martha Custis. After one ball he wrote, "There were about 400 ladies the number and appearance which

Washington in Barbados, a trip he took in 1751 with his half brother Lawrence, from a circa 1895 engraving, artist unknown

exceeded anything of the kind I have ever seen," and after another he wrote, "There were about 75 well dressed, and many of them very handsome ladies."

In the midst of his early flirtations, Washington made his first sea voyage when he sailed to Barbados with his half brother Lawrence. They hoped the warm winter climate there would cure Lawrence's tuberculosis.

On September 28, 1751, the brothers left Virginia. "Calm smooth Sea and fair Weather," Washington wrote in his journal several days later. "Saw many fish swimming abt. us of which a Dolphin we catchd. . . . We had it dressed for Supper."

Yet the sea wasn't always calm and smooth. "Met with a brisk Trade Wind," Washington wrote later, "and pretty large Swell which made the Ship roll much and me very sick." And he wrote of vermin on board, "almost Eaten up by Weavel and Maggots." He was surely glad on November 2, when they sighted land.

"This morning received a card from Major Clarke," Washington wrote two days later, "with an invitation to breakfast and dine with him. We went,—myself with some reluctance, as the smallpox was in his family."

Washington was right to be worried. He caught the disease and was bedridden for three weeks. Luckily he survived and was left with a lifelong immunity to smallpox, a disease that would kill more American soldiers during the Revolution than the British did. He was not unscathed, however—it left his face covered with pockmarks.

When the hot Barbados climate did not cure Lawrence Washington, he decided to go to Bermuda, while George would return home. In Bermuda, Lawrence exercised and followed a strict diet. "These are the only terms on which I am to hope for life," he wrote to a friend. At first, he asked his wife and George to join him there, but later changed his plans. After he lost any hope of recovery, he wrote, "I shall hurry home to my grave."

On June 16, 1752, the very ill Lawrence arrived in Virginia. A short while later, surrounded by friends and family, at the age of thirty-four, he died, a painful loss for young George, who had grown very close to his half brother.

Lawrence Washington had fathered four children, but three died as infants. Only his wife, Anne, and their daughter, Sarah, survived him. Lawrence Washington left them Mount Vernon, his many slaves, and more than two thousand acres of land. If Anne died and Sarah died without children, it would all go to George.

Sarah died a short while later. Within five months of Lawrence's death, his widow married George Lee. Anne and George Lee leased the property to George. Then, upon their deaths in 1761, George Washington became the master of Mount Vernon.

6. Washington's Journal,
My Journey to the French

Before leaving for Barbados, Lawrence Washington had brought two old soldiers to Mount Vernon to train George: one, a Virginian who taught George about guns and strategy, and the other a Dutchman who taught him swordplay. In 1751 Lawrence had his nineteen-year-old half brother appointed as a major in the Virginia militia.

For a young soldier, these were exciting times.

There were more than one million English settlers in North America and fewer than one hundred thousand French. The English were mostly planters with settlements, the thirteen colonies, all along the

Nineteen-year-old Major George Washington of the Virginia militia, from a circa 1910 engraving by J. B. Forrest, based on a 1772 painting by Charles Willson Peale, the earliest known portrait of Washington

Virginia Lieutenant Governor Robert Dinwiddie, who in 1753 sent Washington on a military mission to Fort Le Boeuf at the site of present-day Pittsburgh, from a circa 1900 engraving, artist unknown

Atlantic seaboard. The French were mostly traders with large settlements in Montreal and Quebec. The French claimed the Great Lakes area, the Mississippi Valley, and everything west of the Appalachian Mountains. Both England and France claimed the Ohio Valley.

Lieutenant Governor Robert Dinwiddie of Virginia hoped to settle the matter. "SIR," he wrote to the French commander in the Ohio Valley. "The Lands upon the River Ohio, in the Western Parts of the Colony of Virginia, are so notoriously known to be the Property of the Crown of Great Britain; that it is a Matter of equal Concern and Surprise to me, to hear that a Body of French Forces are erecting Fortresses, and making Settlements upon that River, within his Majesty's Dominions. . . . It becomes my Duty to require your peaceable Departure."

George Washington's mentor Lord Fairfax, among others, convinced Governor Dinwiddie that the twenty-one-year-old Washington should deliver the note. He was ordered to wait no longer than one week for the French commander's answer, and while waiting, he was to do a bit of spying, to see how many French soldiers were stationed along the river and the condition of the French forts.

On October 31, 1753, Washington and a team of eight soldiers began the five-hundred-mile journey, traveling through wilderness and forests, over mountains and across streams, in rain and snow. On December 12 they reached Fort Le Boeuf.

Washington presents Dinwiddie's letter to French commander Legardeur de St. Pierre, December 1753, from a circa 1895 engraving, artist unknown.

Washington put on his dress uniform and met the French commander, Legardeur de St. Pierre, Knight of the Military Order of St. Louis. The Frenchman was a courteous, elderly man and Washington waited as he read Dinwiddie's note. "As to the summons you send me," St. Pierre replied, "I do not think myself obliged to obey it."

Knowing this reply meant war, Washington left to deliver it to Dinwiddie.

Washington described his trip back to Virginia with St. Pierre's reply as a perilous journey. "Our Horses were now so weak and feeble, and the Baggage so heavy," he wrote in his journal, "therefore myself and others . . . gave up our horses. . . . The Cold increased very fast; and the Roads were becoming much worse by a deep Snow, continually freezing. . . . I determined to prosecute my Journey the nearest Way through the Woods, on Foot."

Washington took off all his clothes and put on an American Indian coat. Then, with a gun and a knapsack filled with papers and food, Washington, frontiersman Christopher Gist, and an American Indian guide went off

Washington, dressed in American Indian clothes, walks toward the Allegheny River on his return home from his mission to Fort Le Boeuf, from a circa 1895 engraving, artist unknown.

toward the Allegheny River. On December 27 they came to a meadow.

"It was very light, and snow was on the ground," Gist wrote in his journal. Their guide suddenly stopped, turned, and took a shot at them. Gist wrote, "Said the Major [Washington], 'Are you shot?' 'No,' said I; upon which the Indian ran forward at a big standing white oak, and began loading his gun. . . . I would have killed him, but the Major would not suffer me. . . . I said to the Major, 'As you will not have him killed, we must get him away, and then we must travel all night.'"

Washington's journal entries describe the encounter as even more frightening, that they were attacked not by one, but by "a party of French Indians." Whatever their number, Washington wrote that he and Gist "walked all the remaining part of the night without making any stop . . . to be out of the reach of their pursuit."

The next day they came to the Allegheny River. Blocks of ice floated in the water. "There was no way of getting over," Washington wrote, "but on a raft." It took a full day's work to make one. The next morning they boarded it, but halfway across the river they got caught in the ice and Washington was thrown into the freezing water. "I fortunately saved myself by catching hold of one of the raft logs. Notwithstanding all our efforts we could not get the raft to either shore, but were obliged, as we were near an island, to quit our raft, and make to it."

Washington and Christopher Gist on the raft they made to cross the Allegheny, from a circa 1895 engraving, artist unknown

The weather that night was terribly cold. Gist's hands and feet froze, and so did the river. The next morning, Washington and Gist walked across the frozen Allegheny. On January 16, they reached Williamsburg.

Washington gave St. Pierre's answer to Governor Dinwiddie and told him everything that had happened. Dinwiddie insisted Washington write it all down. Then he had the journal printed and sent to the governors of all the American colonies and to London.

The *Boston Gazette* published Washington's *My Journey to the French* as a serial, in six issues. It was printed in London, too, and people on both sides of the Atlantic Ocean were introduced to the rising young soldier, George Washington.

The journal described wild adventure and clever diplomacy. It showed Washington's leadership abilities, courage, and wisdom in dealings with his American Indian neighbors. But George Washington wrote almost nothing of his thoughts or feelings. Throughout his life, although he wrote many letters and gave many speeches, he never wrote about himself. He was a quiet man of action.

7. "I Have Heard the Bullets Whistle"

Governor Dinwiddie ordered Captain William Trent, who was already in the Ohio Valley, to begin building a fort to protect British interests in the area. Next, he told George Washington to enlist two hundred men, train them, take them to the valley, and help Trent finish the fort. If anyone tried to stop the fort-building, Washington was to "make Prisoners of or kill and destroy them."

Washington had difficulty gathering troops. "I have increas'd my number of Men to ab't 25," he wrote Dinwiddie, "loose, Idle Persons that are quite destitute of House and Home." Some were so poor they had no shoes. Others lacked socks or shirts. Along with his complaints came a request: that he be made a lieutenant colonel. Washington soon received his commission and orders to "March what soldiers you have enlisted immediately to the Ohio."

The march through forests and across swamps, loaded with supply wagons and cannons, was slow and difficult. Before Washington and his men could reach Captain Trent, the French had captured the fort. An urgent message was sent to Washington: "Come soon or we are lost."

Quickly and quietly he led his men, along with some Seneca American Indian warriors, on an overnight march and surprised the French. By the end of the battle, the French commander, Joseph Coulon de Villiers, Sieur de Jumonville, and nine other French soldiers were killed. More than twenty others were taken prisoner. One of Washington's men was killed; three were wounded.

This was the first time Washington had seen action. "I have heard the bullets whistle," he wrote in a letter to his brother John Augustine, "and there is something charming in the sound." This battle marked a turning point in history—it began the French and Indian War, fought between the two great powers of the time, the French and English.

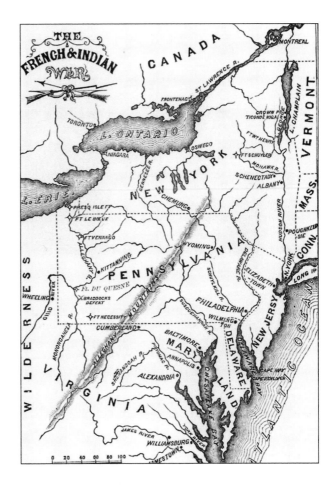

A circa 1875 map of the French and Indian War by Benson J. Lossing

Knowing a few enemy soldiers had escaped and might return with fresh troops, Washington led his men back to a meadow where they built a modest fort by a creek with high ground all around. He called it Fort Necessity.

The French did return a few weeks later, on July 3. Washington assembled his men in a line outside the fort, with their guns loaded—ready to fight.

At six hundred yards, the nine hundred French troops started to shoot. The noise was frightening, but at that distance there was no danger. As the French marched closer, Washington ordered his men to the trenches. Then, just as Washington's men were about to open fire, the French scattered and hid behind trees and rocks. Washington's men, all in one place, were easy targets.

By midafternoon there was a drenching rain. At first Washington welcomed the downpour, since his men were greatly outnumbered and the rain slowed the fire. But Washington had chosen a poor location for his fort. Water poured down the hills into the trenches, trapping his men in deep pools. Soon their open wounds turned the water red.

Tanacharison, a Seneca chief, witnessed the battle and said later, "The French in the engagement acted like cowards, and the English like fools." He wrote that Washington "was a good natured man, but had no experience. . . . He lay in one Place from one Full-Moon to the other, without making any Fortifications, except that little Thing on the Meadow."

At eight that night the French shouted, *"Voulez-vous parler?"* They wanted to talk. At first Washington refused, but there was little food left in Fort Necessity and the rain had ruined their gunpowder. More than one hundred of his men were dead or wounded. Many of the others, wet and discouraged, had broken into the rum and were drunk. Washington had no choice—he knew he was beaten, so he sent a French-speaking soldier to meet the enemy.

The soldier returned with a damp paper written in French.

The surrender terms were generous. Washington and his men could

Washington's first battle ended with ten French soldiers killed, including their commander,
Joseph Coulon de Villiers, Sieur de Jumonville, from a circa 1910 drawing by Davis.
Washington's call to fire here marked the beginning of the French and Indian War.

leave unharmed beneath an English flag, with their drums playing and all their belongings. Only the artillery would have to be left behind. The French commander, Louis Coulon de Villiers, who was Jumonville's older brother, also wrote that the siege of Fort Necessity had been provoked by the *murder* of the diplomat Jumonville, but this part of the letter wasn't properly translated to Washington.

Washington and James Mackay signed for the English. De Villiers signed for the French.

The next morning was July 4. But this was 1754, long before it would become an American day of celebration, and this July 4 was a day of defeat for Washington. The French took over what was left of Fort Necessity and Washington led his men home.

Washington leads the retreat from Fort Necessity, July 4, 1754, from a circa 1890 illustration by Howard Pyle.

Despite the outcome, Washington was called a hero. Colonial newspaper reports of the surprise attack on Jumonville described him as a courageous leader. His later defeat at Fort Necessity was explained away as a problem of bad weather and too few troops.

Later that summer, on August 30, the House of Burgesses voted to give Washington and his officers their thanks "for their brave and gallant defense of their country." Each soldier also received a bonus of almost four dollars. But along with the praise came a demotion. With the threat of more fighting over the Ohio Valley, Dinwiddie had petitioned London for a professional army of British officers and soldiers, and, when he was told it was coming, reduced Washington's rank from colonel to captain. Rather than accept a lower rank, Washington resigned.

Early the next spring Washington watched from Mount Vernon as British ships sailed up the Potomac River with cannons, red-coated soldiers, and Major General Edward Braddock, the newly appointed com-

Major General Edward Braddock, who arrived in Virginia in February 1755 to take command of English forces in North America, from an 1895 drawing by L. Hitchcock

mander in chief of English forces in North America. Braddock's mission was to chase the French from the Ohio Valley all the way to Canada. The stubborn, quick-tempered old soldier set up camp in nearby Alexandria.

Washington rode to the camps, watched the well-trained troops drill, and longed to join them. Braddock was told about Washington's military experience, and an aide wrote to him that Braddock "would be very glad of your Company." Washington wrote back of his desire to serve "my King and country," and on May 10, 1755, his appointment as "Aide-de-Camp to His Excellency General Braddock" was announced.

George Washington's retirement from soldiering had been short-lived. For the rest of his life all things military attracted him. This great attraction surely began at the home of his half brother Lawrence, with all the talk of heroism in the War of Jenkins's Ear. Now, in place of his brother, Washington had a new role model, Major General Braddock.

Braddock pampered himself. He had personal cooks who were rumored to be so talented they could take an old pair of leather boots, mix them with some vegetables, and cook them into a tasty stew. But he was strict with his men, a rough bunch, some of them convicted criminals who chose the military over prison. A soldier found drunk would be severely punished, while one found guilty of theft would be sentenced to numerous lashes administered in front of the troops, after which the thieving soldier would be sent home.

Soon after Washington signed on, Braddock's troops began their five-hundred-mile march to the Ohio Valley. Three hundred men went ahead with axes, chopped down trees, and created a path. Then came a four-mile line of soldiers, packhorses, wagons, and cannons.

Benjamin Franklin visited the camp to warn Braddock that a long thin line of soldiers would be exposed to ambush by American Indians, who were allies of the French. Braddock told Franklin they "may indeed be a formidable enemy to raw American militia, but upon the king's regular and disciplined troops, sir, it is impossible they should make an impression."

On May 19, 1755, the troops reached the British-held Fort Cumberland. On June 19 they started their final march to battle.

Washington was frustrated by their slowness—the troops traveled just three miles a day. "Instead of pushing on with vigor," he wrote, "they were halting to level every molehill, and to erect bridges over every brook."

When they were a few miles from the French at Fort Duquesne, the site

Benjamin Franklin, who helped supply Braddock's army with wagons and horses and warned that a long line of marching soldiers would leave them vulnerable to attack, from a circa 1900 engraving, artist unknown, based on an earlier portrait

of present-day Pittsburgh, Washington suggested his Virginian troops be sent ahead, since they were accustomed to frontier fighting. General Braddock would not consider it.

On July 9, at sunrise, the red-coated troops assembled. English flags were at the head of the line; behind them stood nearly two thousand men. A bugle call and drumroll started the men on their march.

At two o'clock, before they reached Fort Duquesne, where they expected to engage the enemy, gunshots came from the surrounding forest, from behind rocks and trees in what would be called the battle of Monongahela. "We would fight," an officer told Braddock, "if we could see the enemy." Whenever some of the British tried to take cover, Braddock shouted at them, called them cowards, and even hit them with the back of his sword.

When an English officer fell, the French and American Indians ran out of the woods and grabbed his horse. Braddock's troops shot wildly, often hitting their own men. Two of Washington's horses were shot while Washington was riding them. Four bullets went through his coat, but Washington was not hurt.

Braddock was in the middle of it all. One after another, as five horses were shot under him, he mounted another. Then a bullet tore through his right arm and settled in his lung. General Braddock fell from his horse. He was carried to a cart and taken off the battlefield. The injured Braddock continued to shout orders, but now no one was listening. Most of the officers and more than seven hundred of the regular troops were killed or wounded; the others ran off.

Washington hurried to a British camp forty miles away to bring help for the wounded. Two days later he returned and found Braddock near death. According to some reports, just before he died on July 13, Braddock apologized to Washington for ignoring his advice on fighting frontier-style. The

Braddock's men march into battle, from a circa 1900 engraving, artist unknown.

lesson of this defeat was not lost on the young officer. Washington would later adapt his battle strategy to the enemy and the situation. At times during the Revolution, he even chose to retreat to save his troops, having learned that pride was not as important as the lives of his men and an ultimate victory.

On July 14 Washington led the funeral service for Braddock, which was done without the usual military honors, such as the gun salute. They didn't want the enemy to know their position.

In Virginia, news of the terrible defeat arrived, including rumors that Washington had been killed. There were even reports of his last words. "I take this early opportunity of contradicting the first, and of assuring you that I have not composed the latter," he wrote his brother John Augustine. "I have been protected beyond all human probability . . . though death was

Washington leads Braddock's funeral service, July 14, 1755, from a circa 1860 engraving, artist unknown.

leveling my companions on every side of me."

His uncle Joseph Ball, who had once advised keeping Washington out of the British navy, was now proud of his battling nephew. "It is a sensible pleasure to me to hear that you have behaved yourself with such a martial spirit in all your engagements with the French," he wrote in September. "We have heard of General Braddock's defeat. Everybody blames his rash conduct."

Braddock's humiliating defeat was a turning point in America's march to independence. "This whole transaction," Benjamin Franklin wrote later, "gave us Americans the first suspicion that our exalted ideas of the prowess of British regulars had not been well founded."

The powerful English army could be beaten.

8. "Such Deadly Sorrow"

"I have been on the losing order," Washington wrote his brother John Augustine, "ever since I entered the service." He may have been discouraged, but he didn't leave the military. In August 1755 he took command of Virginia's troops and was in charge of protecting settlements in the valley between the Allegheny and Blue Ridge Mountains, the 360-mile Virginia frontier.

Washington set up recruiting stations in Alexandria, Fredericksburg, and Winchester. Then he went to the still unfinished Fort Cumberland and started to institute the strict control he had seen Braddock hold over his troops. Washington ordered his men to line up for roll call three times a day, to exercise twice a day, and to refrain from foul language and alcohol. He ordered all sorts of supplies—uniforms, shirts, socks, shoes, pots, blankets, tents, and rum.

Among Washington's strengths as a military man was that he learned from past mistakes. To enable his troops to move more quickly than Braddock's had, he had gunpowder barrels made small, so a horse easily could carry two of them. Washington proposed a line of twenty-two forts be built and manned by two thousand men taken from Virginia farms and towns. The first one built was Fort Dinwiddie. He ordered that the trees near the fort be cut down so that the enemy couldn't hide in the forest and shoot at it. He also hoped to enlist the help of friendly American Indians. Governor Dinwiddie, however, did not approve his plan.

Washington spent more than two years protecting the frontier. During that time, he felt responsible for the suffering of the people living there. He wrote Dinwiddie, "The supplicating tears of the women, and moving petitions from the men, melt me into such deadly sorrow." And he wrote, "What to do? . . . Three families were murdered the night before last at a distance of less than twelve miles from this place." With each American Indian attack, some of Washington's men deserted, usually twenty or more at a time.

In fall 1757, Washington fell sick with fever and severe stomach pains. The camp doctor "bled" Washington, a common remedy in colonial times, but it didn't help. The doctor recommended he go somewhere quiet to rest.

That November, Washington went home to stay, sometimes so sick he

Frightened settlers speak with Washington, 1756, from a circa 1855 engraving by M. Nevin.

thought he would die. By April, however, he had recovered and returned to his headquarters in Winchester.

British General John Forbes had come to America from England with orders to take Fort Duquesne from the French. Washington busied himself enlisting and training men, and getting horses, wagons, and supplies ready for the attack. Then he and his troops marched ahead, cut through the forest, and prepared the way for Forbes's main army.

Forbes had six thousand men under his command and they traveled slowly. When Washington's advance regiment approached the site of Fort Duquesne, they found the scattered bones of the English soldiers who had died with Braddock. When they came to the fort, there were no French flags—the fort was deserted. The buildings inside the stockade had been set on fire and only smoke and ashes remained. Rather than lose it in battle to superior forces, the French had destroyed the fort. There was no battle, no surrender, but there was victory. Washington planted an English flag and claimed Fort Duquesne for the king.

The bones of Braddock's men were collected and buried in a solemn ceremony. The fort was rebuilt and renamed Fort Pitt after the English statesman William Pitt.

With the French gone, Washington felt his job was done and resigned from the military. Before he returned to Mount Vernon, his officers held a testimonial. "You took us under your tuition, trained us up in the practice of that discipline, which alone can constitute good troops. . . . We must be affected," they said, "by the loss of such an excellent commander, such a sincere friend and so affable a companion."

In late 1758 the English securely held the Ohio Valley, and Washington held the affection of his officers and the many American people who read of his military adventures.

Pennsylvania Gazette
December 14, 1758

On Sunday last an Express arrived here from General Forbes, at *Fort Duquesne*, with the agreeable News of the Enemy's having blown up and abandoned that important Fortress on the Approach of the Army under his Command.

The following Letter from that General's Army, being wrote by one, who seems to be no stranger to the true Interest of these Colonies, nor to Indian *Affairs, we hope will not be unacceptable to our Readers.*

Sir, I HAVE the Pleasure to write this Letter upon the Spot where *Fort Duquesne* once stood, while the *British* Flag flies over the Debris of its Bastions in Triumph.

Blessed be God, the long look'd for Day is arrived that has now fixed us on the Banks of the *OHIO!* ...

It deprives our Enemies of the Benefits they expected from their deep laid Schemes, and breaks asunder the Chain of Communication betwixt *Canada* and *Louisiana*, a Chain that threatened this Continent with Slavery, and therefore the chief Favourite and Mistress of the *French* Court. These Advantages have been procured for us by the Prudence and Abilities of General Forbes, without Stroke of Sword, tho had they been purchased at the Price of much Blood and Treasure, every Lover of his Country must have allowed that they would have been cheaply bought.

The Difficulties he had to struggle with were great. To maintain Armies in a Wilderness, Hundreds of Miles from the Settlements; to march them by untrodden Paths, over almost impassable Mountains, thro' thick Woods and dangerous Defiles, required both Foresight and Experience, especially if you consider the Efforts of an active Enemy, frequently attempting to cut off our Convoys ... He has conquered all this Country, has driven the *French* from the *Ohio*, and obliged them to blow up their fort (when we within a few Miles of it we heard the Explosion) ... To-day a great Detachment goes to *Braddock's* Field of Battle, to bury the Bones of our slaughtered Countrymen, many of whom were butchered in cold Blood by (those crueller than Savages) the *French*, who to the eternal Shame and Infamy of their Country, have left them lying above Ground ever since. The unburied Bodies of those killed since, and strewed round this Fort, equally reproach them, and proclaim loudly, to all civilized Nations, their Barbarity.

Beyond the details of the capture of Fort Duquesne, this letter is included here for the bitter words at the end aimed at the French, an indication of the strong feelings many English felt for them. The editors of the *Pennsylvania Gazette* did not identify the author of this letter.

9. Martha Dandridge Custis Washington

In 1756, while Washington was still commander of the Virginia militia, Captain Dagworthy, a British soldier, had refused to obey him. As an Englishman, Dagworthy felt he should not take orders from an American. Washington traveled to Boston to discuss the problem with William Shirley, the governor of Massachusetts and commander of all British troops in North America. Shirley took Washington's side. "In case it should happen, that Colonel Washington and Captain Dagworthy should join at Fort Cumberland," he wrote, "it is my order that Colonel Washington shall take command."

After his meeting with Shirley, Washington left Boston. He would not return to the city for nineteen years, until he came as the head of the Continental army fighting the British. On his way back to Virginia, he stopped in New York City. According to one story, a regiment of soldiers had just come from England. Someone at New York Governor Charles Hardy's

Governor William Shirley of Massachusetts, in 1755 appointed commander in chief of British forces in North America, from a circa 1900 engraving, artist unknown

table said that these officers were the finest-looking men anywhere.

"I wager," one of the governor's female guests said, "I will show your Excellency a finer man in the procession tomorrow than your Excellency can select from your famous regiment."

The governor agreed to the bet.

The next day there was a parade in honor of the king's birthday. In the front was the British regiment and behind it some colonial officers. The woman pointed to one of the Americans and asked, "What do you think of your wager now?"

"Lost," he answered. "When I laid my wager I was not aware that Colonel Washington was in New York."

George Washington was a handsome man, tall and broad-shouldered. Captain George Mercer, a friend of his and an officer in the Virginia regiment, wrote of Washington in 1760, "His head is well shaped though not large, but is gracefully poised on a superb neck. A large and straight rather than prominent nose; blue-gray penetrating eyes which are widely separated and overhung by a heavy brow." Mercer wrote of his high cheekbones and good firm chin. Of course, Washington was not without imperfections. Mercer wrote, "His mouth is large and generally firmly closed, but which from time to time discloses some defective teeth."

Washington was good company. "In conversation," Mercer wrote, "he looks you full in the face, is deliberate, deferential, and engaging. His voice is agreeable rather than strong. His demeanor at all times composed and dignified."

In the spring of 1758, Washington stopped in Virginia and dined at his friend Major Chamberlayne's house. There he met Martha Dandridge Custis, a rich widow about his age who had two small children. She was a small woman with light brown hair, hazel eyes, and good manners—though at times she could be somewhat hot-tempered and stubborn. She

Washington visits with widow Martha Dandridge Custis, 1758, from a circa 1910 engraving, based on an earlier piece by Alonzo Chappel.

played the piano, danced, and was an especially good weaver and seamstress who often made her own clothes. She also knew how to manage a colonial kitchen and supervise staff, including slaves and servants. Although she was not well read nor well educated, neither was George Washington.

Later that afternoon, Washington's servant, Bishop, came by with his master's horses. But the usually prompt Washington wasn't ready to leave. "'Twas strange, 'twas passing strange," Bishop later remembered. Washington had an early appointment the next morning in Williamsburg, and "he was the most punctual of all punctual men." At sunset, Bishop was told to put the horses in for the night.

The next morning, Washington and Bishop rode off to Williamsburg, but returned that afternoon. Washington proposed marriage to Martha Custis and she accepted.

When they met, Washington was accustomed to lengthy tours in army camps, the horrors of battle, without being able to look forward to the joyous homecoming of a married, family man. In Martha he found a stable,

Martha Dandridge Custis near the time of her marriage to George Washington, from a circa 1910 engraving by J. Rogers, based on an earlier painting by John Woolaston

cheerful homemaker, wealthy enough to relieve him of his debts; and Martha had found a gallant, handsome man, a good manager for her land, money, and slaves.

How did Washington feel about Martha? Shortly before he married, he wrote to Sally Fairfax, "I confess myself a votary of love. . . . I feel the force of her amiable beauties in the recollection of a thousand tender passages that I wish to obliterate till I am bid to revive them. But experience, Alas! sadly reminds me how impossible this is." Impossible because according to most historians he was writing not of his feelings for Martha but for Sally, up to that time the great love of his life.

Washington's later letters indicate a change in his feelings for Martha, that what began as a practical, comfortable marriage, characterized at first by fondness, loyalty, and respect, grew into love. •

The site of Martha and George Washington's marriage, her house, The White House, from an 1896 drawing, artist unknown

Washington resigned from the military in late December 1758. On January 6, 1759, he married Martha Custis in her home. Grand homes at this time had names, and, in a bit of irony, hers was called The White House.

The night before the wedding, the bride, groom, and their friends and families danced and partied by candlelight. At one o'clock the next afternoon, the guests crowded into the large drawing room. George and Martha walked slowly toward the Reverend David Mossom of St. Peter's Church, who performed the ceremony.

The bride wore a white silk skirt and satin top; purple satin high-heeled shoes trimmed with silver lace and diamond buckles; and a pearl necklace, bracelet, and earrings. Strings of pearls were woven in her powdered hair. The groom wore a blue jacket lined with red silk and trimmed with silver, a white satin shirt, white gloves, white silk stockings, gold buckles on his

The Washington wedding, an elegant affair with the bride in a silk skirt and satin top, the groom in a silk-lined jacket, and English military officers in dress uniforms, from a circa 1858 wood engraving, artist unknown

shoes, and a dress sword. His hair was powdered, too. The guests also looked elegant. English army and navy officers were there in full dress uniforms. Virginia Lieutenant Governor Francis Fauquier wore a gold and scarlet suit and dress sword.

After the ceremony the forty guests stayed for dinner, tea, and supper. The next day, Martha and George Washington rode to church. She rode in a carriage and he rode alongside on his horse.

Mrs. Mary Washington, George's mother, was not at the wedding and was never close to Martha. Nonetheless, she was delighted that her son was married, convinced it meant he was done with the military. "There was no end to my troubles while George was in the army," Mary Washington wrote her brother Joseph Ball in July 1759, "but he has now given it up."

George, Martha, and Martha's two children, four-year-old John "Jacky" Parke Custis and two-year-old Martha "Patsy" Parke Custis, lived in Martha's homes, The White House and Six Chimneys, for the next three months. After that they moved to Mount Vernon.

10. Sell Him "for Whatever He Will Fetch"

When Daniel Parke Custis, Martha's first husband, died, she and her two children inherited money, slaves, cattle, and more than seventeen thousand acres of Virginia land, much of it in and around Williamsburg. When Martha remarried, her share belonged to her new husband. Washington also controlled the property left to her children, so with his marriage, George Washington became one of the richest men in the American colonies.

At the time, the practice in Virginia was to clear some land and plant first tobacco and then Indian corn, two crops that quickly deplete the soil of nutrients. When the exhausted land no

The western front of Mount Vernon, Washington's Virginia estate, from a circa 1870 engraving by Lossing and Barritt, based on a drawing by Benson J. Lossing

A southern plantation slave cabin, from a circa 1900 engraving by Hoskin

longer produced a decent crop, farmers would move on to clear another field and again plant tobacco and Indian corn.

Washington read books on agriculture. After checking his own fields in 1765, he decided, except for some land along the York River, to plant wheat. He also set up three mills to grind his wheat into flour. Washington, a fine horseman, had at one time, as many as one hundred thirty horses. He also kept chickens, turkeys, ducks, geese, swans, pheasants, hogs, sheep, and cows.

Washington woke early each morning, often before sunrise; ate a light breakfast of corn cakes, honey, and tea; and then got on a horse and rode across his property. He checked his fences, fields, and workers, some of whom were white indentured servants, but most were African-American slaves. Washington had inherited some slaves and bought many others, including thirteen in 1759, his first year back at Mount Vernon.

Living conditions for slaves on Virginia plantations were horrid, with small, drafty, dirt-floor cabins. Washington wasn't always a benevolent slaveholder: one letter from a farm manager complained that his slaves' children had no clothes for the winter, another that they had no blankets. In

October 1760, when a slave ran off, Washington paid a printer seven shillings to advertise for his return.

Washington's letters show him to have been a hard taskmaster. "Doll at the Ferry," he wrote, "must be taught to knit, and *made* to do a sufficient day's work." He complained his "sewers" made only six shirts a week and "the last week Carolina (without being sick) made only five." He wrote that his blacksmiths were "two very idle fellows." In 1766 he sent an unruly slave to the West Indies and instructed the captain of the ship to sell him "in any of the islands you may go to, for whatever he will fetch."

Yet, at times, he did show compassion. In a contract with Nelson Kelly, one of his overseers, he had him agree to "take all necessary and proper care" of his slaves, "treating them with humanity and tenderness when sick."

Later in life, Washington saw the evil in slavery and was careful not to break up families. In 1787 he contacted a slave agent about a bricklayer who was for sale. "If he has a family," Washington wrote, "from whom he would reluctantly part, I decline the purchase."

Inside a typical slave cabin, from a circa 1900 engraving by C. Graham

In 1791, when he was president, Washington declared he would never buy another slave. But after his cook ran off, he wrote, "I had resolved never to become the master of another slave by purchase, but this resolution I fear I must break." Also during his presidency, he wrote bitterly about one of his slaves, that for "every day Betty Davis works she is laid up two." One month later, when she was still not at work, he wrote that she was "lazy deceitful and impudent . . . I shall get no service from her." In his last will, Washington directed that "upon the decease of my wife," all his slaves be set free, but in 1796 Ona Judge, Martha's household slave, ran off, and Washington sought her return. Perhaps, with his authoritarian personality, he could only accept that his and Martha's slaves be free when *he* released them.

In many ways, Washington's attitude seems similar to another Virginian, Patrick Henry, who called slavery "an abominable practice," yet had many slaves, more than sixty at the time of his death. Henry explained he kept slaves because it would be just too difficult "living here without them." Washington and Henry were slaveholders, each with a conscience, but slaveholders nonetheless.

There were others among the founding fathers who saw the evils of slavery. Benjamin Franklin was president of a Pennsylvania abolition society. When Samuel Adams and his second wife, Betsy, were given a slave as a wedding gift, they immediately set her free. But neither Franklin nor Adams lived in the agrarian south. And while Washington only let his slaves go at his and Martha's death, for those he set free it was no empty gesture.

Beyond his slaves and other farm business, during his time at Mount Vernon, Washington busied himself with church business and politics.

His local Episcopal church was old and rundown and needed to be replaced. At a meeting he listened to his friend George Mason give a long, impassioned speech to build the new church where the old one stood, the place of so many celebrations, and sadness, too. Mason didn't want it moved away from the cemetery that was just outside.

While Washington listened, he quietly drew a map of the parish, showing all the houses, the site of the old church, and where he thought a new one should be built. When Mason was finished talking, the always practical Washington showed his map and asked which was the better spot. Mason's long speech lost to Washington's simple drawing.

Washington served in Williamsburg as a member of the state assembly, the House of Burgesses, and his fellow members were proud to have him. In 1759, on his first day as a burgess, a vote was taken to thank him for his "faithful services to his Majesty and this colony and his brave and steady behavior from the first encroachments and hostilities of the French."

Washington stood and blushed. "Mr. Speaker," he said. "Mr. Speaker." Then he stopped—he didn't know what to say next. The Speaker smiled. "Sit down, sir," he told Washington. "Your modesty equals your valor."

Washington served in the House of Burgesses with such Patriots as Thomas Jefferson and Patrick Henry. He was elected for fifteen straight years and served on various committees, including one to reduce the number of stray hogs. As a burgess, Washington mostly sat and listened. At night, when the meetings were over, he played cards, often at Williamsburg's

The House of Burgesses, Williamsburg, Virginia, from a circa 1895 engraving, artist unknown

Raleigh Tavern. He attended cockfights, boxing matches, horse races, the theater, and dinner with friends.

On his way home from Williamsburg, Washington often stopped in Fredericksburg to visit his mother and his sister, Betty Lewis. When he arrived there, a dinner party was usually given for him at the Indian Queen Tavern. At one such party a British officer got up and sang a funny but bawdy song. Washington laughed until tears ran down his cheeks, proving to some that he *did* have a sense of humor.

Washington sometimes went alone to Williamsburg. Other times Martha and her children accompanied him.

Martha and George Washington had hoped to have children together, but it is very likely that they couldn't. As a young man, George had suffered a bad case of mumps, and at nineteen, smallpox. Either illness may have left him infertile. Soon after Martha married George she had a serious case of measles, which could have left her unable to conceive a child as well. But in 1786, after more than twenty-seven years of marriage, Washington still thought about having children.

"If Mrs. Washington should survive me," he wrote to his nephew George Augustine Washington in a letter that shows how Washington carefully thought about things, "there is a moral certainty of my dying without issue, and should I be the longest liver, the matter in my opinion is almost as certain; for whilst I retain the reasoning faculties I shall never

Jacky and Patsy Custis, Washington's stepchildren, from a circa 1870 engraving by Lossing and Barritt, based on a drawing by Benson J. Lossing

marry a girl; and it is not probable that I should have children by a woman of an age suitable to my own, should I be disposed to enter into a second marriage." This letter implies that Washington didn't believe himself to be infertile.

Washington was a good stepfather to Martha's children. Soon after he married, among his orders for goods from London were "ten shillings worth of toys," "six little books for children beginning to read," a Bible and prayer book for each of the children with their names printed on the covers in gold, and a box of gingerbread cookies. He hired tutors and dancing teachers for the children, and when he sent Jacky off to boarding school, he offered the teacher, the Reverend Jonathan Boucher, extra pay to give Jacky special attention. Washington wrote that he wanted to make the boy fit for "something more useful than horse racing."

When Patsy was about eleven, she began having seizures. The Washingtons took her to doctors and to a spa, but she didn't improve. Then, on June 19, 1773, just after dinner, sixteen-year-old Patsy fell off her chair. Washington hurried to her, but there was nothing he could do. Within just two minutes, she was dead, "without," Washington wrote in a letter, "uttering a word, a groan, or scarce a sigh."

"If we mortals can distinguish those who are deserving of Grace & who are not," Jacky wrote from school when he heard of his sister's death, "I am confident she enjoys the Bliss prepar'd only for the Good & virtuous."

Soon after that, on February 3, 1774, nineteen-year-old Jacky married Eleanor "Nelly" Calvert, a direct descendant of Lord Baltimore, who had founded the first British settlement in Maryland.

Washington's Changing Attitude Toward Slavery
from his writings

Letter To Captain Josiah Thompson
July 2, 1766

With this Letter comes a Negro (Tom) which I beg the favour of you to sell, in any of the Islands you may go to, for whatever he will fetch, and bring me in return from him

One Hhd of best Molasses

One Ditto of best Rum

One Barrl of Lymes, if good and Cheap

One Pot of Tamarinds, contg. About 10 lbs.

Two small Do of mixed Sweetmeats, abt. 5 lb. each

And the residue, much or little, in good old Spirits.

That this Fellow is both a Rogue and a Runaway (tho' he was by no means remarkable for the former, and never practiced the latter till of late) I shall not pretend to deny. But that he is exceedingly healthy, strong, and good at the Hoe, the whole neighborhood can testifie and particularly Mr. Johnson and his Son, who have both had him under them as foreman of the gang; which gives me reason to hope he may, with your good management, sell well, if kept clean and trim'd up a little when offered for Sale.

Letter To Lund Washington
February 24, 1779

The advantages resulting from the sale of my negroes, I have very little doubt of ... My scruples arise from a reluctance in offer-ing these people at public vendue, and on account of the uncertainty of timeing the sale well. In the first case, if these poor wretches are to be held in a state of slavery, I do not see that a change of masters will ren-der it more irksome, provided husband and wife, and Parents and children are not sepa-rated from each other, which is not my intentions to do. And with respect to the sec-ond ... if a sale takes place while the money is in a depreciating state, that is, before it has arrived at the lowest ebb of depreciation; I shall lose the difference, and if it is delayed, 'till some great and important event shall give a decisive turn in favor of our affairs, it may be too late.

General Orders to the Troops
October 25, 1781

It having been represented that many Negroes and Mulattoes the property of Citi-zens of these States have concealed them-selves on board the Ships in the harbour, that some still continue to attach themselves to British Officers and that others have attempted to impose themselves upon the officers of the French and American Armies as Freemen and to make their escapes in that manner, In order to prevent their succeeding in such practices All Officers of the Allied Army and other persons of every denomina-tion concerned are directed not to suffer any such negroes or mulattoes to be retained in their Service but on the contrary to cause them to be delivered to the Guards . . .

Letter To Marquis de Lafayette
April 5, 1783

The scheme, my dear Marqs. Which you propose as a precedent, to encourage the emancipation of the black people of this Country from that state of Bondage in wch. They are held, is a striking evidence of the benevolence of your Heart. I shall be happy to join you in so laudable a work; but will defer going into a detail of the business, 'till I have the pleasure of seeing you.

Letter To Robert Morris
April 12, 1786

I give you the trouble of this letter at the instance of Mr. Dalby of Alexandria; who is called to Philadelphia to attend what he conceives to be a vexatious lawsuit respecting a slave of his, which a Society of Quakers in the city (formed for such purposes) have attempted to liberate. . . . I can only say there is not a man living who wishes more sincerely than I do for the abolition of it; but there is only one proper and effectual mode by which it can be accomplished, and that is by Legislative authority; and this, as far as my suffrage will go, shall never be wanting. But when slaves who are happy and contented with their present masters, are tampered with and seduced to leave them; when masters are taken unawares by these practices; when a

conduct of this sort begets discontent on one side and resentment on the other, and when it happens to fall on a man whose purse will not measure with that of the Society, and he loses his property for want of means to defend it; it is oppression in the latter case, and not humanity in any; because it introduces more evils than it can cure.

Letter To John Francis Mercer
September 9, 1786

I never mean (unless some particular circumstances should compel me to it) to possess another slave by purchase; it being my first wish to see some plan adopted, by which slavery in this country may be abolished by slow, sure, and imperceptible degrees.

From His Last Will and Testament

Upon the decease of my wife, it is my Will & desire that all the Slaves which I hold in my own right, shall receive their freedom— To emancipate them during her life, would, tho' earnestly wished by me, be attended with such insuperable difficulties on account of their intermixture by Marriages with the Dower Negroes . . .—And whereas among those who will receive freedom according to this devise, there may be some, who from old age or bodily infirmities, and others who on account of their infancy, that will be unable to support themselves it is my will and desire that all who come under the first & second description shall be comfortably cloathed & fed by my heirs while they live.

II. "If This Be Treason, Make the Most of It!"

On October 25, 1760, seventy-seven-year-old King George II died. The next day, his twenty-three-year-old grandson ascended the throne as King George III.

Kings George I and George II had been born in Hanover, Germany. King George I didn't speak English at all, and King George II spoke it poorly. They left the ruling of their country mostly to their ministers. But King George III was born in England and spoke the language of his subjects. His people were delighted when he ascended the throne.

George III helped restore powers to the monarchy and, with the 1763 Treaty of Paris, brought a successful end to the

King George III of England, whose policies regarding the American colonists led to revolution, from a circa 1900 engraving, artist unknown

Seven Years' War with France. England emerged as the most powerful nation in Europe.

King George III had failures, too. During his more than fifty-year reign, the government's spending would increase seven-fold, the nation's debt would get out of hand, and England would lose the greatest holding in its empire, the thirteen American colonies. George III also had a personal battle with what was thought to be mental illness but may have been porphyria, a genetic condition that can cause depression, hallucination, anxiety, and physical pain. In 1811, because of his illness, Parliament put his son, George IV, on the throne of England. George III died nine years later in 1820.

With the February 1763 signing of the Treaty of Paris, England controlled all of French Canada and most of the Mississippi Valley. People in the American colonies hoped this would bring them peace, but it didn't. The French had rented land from American Indians for their forts. These became British forts, but the British refused to pay the land owners.

Chief Pontiac told leaders of western tribes that the Great Spirit wanted them to declare war against the British. "I am the Lord of life. It is I who made all men," Chief Pontiac said in the name of the Great Spirit. "If you suffer the Englishmen to dwell in your midst, their diseases, their poisons, shall destroy you utterly and you shall die."

In June 1763, "Pontiac's War" broke out. The Delaware, Shawnee, Hurons, Mingos, and other American Indian tribes attacked British forts from Detroit through New

Pontiac, chief of the Ottawas and ally of the French, from a circa 1900 engraving, artist unknown

York, Pennsylvania, Maryland, and Virginia. Farmhouses were set on fire and settlers were murdered. By the fall, some two thousand soldiers, traders, and settlers had been killed.

The British government needed to protect its colonies against such attacks and to be ready in case the French returned. In October 1763 the king's cabinet ordered British warships to America. The cabinet also ordered a line drawn from north to south. The land to the east of the line would be reserved for white settlers, while the land to the west would be for fur traders and American Indians. Ten thousand British soldiers would keep the peace, but at a cost of £250,000 to £300,000 a year.

Also, in 1763 the British navy was charged to enforce the long-standing Navigation Act, which limited the important American market to only English goods. Navy ships cruised along the coast and seized anything that did not come from England. This so enraged the American colonists that they began a boycott, a hardship on the mother country, but a hardship on America, too. Clothes and cloth had made up much of what was purchased from England. Now colonists had to get busy spinning, weaving, and sewing to replace what they refused to buy.

George Grenville, who in 1764 as British first lord of the treasury proposed the infamous Stamp Act, from a circa 1900 engraving, artist unknown

In 1764 the already poor relations between England and its colonies worsened. With the Empire reeling from higher military costs, Prime Minister George Grenville decided the American people should pay for their own defense. In April Parliament passed the Revenue Act, also called the Sugar Act, which taxed coffee, tea, sugar, molasses, rum, wine, and tobacco. This infuriated the colonists even more.

The next year, in March 1765, while King George III was undergoing treatment for his illness—his butler whipped him daily in an attempt to beat the devils out of him—Parliament passed another new tax on the American colonies, the Stamp Act. Some fifty items, including newspapers, marriage licenses, wills, mortgages, playing cards, and pamphlets, had to be printed on specially stamped paper. The stamp was proof a tax had been paid.

The colonists hated this tax. On May 29, in the Virginia House of Burgesses, George Washington listened as Patrick Henry spoke out against it. "Caesar had his Brutus," Henry said of the Roman ruler and the man who killed him, "Charles the First had his Cromwell," he said of the English king who was beheaded by his own people, "and George the Third may profit from their example."

"Treason!" the Speaker called out.

"If this be treason," Henry answered, "make the most of it!"

Henry proposed seven resolutions and the House passed four of them,

A tax stamp printed in embossed letters on coarse blue paper with a narrow strip of tin foil just beneath the right side of the crown, from a circa 1875 engraving by Benson J. Lossing

Patrick Henry in the Virginia House of Burgesses speaks out against the Stamp Act, from a circa 1875 engraving by Benson J. Lossing.

declaring that King George III and his Parliament had no right to pass laws for the American colonies.

Washington did not take part in the stormy debate over Patrick Henry's resolutions. He displayed a soldier's disposition, calm in times of crisis, but he knew this was a turning point. "The eyes of our people already begin to be opened," he wrote. And it appeared they were. Colonists formed associations both to boycott British goods and to support the boycott. People in Philadelphia refused to eat lamb stew. By not killing the sheep, they could use their wool and make yarn to replace English cloth. In Boston people broke with custom and stopped wearing gloves at funerals, since gloves came from England.

"Taxation without representation is tyranny," James Otis of Boston wrote in his pamphlet, *The Rights of the British Colonies Asserted*. Soon, protests erupted throughout the colonies. Groups calling themselves the Sons of Liberty were formed.

Despite these protests, stamps continued to be printed in England and sent to agents in the colonies, who were to sell them.

In Boston, on August 14, 1765, protesters smashed the windows of stamp agent Andrew Oliver's house, broke in and drank his wine, destroyed the building meant to be his stamp office, and hung Oliver in effigy. The next day Oliver resigned. Several days later protesters destroyed Lieutenant Governor Hutchinson's home. In Connecticut a mob on horseback chased the stamp agent from his house. He also resigned. "It's not worth dying for," he said.

In October delegates from nine colonies attended a Stamp Act Congress in New York. They denounced the tax and wrote a Declaration of Rights and Grievances, which declared that only the governments of the colonies themselves could tax them. In cities throughout the colonies, more citizens and merchants pledged to boycott English goods until the taxes were repealed.

The day the Stamp Act was to become law, November 1, 1765, was declared a day of fasting and mourning. Bells tolled. Flags were set at half-mast. Courts were closed. Business stopped. Ships didn't sail. There were funeral processions in the streets and thick black lines bordered the columns of newspapers.

Finally, in response to all the protests, in March 1766, Parliament repealed the tax.

The colonists were delighted. In New York City a statue of King George III was set in Bowling Green and one of William Pitt, a member of Parliament who spoke against the tax, was set on Wall Street.

Washington was also pleased. "The repeal of the Stamp Act," he wrote in a letter, "ought much to be rejoiced at; for had the Parliament of Great Britain resolved upon enforcing it, the consequences, I conceive, would have been more direful than is generally apprehended, both to the mother country and her colonies."

Still, it wasn't a complete victory. Parliament added a clause to its repeal of the Stamp Act that declared it had "the sole and exclusive right of imposing duties and taxes" in the colonies. A year later Parliament asserted that right. In June 1767 it passed the Townshend Acts, new taxes on glass, lead, paper, paint, and tea.

"Our lordly masters in Great Britain," Washington wrote to his neighbor George Mason, "will be satisfied with nothing less than the deprivation of American freedom."

"I entirely agree with you," Mason replied. "Our all is at stake."

Washington met with other members of the House of Burgesses in Williamsburg, at the Raleigh Tavern, and proposed a broader boycott of goods from England, this time

Washington's Virginia neighbor, Patriot, and statesman George Mason, who drafted Virginia's Declaration of Rights and state constitution, from a circa 1898 illustration, artist unknown

Lord Frederick North, English prime minister from 1770–1782, from a reprint of a circa 1870 engraving by Lossing and Barritt, based on a drawing by Benson J. Lossing

including hats, shoes, boots, clocks, axes, beef, beer, wines, pickles, sugar, and cloth. Also included in the boycott was a pledge not to buy slaves brought to the colonies after November first. Washington collected signatures from his neighbors to honor the boycott.

By 1770 the boycott had cost England millions of British pounds in sales, while the tax had brought in only about twenty thousand pounds in revenue. On March 5, 1770, the new prime minister, Lord Frederick North, called for a repeal of the Townshend Acts. All but the tax on tea was dropped.

Yet it wasn't just the tax that American colonists resented. The presence of large numbers of British soldiers on their soil further inflamed them. On the same day the Townshend Acts were repealed, a rowdy group of colonists crowded around a few British soldiers on King Street in Boston. They called the soldiers names and threw snow and chunks of ice. Then Edward Garrick, a young barber, accused one soldier of hitting him with a gun.

"Attack the main guard!" Crispus Attucks shouted to the colonists. "Shoot if you dare!" he called to the soldiers. They did shoot, killing five colonists, including Attucks, in what became known as the Boston Massacre.

Other confrontations between the colonists and the British took place.

The Boston Massacre, March 5, 1770, from a circa 1890 illustration by Howard Pyle

In June 1772, near Providence, Rhode Island, colonists led by Abraham Whipple dressed as American Indians, boarded the British ship *Gaspee,* and set it on fire.

In late November 1773 three ships loaded with tea, which still required the hated tax to be paid, arrived in Boston. Massachusetts colonists told Thomas Hutchinson, their governor, to send the ships and their tea back to England. He refused and plans were set to unload the tea on Friday, December 17.

That Thursday, people from Boston and nearby towns walked to Griffin's Wharf, looked at the three ships, and then gathered at the Old South Meeting House to debate what should be done. Some of their leaders suggested that they not

Abraham Whipple, commander of the Patriots who in 1772 burned the Gaspee; *later he was a commodore in the Continental navy, from a circa 1900 engraving, artist unknown*

The burning of the Gaspee, *an armed British ship, June 9, 1772, from a circa 1900 engraving, artist unknown. A large reward was offered for the name of the leader of the attack, but no one betrayed Captain Abraham Whipple.*

allow the chests of tea to be unloaded. "Let us look to the end," Josiah Quincy said. "Let us weigh and consider before we advance to those measures which must bring on the most and terrific struggle the country ever saw."

Quincy's warning was prophetic, for the measures taken that day led to the Revolution.

After the meeting, a committee visited Governor Hutchinson and requested that he stop the tea from being unloaded. The governor asked them to return at five o'clock for a definite answer, but when they returned, he was gone. When the people waiting back at the meetinghouse heard this, they cried out, "Let every man do his duty and be true to his country."

"It was now evening, and I immediately dressed myself in the costume of an Indian, equipped with a small hatchet," George Hewes remembered many years later. "After having painted my face with coal dust in the shop of a blacksmith, I repaired to Griffin's Wharf, where the ships lay that contained the tea." Hewes and others marched to the wharf, where they divided into three parties. "The commander of the division to which I belonged, as soon as we were on board the ship, appointed me boatswain, and ordered me to go to the captain and demand of him the keys to the hatches and a dozen candles. I made the demand accordingly, and the captain promptly replied, and delivered the articles; but requested me at the same time to do no damage to the ship or rigging. We were then ordered by our commander to open the hatches and take out all the chests of tea and throw them overboard, and we immediately proceeded to execute his orders." Together the three groups dumped 342 chests of tea into the harbor in what became known as the Boston Tea Party.

Many Americans, even future leaders of the Revolution, were shocked by what had happened in Boston Harbor. Benjamin Franklin called it "an Act of violent Injustice on our part." Gouverneur Morris of New York, later

The December 16, 1773, Boston Tea Party, during which about fifty Patriots boarded three British ships, the Dartmouth, *the* Beaver, *and the* Eleanor; *broke 342 chests of tea; and threw them into the harbor, from a reprint of a circa 1870 engraving by Lossing and Barritt, based on a drawing by Benson J. Lossing*

a member of the Second Continental Congress, wrote how these Patriots "grow dangerous to the gentry and how to keep them down is the question." Others felt nothing was safe.

Members of Parliament were angry. One declared, "Boston ought to be knocked about their ears and destroyed." In retaliation, Parliament passed a series of bills known in the colonies as the Intolerable Acts. The first, the Boston Port Bill, which was signed in March 1774, closed Boston Harbor until the people there paid for the tea. Later bills outlawed town meetings and forced colonists to house British soldiers.

On May 5 in Williamsburg, the House of Burgesses met to discuss the Boston Port Bill. "We cooked up a resolution," Thomas Jefferson wrote, "for appointing the 1st day of June, on which the port-bill was to commence, for a day of fasting, humiliation, and prayer, to implore Heaven to avert us the evils of civil war."

Lord Dunmore, the royal governor of Virginia, thought the resolution was an insult to King George III. To stop any further resolutions, on Wednesday, May 25, Lord Dunmore dissolved Virginia's assembly.

At the time, Washington clearly didn't sense that the colonies were headed toward revolution. On the night of the twenty-fifth, just after Dunmore had dissolved the House of Burgesses, Washington dined with him. The next morning they had breakfast together. Two nights later Washington went to a ball given by the House of Burgesses in honor of Lady Dunmore.

Two days after the ball, Washington attended a protest meeting in Raleigh Tavern. The social niceties with the king's chief representative in Virginia, followed by this meeting, reflected the mixed feelings of Washington and others toward England.

In 1774, when Governor Dunmore dissolved Virginia's House of Burgesses, its members met here, in the Apollo Room of Williamsburg's Raleigh Tavern, from a reprint of a circa 1870 engraving by Lossing and Barritt, based on a drawing by Benson J. Lossing.

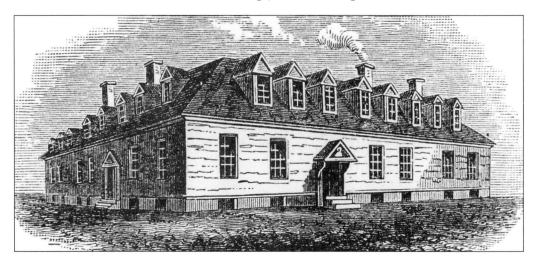

On Sunday, May 29, Washington and other members of the House of Burgesses who were still in Williamsburg met and called the port bill dangerous, stating that an attack on the liberty of one colony was an attack on them all. They proposed that representatives from each colony meet annually in a General Congress to discuss their rights, and agreed to expand the boycott of British goods and to meet again in August.

Many people in Virginia owed large amounts of money to England. Some members of the House of Burgesses called for a boycott on repaying those debts, but Washington had a strong sense of right and wrong and he protested, "Whilst we are accusing others of injustice," he wrote a few weeks later, "we should be just ourselves."

George Washington was still in Williamsburg on June 1, the day the port of Boston was to be closed. The day began with church bells ringing. "Went to church," Washington noted in his diary, "and fasted all day." People throughout Virginia observed the fast. "The effect of the day," Thomas Jefferson later said, "was like a shock of electricity, arousing every man."

At noon that day, General Thomas Gage, now the governor of Massachusetts, closed Boston Harbor and all business there stopped. Gage was sure this show of strength would tame the rebels. "The Americans," he told the king, "will be lions only as long as the English are lambs."

In July Washington chaired a meeting in Fairfax County to discuss the Intolerable Acts. His neighbors recommended a petition be sent to King George III to assert their rights but still declare their loyalty to the king, his family, and his government.

Washington supported the petition, but he didn't think it would do much good. His hope was that the boycott of

Major General Thomas Gage, British military leader and governor of Massachusetts, from a circa 1900 engraving, artist unknown

Peyton Randolph of Virginia, president of the First Continental Congress, from a circa 1900 engraving, artist unknown

English goods would get the attention of Parliament. "There is no relief for us but in their distress," he wrote in a letter. "I think—at least I hope—that there is public virtue enough left among us to deny ourselves everything but the bare necessaries of life to accomplish this end."

On August 1 there was a meeting in Williamsburg of representatives from all parts of Virginia. Washington spoke there and at last gave a hint that he knew what was in store for the American people. "I will raise a thousand men," he said, "subsist them at my own expense, and march them to the relief of Boston." At that meeting Peyton Randolph, Richard Henry Lee, Patrick Henry, Richard Bland, Edmund Pendleton, Benjamin Harrison, and George Washington were chosen to represent Virginia at the First Continental Congress to talk about Great Britain and the rights of Americans.

12. "I Do Not Think Myself Equal to the Command"

More than fifty delegates came to the First Continental Congress in Philadelphia in September 1774, representing twelve of the American colonies, all but Georgia. "Here is a diversity of religions, educations, manners, interests," John Adams wrote in his diary, "such as it would seem impossible to unite in one plan of conduct." But their dispute with England brought them together, moving Patrick Henry to declare, "The distinctions between New Englanders and Virginians are no more. I am not a Virginian, but an American."

The Congress opened with a reading from

Carpenter's Hall, Philadelphia, where the First and Second Continental Congresses met, from a circa 1898 engraving, artist unknown

the thirty-fifth Psalm. "Strive, O Lord with those who strive against me. Fight with those who fight against me. . . . Rise and help me." After much discussion, the delegates voted to cease all trade with England, but they stopped short of declaring independence. The Congress agreed to meet again in May 1775.

Washington didn't participate in the public debate, but he spoke privately with other members of the Congress, and impressed them. "If you speak of solid information and sound judgement," Patrick Henry said, "Colonel Washington is unquestionably the greatest man on the floor."

While he was in Philadelphia for the Congress, Washington did some shopping. He bought a satchel for Martha, a cloak and riding chair for his mother, and a chain for his sword. He also went to various teas and dinners—the grandest was one given for the delegates by the city of Philadelphia at the State House. Among the thirty-six toasts made were tributes to King George III; his queen, Charlotte Sophia; and their eldest son, the Prince of Wales. In 1774 there were frenzied, angry speeches against English policies, but many people in America still loved their king.

On Washington's way home, he stopped in Williamsburg, where he received a letter from a fellow Virginian. Captain Robert Mackenzie had served with him in the French and Indian War and now served in Boston, under General Gage. He wrote against the call for independence. George Washington's response to his letter indicates the struggle many Americans had in breaking with their Mother Country.

"That the people of Massachusetts are rebellious, setting up for Independency, and what not, give me leave, my good friend, to tell you that you are abused." Despite his earlier declaration, "I would raise a thousand men," it seems that now he did not seek to break with England and was sure no one else did either. "I am well satisfied, that no such thing is desired by any thinking man in all North America."

Perhaps Washington was right, that at the time the colonists did not seek independence, or perhaps he misread the intensity of the changing mood of his countrymen. He attended the second Virginia Convention. On March 23, Patrick Henry addressed the assembly.

"For my own part," Patrick Henry said, "I consider it as nothing less than a question of freedom or slavery." He spoke of the many soldiers sent from England to the colonies. "Has Great Britain any enemy in this quarter of the world to call for this accumulation of navies and armies? No, sir, she has none. They are meant for us; they can be meant for no other. They are sent over to bind and rivet upon us those chains which the British ministry have been so long forging. . . . We have done everything that could be done to avert the storm which is now coming on. We have petitioned; we have remonstrated; we have supplicated. . . . There is no longer room for hope. . . . We must fight! . . . I know not what course others may take; but as for me, give me liberty or give me death!"

Washington saw that the tide was turning and joined a committee to prepare to defend the colonies. If war was unavoidable, even inevitable, he would be sure the colonies were ready for it. His brother John Augustine was already training a troop of volunteers. "I shall cheerfully accept the honor of commanding it," George Washington wrote his brother, "if needful."

It would soon be needful.

General Gage had secret orders from Britain to show some force. He sent troops to Concord, Massachusetts, where the colonists had stored guns and ammunition. The troops were planning to take or destroy the entire cache. About seven hundred British soldiers led by Lieutenant Colonel Francis Smith left Boston and marched northwest, to Concord. American Patriots Paul Revere, William Dawes, and Samuel Prescott rode ahead to warn the colonists.

The battle at Lexington, Massachusetts,
April 19, 1775, the first battle of the Revolutionary
War, from a circa 1890 illustration
by Howard Pyle

Then, on April 19, 1775, in Lexington, five miles east of Concord, British red-coated troops came upon some seventy armed colonists, among them John Robbins. "I being in the front rank," Robbins later reported, "there suddenly appeared a number of the King's troops, about a thousand, as I thought, at the distance of about sixty or seventy yards from us, buzzing, and on a quick pace toward us, with three officers in their front on horseback, and on full gallop toward us, the foremost of which cried, 'Throw down your arms, ye villains, ye rebels.'"

It's not certain who fired the first shot, the British or the Americans. According to Robbins, it was the British.

British soldiers on North Bridge, on their way from Lexington to Concord, fire at Patriot soldiers, from a circa 1900 engraving, artist unknown.

"The foremost of the three officers," Robbins reported, "ordered his men to, 'Fire, by God fire,' at which moment we received a heavy and close fire from them, at which instant being wounded, I fell, and several of our men were shot dead."

John Parker, the American commander, reported the next month in the *Pennsylvania Gazette* that when he saw the Redcoats approach, "I immediately ordered our militia to disperse, and not to fire; immediately said troops made their appearance and rushed furiously, fired upon us and killed eight of our party, without receiving any provocation therefore from us."

That first shot has been called "the shot heard round the world." It was the beginning of the American Revolution.

The British troops marched on to Concord, where they were met by American Patriot soldiers ready to fight. At North Bridge the Patriots fired and killed three of the British. The Redcoats retreated, but the Patriots were not done. Hundreds hid behind rocks, trees, and bushes and fired at the

The battleground at Concord, Massachusetts, from a circa 1910 engraving, based on an earlier painting by Alonzo Chappel

British. In the fighting, almost three hundred Redcoats and about ninety colonists were killed or wounded.

The next month, the delegates gathered in Philadelphia for the Second Continental Congress. It was now too late to talk of petitions and boycotts—it was time to talk of war. "Americans will fight for their liberty and property," Washington wrote to a friend in England. But his experience in battle had taught him the realities of war. "Unhappy it is," he wrote, "that a brother's sword has been sheathed in a brother's breast, and that once happy and peaceful plains of America are either to be drenched in blood, or inhabited by slaves. Sad alternative!"

The Congress opened on May 10, 1775. Earlier that day, Ethan Allen, Benedict Arnold, and a troop of Allen's Green Mountain Boys had stormed New York's Fort Ticonderoga. Ethan Allen had climbed the outer staircase of the fort and banged the handle of his sword on the door of the British commander, who came out with his uniform shirt on, but not his pants. His terrified wife stood behind him.

Ethan Allen demanding the surrender of Fort Ticonderoga, from a circa 1910 engraving by T. Phillibrown, based on an earlier painting by Alonzo Chappel

"I demand an instant surrender!" Allen said and waved his sword over the head of the frightened commander.

The commander complied.

Fort Ticonderoga was at the southern end of Lake Champlain, an important position between the American colonies and Canada. Along with the fort came all its weapons, among them more than one hundred cannons, two mortars, and lots of ammunition. Two days later Patriots took the fortress at nearby Crown Point.

At the Congress, New England delegates, led by Sam and John Adams, wanted a declaration of independence. Others, led by John Dickinson of Pennsylvania, later a representative of Delaware, still hoped they could reach a peaceful agreement with England. But they all agreed that the colonies had to prepare to defend themselves, to raise money for guns and ammunition, and to establish a united army.

Washington knew the colonies must fight. He made his opinion known in his own quiet way, by sitting in the Congress dressed in his Virginia militia blue-and-beige uniform.

John Adams of Massachusetts proposed that the troops already in place in Boston be made the beginnings of the Continental army and asked Congress to name a commander in chief.

General Artemas Ward commanded the New England troops outside Boston and was currently holding off British forces. Since the Continental army was at the time an all–New England army, it made sense to some to put Ward in charge of it. John Hancock of Massachusetts was also interested in the post. But John Adams felt that the southern colonies would only join the fight if a southern general were to lead it. Some wanted Colonel William Byrd, who followed Washington as commander of the Virginia militia. Others wanted Colonel Andrew Lewis, who, in October 1774, led victorious Virginia troops in a fierce battle against American Indians. Another candidate was the boastful, quarrelsome General Charles Lee—the Mohawks named him Ounewaterika, "Boiling Water." But Lee had been born in England.

Major General Charles Lee of the Continental army, a difficult man and overrated soldier whose jealousy of Washington caused him to be untrustworthy, from a reprint of a wood engraving by Lossing and Barritt, based on a drawing by Benson J. Lossing, circa 1870

"I had but one gentleman in my mind for that important command," Adams later wrote, "and that was a gentleman from Virginia." He meant George Washington.

Washington sat near the door, but when he heard himself being discussed, he left the room. Some delegates were against naming him commander in chief, among them fellow Virginian, Edmund Pendleton. The Congress decided that whoever was chosen, the vote should be unanimous and it was. On Thursday,

June 15, 1775, Thomas Johnson of Maryland nominated Washington for the post. The ballots were cast, every one for Washington.

The next day, Washington stood before the Congress. He did not boast that he would defeat the British. Instead he humbly said, "Though I am truly sensible of the high honor done me, in this appointment, yet I feel great distress. My abilities and military experience may not be equal to the extensive and important trust." He accepted the post, "But, lest some unlucky event should happen," he said, "I beg it should be remembered by every gentleman in the room, that I do this day declare, with the utmost sincerity, I do not think myself equal to the command I am honored with."

"There is something charming to me in the conduct of Washington," John Adams wrote to his wife, Abigail, "leaving his delicious retirement, his family and friends, sacrificing his ease, and hazarding all in the cause of his country!"

As commander in chief, Washington would do more than plan for battle—he would be responsible for recruiting soldiers and acquiring weapons and supplies. In the end, Washington would deserve much credit for not only defeating the British, but also for building the Continental army.

Washington refused to be paid. "I do not wish to make any profit from it," he said, only that he be reimbursed for his expenses.

On June 18, Washington wrote to his wife. "I am now set down to write you on a subject which fills me with inexpressible concern. . . . It has been determined in Congress that the whole army raised for the defense of the American cause shall be put under my care. . . . You may believe me, my dear Patsy, when I assure you, in the most solemn manner, that, so far as seeking this appointment, I have used every endeavor in my power to avoid it."

The next day he wrote to his stepson, Jacky. "My greatest concern upon this occasion is the thought of leaving your mother. . . . I therefore hope, expect, and indeed have no doubt, of your using every means in your power to keep up her spirits."

Women were not expected to fight the British, but they would still play important roles in winning the Revolution. During the boycotts that preceded the war, they wove cloth to replace English fabric, which Patriots refused to import. Once war broke out, with the men away, women took charge of running the farms and managing the family finances. Often, they also had to house troops: Americans, British, and German Hessian soldiers hired to help the Redcoats. A few women, including Deborah Sampson of Massachusetts and Mary Hayes of New Jersey, even took up arms and fought alongside the men.

On June 23 Washington rode out of Philadelphia and north to Boston. Soon after he got on his way, news came to him of the battle of Bunker Hill. British ships had fired

Citizens of Boston watch the battle of Bunker Hill from the safety of their rooftops, June 1775, from a circa 1890 illustration by Howard Pyle.

Washington, on his way to take command of the Continental army, learns of the battle of Bunker Hill, from a circa 1895 engraving, artist unknown.

their big guns at Patriots, and British troops made three assaults on the hill. Since the American troops were short of ammunition, General Israel Putnam told his men not to fire at the enemy "until you see the whites of their eyes." British troops stormed the hill twice, met with a hail of gunfire, and retreated. By the third assault, the Patriots had run out of ammunition and retreated.

The British won the battle, but at great cost. More than one thousand of their troops, including ninety-two officers, were killed or wounded, against some four hundred American soldiers, making it one of the bloodiest battles of the Revolution.

Perhaps the greatest loss to the British, in Boston and at Concord, was the feeling that they could easily defeat the Americans. The Patriots had no use for drills and military formations. Fighting to them simply meant shooting the enemy. And the Americans were great marksmen.

"Did the militia fight?" Washington asked when he heard of the battle. He was told they did and was reported to have replied, "Then the liberties of the country are safe."

Excerpts from

Virginia Gazette

With the Freshest Advices Foreign and Domestic

July 8, 1775

Philadelphia,

The Hon. Congress have appointed George Washington, Esq; of Virginia, Generalissimo of the American forces

Yesterday the three battalions, with artillery, light horse, and ranges of this city and liberties, were reviewed by General Washington, attended by the Honourable the members of the Congress.

We hear the schooner Bonaventure, Capt. Waterman, from this port for Nantucket, is taken by an armed ministerial plunderer, and carried to Boston.

Williamsburg,

On the 18th printed hand-bills were published at Philadelphia, giving an account of a late engagement near Boston. We have not been able to procure a copy, but we have good authority to assure the public, that the following are the most material circumstances mentioned in the hand-bill:

"Three thousand regulars landed at Charlestown, set that place on fire, and immediately marched towards Bunker's hill. The provincial army soon being apprized of their approach, 1400 men posted themselves at the corner of a fence, upon the right or left of which the King's troops were obliged to pass, and when they came within 15 rods, gave two brisk fires, which did wonderful execution. The provincials were immediately reinforced with 400 men, and under command of General Putnam, pursued the enemy, who retreated to an adjacent lane, where a very bloody engagement ensued, and was continuing when the express came away. It was imagined that the regulars lost 800 men at the fence, and in the whole 1000, besides about 60 officers. Only 160 of the provincials were killed."

Extract of a letter from LONDON, dated April 25, 1775.

"A steady friend to America called upon me this afternoon to acquaint me with the following intelligence, communicated to him by ———— this day, which you may rely upon as fact.

"———— said, that Administration on Friday received advices from General Gage to the 18th of March, wherein he acknowledges the receipt of the King's orders to apprehend Messrs. Cushing, Adams, Hancock, &c. and send them over to England to be tried; but that the second orders, which were to hang them in Boston, he said the General had not received. The General expressed his fears on the occasion and in hopes of their being reversed, he should delay the execution a while longer; because he thought, if the orders were fulfilled, come to an engagement—the event of which, he had every reason to apprehend would be fatal to himself and the King's troops, as the Massachusetts Government had at least 15,000 men ready trained for the onset, and besides, had every public and private road occupied by the militia, so as to prevent his marching into the country, and which were at the same time ready to facilitate any attempts against the army; in which unwelcome situation he earnestly withheld for a reinforcement, if that disagreeable order must be effected.

Anecdote of the late Sir JOHN RUSHOUT.

AS Sir John was traveling once in his carriage from London to his seat at Northwich in Gloucestershire (his servant loitering behind) he was attacked and robbed by a single highwayman; when the servant came up, Sir John reprimanded him for his absence, and told him he had been robbed. The servant impatiently desired to know the road the robber took, adding, that he would instantly pursue and take him. Sir John told him, and away the man galloped; and on his return in a short time, Sir John asked him if he had taken the highwayman? "No, Sir John (says the servant) but I overtook him, and he robbed me too," which made Sir John very merry, as well then as often afterwards, when he recounted the adventure to his friends.

13. "The Ragged Fellows Are the Boys for Fighting"

The British faced problems fighting in America. Three thousand miles of ocean separated England from the colonies. Sailing ships had to be sent loaded with soldiers, horses, large and small guns, ammunition, and other supplies. In good weather the trip took five weeks. In bad weather it often took ten weeks or more.

Many British soldiers died of disease on their way across the Atlantic. Storms rocked the ships and pirates robbed them. And when they reached the colonies, the Redcoats had to fight along a seacoast of more than one thousand miles, with settlements six hundred miles deep, across plenty of hills, mountains, and forest with few decent roads. In addition, the British army was also facing revolt in Ireland, French forces in India, and battles in the West Indies.

On the American front, the British commander, General William Howe, knew that American troops were short of ammunition. July 1775 in Boston would have been a good time and place for the British to attack. But Howe didn't. Perhaps he expected a quick diplomatic settlement between Parliament and the American colonies.

On July 2, 1775, General George Washington arrived in Cambridge, Massachusetts. The next day he took command of the Continental army, a ragtag bunch with no real sense of order. Its soldiers were farmers, woodsmen, and clerks, sure to be around when provisions were given out, and likely to be gone when it was time to drill. Their uniforms were mostly homemade, cheap round hats and long shirts, belted at the waist and left hanging. Their bunks varied from soldier to soldier, some made of wood and canvas, others of stone. And there was a foul odor in the camp. It was clear the men hadn't dug latrines. Desertion from the Continental army was widespread. Some men would sign up merely to get the enlistment bonus and then desert, only to enlist for a bonus somewhere else. Hundreds would leave just before battle. To complicate Washington's job even more, throughout the Revolu-

General William Howe, commander of British forces in America from May 1777–May 1778 and credited with Redcoat victories at the battles of Bunker Hill, Brandywine Creek, and New York City, from a circa 1910 engraving, artist unknown

Washington in Cambridge, Massachusetts, takes command of the Continental army on July 3, 1775, from a circa 1895 engraving, artist unknown.

tion an estimated one third of the American population remained loyal to the king.

When Washington arrived, discipline was loose, with soldiers not trained to obey orders and officers not prepared to command. Many of the officers were elected to their posts by their own troops and felt that they answered to them. Washington found some officers cutting their men's hair and shining their shoes. Beyond the failings of the troops, there were shortages of guns, ammunition, and supplies.

"There is a great overturning in the camp," Reverend William Emerson, a chaplain in the Continental army wrote a few days after Washington arrived. "New lords, new laws . . . The strictest government is taking place, and great distinction is made between officers and soldiers."

General Braddock had set an example for Washington on proper discipline and punishment, but the men under his command had been very different from Washington's Continental army. Many of Braddock's men were rogues—Washington's were mostly farmers. On July 4, his second day in command, Washington ordered that all soldiers and officers attend religious services, "to implore the blessings of heaven." There would be no cursing, swearing, or drunkenness. He later ordered there be no card playing. All officers were to keep their men neat and clean, be sure that no more than two men at a time from any company be allowed out of camp, that no soldier be allowed to go fishing at Fresh water pond, "as there may be danger of introducing the small pox into the army." He demanded that there be no wasteful firing of guns.

General Washington ordered "the Necessarys [privies] be filled up once a Week, and new ones dug," that the camp be swept daily, and the leftovers from animals killed for meat be buried. "Next to Cleanliness, nothing is more conducive to a Soldier's health." He also ordered that none of his men bathe near the bridge in Cambridge, "where it has been observed and complained of, that many Men, lost to all sense of decency and common modesty, are running about naked upon the Bridge, whilst Passengers, and even Ladies of the first fashion in the neighborhood, are passing over it."

Soon after Washington took command, he ordered that in time of battle officers show "an Example of Bravery and Courage to their men . . . do their duty in the day of Battle, as brave and good Officers." Those who do "shall be honor'd with every mark of distinction and regard." Those who don't "shall be held up as an infamous Coward and punish'd as such."

Later that winter he ordered that his regular soldiers be brave in battle. "It may not be amiss to the troops to know, that if any man in action shall presume to skulk, hide himself, or retreat from the enemy without the orders of his commanding officer, he will be instantly shot down as an example of cowardice."

After Washington reviewed his new troops and conditions of the camp, he went up the hill and looked through a spyglass across the bay at more than ten thousand Redcoats. Boston Harbor was crowded with British ships armed with heavy guns.

Through the summer of 1775 and the winter of 1775–1776, the British held Boston, but the Continental army surrounded them.

Washington found this a difficult time. He tried to encourage his troops, to keep their spirits up, but his letters tell how he truly felt. "Search the volumes of history," he wrote in January, "and I much question whether a case similar to ours is to be found, namely, to maintain a post against the power of the British troops for six months together without powder [gunpowder]. . . . The reflection on my situation and that of this army produces me many an unhappy hour when all around me are wrapped in sleep. . . . I have often thought how much happier I should have been, if, instead of accepting the command under such circumstances, I had taken my musket on my shoulder and entered the ranks." What about the outcome of the Revolution? "God in His great goodness will direct," Washington wrote. "I am thankful for his protection to this time."

Washington kept his prayer book with him. He went to church regularly and often stopped to pray in his quarters, both mornings and evenings.

On December 11, 1775, Washington's wife, Martha, arrived in camp—her first trip outside Virginia. "Every person seems to be cheerful and happy here, some days we have a number of cannon shells from Boston and Bunker Hill, but it does not seem to surprise anyone but me," Martha wrote to a friend. "There seems to be a number of fine buildings in Boston, but God knows how long they will stand; they are pulling up all the wharfs for fire wood." While Martha Washington was in Cambridge, she gave dinner parties for the officers and when she entertained, her fingers were ever-busy with her favorite pastime—knitting.

General Israel Putnam in 1775 led Patriot forces in Connecticut and later in New York, from a reprint of a circa 1870 engraving by Benson J. Lossing.

George Washington formed the army into three divisions, one under each of his subordinates, Generals Artemas Ward, Charles Lee, and Israel Putnam. He made Henry Knox, a twenty-five-year-old bookseller from Boston, his chief of artillery. In a bit of irony, or perhaps a reflection of the inexperience of Washington's troops, the chief of artillery had lost two fingers in an earlier tragic accident when his hunting gun exploded.

On January 1, 1776, Washington declared the army prepared. On January 3 he read King George III's speech before Parliament to his men. The king had called on Americans to put down their arms. Washington's men responded by burning copies of the speech.

One night, many of the British soldiers were in a theater that they had set up, watching a comedy on the war entitled *The Blockade of Boston*. In it, a soldier with an oversized wig and a long rusty sword played Washington. Just as the curtain went up a sergeant ran in and announced an attack on the guardhouse. At first, everyone thought this was part of the show, but then General Howe called out, "Officers, to your alarm posts." There were screams. A few of the women in the audience fainted. The war comedy was suddenly not very funny.

Washington had sent one of his favorite officers, Major Thomas Knowlton, with about two hundred men to attack a guardhouse in Charlestown. Knowlton led his men just below the house, set fire to it, and took some prisoners, all without any casualties.

Despite this attack and some other skirmishes, it was a quiet winter. But the battle of words became even more militant.

"Tyranny, like hell, is not easily conquered," Thomas Paine, an English-born writer and philosopher who came to Philadelphia in 1774 and quickly became an American Patriot, wrote in his 1776 pamphlet *Common Sense*. "Yet we have this consolation with us—that the harder the conflict, the more glorious the triumph. . . . I am as confident as I am that God governs the world, that America will never be happy till she gets clear of foreign domination."

Thomas Paine, who was born in England, came to America in 1774 and quickly took up the Patriot cause, from a reprint of a wood engraving by Lossing and Barritt, based on a drawing by Benson J. Lossing, circa 1850.

Washington was so moved by Paine's pamphlet that he had it read to his troops. *Common Sense* was reprinted more than twenty times in the first three months of publication and sold about 120,000 copies.

In mid-February Colonel Knox arrived in camp along with fifty cannons, guns, and ammunition, all captured in May 1775 at Fort Ticonderoga and Crown Point. Ten new regiments of Continental soldiers were sent. The Continental army was ener-

General Henry Knox arrives in Boston in February 1776 with cannons taken from Fort Ticonderoga, from a circa 1910 engraving by Halpin based on an earlier illustration by F. O. C. Darley.

gized by its new troops and material. Now seemed a good time to attack.

On Sunday, March 3, 1776, a British officer stationed in Boston wrote to a friend in London, "For these last six weeks or near two months we have been better amused than could possibly be expected in our situation. We had a theater, we had balls, and there is actually a subscription on foot for a masquerade. England seems to have forgotten us, and we have endeavored to forget ourselves." This officer was "roused to a sense of our situation" by rebel bombing, but didn't seem overly concerned.

The night after that letter was written, two thousand of Washington's men quietly set up fortifications on Dorchester Heights, overlooking the British. The next morning, the sixth anniversary of the Boston Massacre, British General Howe woke up and saw the mighty cannons taken from Ticonderoga pointed at his men.

Howe considered either attacking the Americans or setting fire to Boston, but in the end he did neither. Washington allowed him to leave peacefully. On March 17 more than one hundred ships took Howe, nine thousand of his men, and a thousand Tories (Americans who remained loyal to England) out of Boston.

When Washington's men took over the British positions, they found wooden dummies dressed in Redcoat uniforms left to guard the retreat. They also found an enormous amount of supplies—bushels of wheat, barley, and oats—as well as coal, horses, clothing, bedding, gunpowder, muskets, and more than two hundred cannons.

Washington moved into General Howe's old headquarters, where he met the landlady's granddaughter. Washington put the little girl on his knee, smiled, and asked whom she liked better, his troops or the Redcoats.

"The Redcoats," the little girl answered.

"Ah, my dear," Washington said, "they look better, but they don't fight. The ragged fellows are the boys for fighting."

British forces evacuate Boston, March 17, 1776, from a circa 1910 engraving by J. Godfrey, based on a painting by M. A. Wageman

14. "I Think the Game Will Be Pretty Well Up"

The British ships left Boston and anchored offshore. "What they are doing, the Lord knows," Washington wrote at the time. "My opinion of the matter is, that they want to retrieve their disgrace." Washington thought they were headed for New York.

New York City was a major harbor, large enough to hold Howe's British fleet comfortably. It was also strategically important, given its position between the New England colonies and those farther south.

Washington left five regiments in Boston under the command of General Ward. He sent the rest of his men, sixteen regiments, to New York. On April 4, 1776, he headed there to take command. But on April 13, when he arrived, he was surprised. Howe's troops weren't there. The British had gone to Nova Scotia.

During this time, New York was the site of disputes among its own colonists, some of whom were Patriots, supporters of independence, and others who were Tories, supporters of the British Crown. Some Patriots refused to sit in church with Tories or do any business with them. They burned their carriages, ruined their property, and strung up dolls and hung them in front of their homes. In Kinderhook, New York, young women at a quilting party grabbed a Tory, stripped him to the waist, and covered his chest with molasses and leaves. In nearby Connecticut, some of Washington's troops covered a Tory farmer with hot tar and feathers plucked from his own goose.

Tories did mischief, too. A few stopped a Patriot preacher with some Continental paper money, then made him eat the money and promise never to pray for the Continental Congress "or their doer of dirty work, Mr. Washington."

The Tories had more sinister plans for Washington. "Their design was," according to Dr. William Eustis, a surgeon in the Continental Army, "to have murdered, with trembling heart I say it, the best man on earth: Gen. Washington."

The plot began in March 1776, when the Continental army began a search for "good men, such as they can recommend for their sobriety, honesty, and good behavior" to serve as guards for General Washington. Somehow, Thomas Hickey was chosen. A deserter from the British army, he served the Tories as a counterfeiter of Continental money in a plot to wreck its value. In mid-June 1776, Hickey entered Washington's kitchen, laced a dish of green peas with poison, and gave it to the housekeeper, Miss Fraunces. Hickey had thought she was in on the plot, but she wasn't and quietly warned Washington. The dish was thrown in the yard, and if there was any doubt about Hickey's intentions, it was soon gone—a few unfortunate chickens ate the peas and quickly died.

Thomas Hickey was found guilty of mutiny, sedition, and correspondence with the enemy. On the morning of June 28, 1776, thousands of Washington's troops watched as Hickey was led to a tree near Bowery Lane. "He appeared unaffected and obstinate to the last, except that when the chaplains took him by the hand under the gallows," Dr. Eustis wrote, "a torrent of tears flowed over his face." Hickey wiped the tears away with his hand and "assumed the confident look" as the hangman put his head in the noose.

"The unhappy fate of Thomas Hickey," Washington wrote in an order to his men, "will be a warning to every soldier in the army to avoid those crimes and all others."

The assassination of Washington was just the beginning of the plot. After Washington's death, Hickey and his associates had planned to blow up the Patriots' gunpowder, burn New York City, start a mutiny in the troops, and attack the city from warships anchored nearby. If the Tories had been able to do all they planned, the Revolution might have ended then.

Richard Henry Lee of Virginia, who in June 1776 proposed Congress declare the colonies to be free and independent of England, which led to the formation of the committee to write such a declaration, from a circa 1900 engraving by an unknown artist

On June 7, 1776, at the Continental Congress, Richard Henry Lee of Virginia called for full separation from England. A committee made up of Thomas Jefferson, John Adams, Benjamin Franklin, Roger Sherman, and Robert R. Livingston was formed to write a document declaring the colonies' independence from the king.

Jefferson wrote a draft of the document, which was presented to the Congress on July 2. Two days later, on July 4, 1776, the Congress adopted the Declaration of Independence. Its second paragraph begins, "We hold these truths to be self-evident: that all men are created equal; that they are endowed by their Creator with certain unalienable rights; that among these are life, liberty, and the pursuit of happiness." Following that was justification for the Revolution: "That to secure these rights, governments are instituted among men, driving their just powers from the consent of the governed. That, whenever any form of government becomes destructive of these ends, it is the right of the people to alter or abolish it, and to institute new government."

On July 9 Washington received a copy of the Declaration. He sat on horseback and listened as one of his aides read it to his cheering men. That evening, a crowd pulled down a lead statue of King George III in nearby Bowling Green, the one put up to celebrate the repeal of the stamp tax. The broken statue was sent

Thomas Jefferson of Virginia, who wrote the Declaration of Independence, from a circa 1910 illustration by an unknown artist

Washington, on horseback, listens as the Declaration of Independence is read to his troops, July 9, 1776, from an 1897 illustration by R. F. Zogbaum.

Patriots in New York City's Bowling Green tear down a statue of King George III, July 9, 1776, from a circa 1858 wood engraving, artist unknown.

to Litchfield, Connecticut, and made into forty-two thousand bullets for the revolutionary army.

That same day, General William Howe landed on New York's Staten Island with nine thousand men. Five days later, his brother, Admiral Richard Howe, arrived with a powerful fleet of warships, thousands of Hessians (hired German soldiers), and a message of peace. He sent one of his men with a white flag to request a meeting with Washington.

The British envoy met Washington's friend Joseph Reed and tried to give him a letter from Lord Howe addressed to Mr. Washington. Reed, who objected to his commanding officer being addressed as "Mr." and not "General," replied that there was no such person in the army.

A Hessian soldier, from a circa 1895 drawing, artist unknown

A few days later Howe sent a second envoy, Colonel Patterson, with a letter addressed to "George Washington, Esq, &c. &c." Patterson explained that "&c." implied everything. "Everything and anything," Washington said. Nonetheless, he put aside his pride and met the man.

Howe's peace offer was to grant pardons to the rebels, and "any colony, town, port, or place in the peace" would receive the king's protection. Washington declined the offer. "Those who have committed no wrong need no pardon," Washington said. "We are only defending what we deem our indisputable rights."

The war continued.

At daybreak on Tuesday, August 27, the battle of Long Island began. New Yorkers awoke to the frightening sounds of big British guns. Washington stood on a hill, watching the fighting. "Good God," he said in dismay. "What brave fellows I must lose this day." By the end of that day, more than one thousand of his men were killed, wounded, or taken prisoner.

Luckily for the American troops, a rainstorm kept the British from fighting for the next two days. But with the mighty British forces nearby, Washington kept his men on alert. They stood guard in the pouring rain, some up to their waists in water, and waited. Washington stayed on his horse night and day and rode among his troops. He noticed movement among the enemy's ships. Sure they were about to move up the East River and surround his troops, he led them to safety on the night of August 29, under the cover of darkness and fog. Nine thousand American soldiers, along with their horses, cattle, carts, baggage, and artillery, moved in small boats across the East River, from the Brooklyn shore to Manhattan. Washington left in the last boat. He was able to move all but a few cannons.

The next morning when the British troops were called to battle, their enemy was gone. Washington's troops were safe, but Long Island was lost.

Washington's army had suffered terrible losses—more than two thousand soldiers killed, wounded, or taken prisoner—but it had not been destroyed. Surely Washington had taken a lesson from Braddock, who more than twenty years earlier had commanded his troops to stand their ground and die as heroes. Unlike Braddock, Washington chose to forgo futile valor in the hope of ultimate victory.

Benjamin Rush of Pennsylvania, a respected physician who during the yellow fever epidemic of 1793 is said to have saved six thousand lives, was a signer of the Declaration of Independence and an ardent Patriot, from a circa 1910 engraving, artist unknown.

"We have lost a battle and a small island," Dr. Benjamin Rush, a representative from Pennsylvania, reported to the Continental Congress, "but we have not lost a state."

On September 15 British ships again fired on Washington's troops. When Washington saw his men running from the battle, he became enraged and had one of those attacks of anger Lord Fairfax had written about thirty years earlier. Washington shouted, waved his gun and sword, threw his hat on the ground, and cried out, "Are these the men with whom I am to defend America!"

An aide grabbed the bridle of Washington's horse and pulled him away.

The next day, at the battle of Harlem Heights, on the northern end of Manhattan, the Americans fought British and Scottish troops. The fighting went on for five hours when, at last, the enemy retreated.

But the huge force of enemy troops that had invaded New York in June and July remained. Washington wanted to find out what the British planned next and asked for someone to spy on them. Nathan Hale of Connecticut volunteered.

Hale disguised himself as a Dutch schoolmaster, crossed Long Island Sound, and made his way to the enemy's camp in Brooklyn. He sketched the camp, took notes, and hid the papers in his shoes. On September 21, on his way back, he was caught.

That night, Nathan Hale was taken to Howe's headquarters.

It had been a difficult day for General Howe. Early that morning, in New

York City, a fire started in a shed and spread quickly. The British held the city, but now, without enough buildings left standing to house his men, it was of little use to them. That night, without a trial, the distraught General Howe ordered that Hale be hanged.

The next morning, September 22, 1776, Nathan Hale was taken to the tree from which he would hang. Hale asked for a minister and was told he could not have one. He asked for a Bible, but that was also refused. He asked if he could write letters to his mother, sisters, and to the woman he planned to marry. This was allowed, but after he finished, the hangman took the letters and, while Hale watched, destroyed them. Yet in the end, Hale's last words, which showed real courage and patriotism, got the best of the British. "I regret," Hale said just before he was hanged, "that I have but one

Just before his execution, Nathan Hale told British officers, "I regret that I have but one life to lose for my country," September 22, 1776, from an 1880 illustration by Howard Pyle.

life to lose for my country." His brave declaration was a paraphrase from the work of former member of Parliment Joseph Addison's popular tragic play *Cato,* which was first performed in London in 1713.

Washington waited in vain for Nathan Hale to return. Without any advance knowledge of the enemy's plans, he had little hope of defeating them. He lacked supplies and ammunition, his troops were deserting, and there was a huge fleet of British warships in the Hudson River. Washington retreated from Harlem Heights. Some of his men went to Fort Washington on the New York side of the Hudson, others to Fort Lee on the New Jersey side.

On November 15 and 16, British warships attacked Fort Washington from the water, followed by troops who stormed the fort. It quickly fell. With it, the British took 140 cannons, 12,000 rounds of ammunition, 2,800 guns, 400,000 cartridges, and more than 2,600 prisoners.

Four days later the British took Fort Lee.

The future of the Continental army seemed bleak. With all the battle losses, prisoners taken, and desertions, Washington was left with only about three thousand men. Winter was coming. Washington led what was left of his army across the Delaware River, from Trenton, New Jersey, to Pennsylvania.

On December 18 Washington wrote to his brother John Augustine, "Your imagination can scarce extend to a situation more distressing than mine." Without the enlistment of a new army, "I think the game will be pretty well up."

15. The "Old Fox"

The Continental army was in desperate need of a victory. On December 26, 1776, they achieved it.

On Christmas Day, in the late afternoon, Washington led more than two thousand of his troops across snow-covered ground toward the Delaware River. It was a bitterly cold day, with strong wind, hail, and sleet, yet by four o'clock in the morning the poorly clothed troops, many of them in their bare feet, somehow managed to get across the ice-filled river. Then they marched

An engraving of the famous painting of Washington crossing the Delaware River in December 1776—though surely he did not stand in the boat, his troops were not nearly so well dressed, and the flag shown was not yet the nation's standard—from an engraving based on the 1851 painting by Emanuel Leutze

ahead. Washington rode in front, his men following, some leaving trails of reddened snow from the bloody cuts in their feet. When they neared Trenton, Washington stopped and asked a man cutting wood to direct him to the enemy's camp.

"I don't know," the man answered.

"You need not be afraid," the officer riding with Washington told the man. "This is General Washington."

"God bless and prosper you, sir," the man said and pointed the way.

Some of the Hessian troops who were fighting for the British had celebrated all Christmas Day. When Washington and his men reached them, they were in no condition to defend themselves. More than twenty Hessians were killed and nine hundred were taken prisoner. Two Americans were wounded in the brief fighting. One of them was Lieutenant James Monroe, the future president.

General Charles Cornwallis, whose poor judgment allowed Washington and his troops to escape Trenton, January 2–3, 1777, and who four years later surrendered at Yorktown, Virginia, October 19, 1781, from a circa 1910 illustration based on an earlier English print, artist unknown

The entire battle was over in about forty-five minutes. Afterwards, Washington told one of his officers, "This is a glorious day for our country." That feeling was shared among Patriots throughout America.

With this battle, Washington learned a valuable lesson. While his ragtag army could not hope to overcome the powerful, well-armed British head-on, it could win smaller, well-planned attacks. But he could not stop to savor his victory. He was about to encounter the formidable British general, Lord Charles Cornwallis.

Cornwallis was an aggressive, brave commander. At one time an aide to King George III and a member of Parliament, he had been independent enough to oppose the very policies that sparked the American Revolution. But when the fighting started, he led his regiment across the Atlantic, and in June 1776 participated in the unsuccessful attack on Charleston, South Carolina.

Cornwallis began moving north, leading more than five thousand men toward Trenton. By the night of January 2, 1777, his men were in position, and Washington and his troops were trapped. Cornwallis was urged by General William Erskine, one of his officers, to attack immediately, but Cornwallis would not be rushed. He promised his men that in the morning they would "bag the old fox."

It was a good thing for the Patriots that he waited. An attack that night could have ended the Revolution and, for the time, any chance for American independence.

But Washington, the "old fox," would not be bagged. He kept campfires burning and secretly led his men to Princeton, behind the rear guard of the enemy's troops. At sunrise, the Americans attacked. The British fired back and charged with their bayonets, and the Americans began to retreat. Washington rode among his men and rallied them. In all the dust and gun smoke, Colonel Edward Fitzgerald lost sight of Washington and was sure the general was killed. When Fitzgerald saw him, he rushed to his side. "Thank God," the colonel said, "your Excellency is safe."

"Bring up the troops," Washington replied. "The day is our own!"

Washington at Princeton, New Jersey, where he surprised and defeated the British, from a circa 1895 engraving by an unknown artist, based on an earlier work

Meanwhile, Cornwallis had awakened and found that the "old fox" and his troops were gone. When he heard the faint sounds of cannon fire, the fighting at Princeton, he thought it was a far-off thunderstorm.

"To arms, General!" said General Erskine, who knew what was happening, "Washington has out-generalled us!"

In the battle at Princeton, a total of about four hundred thirty British were killed, wounded, or taken prisoner, against about one hundred Americans lost. By the time Cornwallis arrived, Washington and his men and prisoners were well on their way to Morristown, New Jersey, where they camped for the winter of 1776–1777.

In Morristown, the nearby farms provided food for Washington's troops, and the surrounding hills gave him a good view of the area, in case the British approached. But that winter, it wasn't the British who threatened his men—it was the deadly disease smallpox. The very mention of it in the 1700s was frightening. In Boston in 1721, eight hundred fifty people had died from it, more than 7 percent of the population. Many died quickly, some within three to four days of being stricken.

In 1721, information reached Boston of an inoculation that purposely exposed the patient to a light case of the disease so that he would develop an immunity to it. It was tested with great success. Washington turned a local church into a hospital. Since Washington had already had smallpox many years earlier, he was now immune. He visited his suffering soldiers and insisted that his still healthy troops be inoculated.

Marquis de Lafayette, the French noble who came to America in 1777 and volunteered to serve without pay in the Continental army; because of his enthusiasm and illustrious family, he was immediately given the rank of major general, from a circa 1910 engraving, artist unknown.

Thaddeus Kosciusko of Poland came to the United States in 1776 and soon, as Washington's colonel of engineers, planned the construction of fortresses, from a circa 1910 engraving, artist unknown.

Washington spent the winter organizing his army. It wasn't easy. Each of the colonies wanted its men to be officers. Also, that winter and throughout the war, in what proved to be a mixed blessing, some officers came from across the ocean to volunteer. Many sought the adventure of battle and others boasted of experience and talents they did not have. But there were some foreign volunteers who were a great help to Washington, including the Marquis de Lafayette from France, Thaddeus Kosciusko and Casimir Pulaski from Poland, Johann Kalb (Baron de Kalb) from Bavaria, and Frederich Wilhelm von Steuben from Prussia. Lafayette best expressed the feelings of many of them. "The moment I heard of America, I loved her," he wrote in a letter. "The moment I knew she was fighting for freedom, I burnt with a desire of bleeding for her."

Count Casimir Pulaski of Poland came to the United States in 1777 and fought in the battles of Brandywine Creek, Germantown, and Savannah, where he was mortally wounded, from a circa 1875 engraving by Benson J. Lossing.

During the spring there were a few small battles between American and British forces. Then, in the summer, Howe led his troops toward Philadelphia, and Washington led his men south to defend the city. They met on September 11, 1777, at the battle of Brandywine Creek, Pennsylvania.

The night before the battle, the Reverend Jacob Trent spoke to the American soldiers.

"Soldiers!" he said. "We will march forth to battle. . . . Fight for your homesteads, for your wives and children . . . fight by the

Baron Friedrich Wilhelm von Steuben of Prussia came to the United States in 1777 and joined Washington at Valley Forge, Pennsylvania, from a circa 1910 engraving, artist unknown.

galling memories of British wrong. Walton, I might tell you of your father, butchered in the silence of night, on the plains of Trenton. I might picture his gray hairs dabbled in blood; I might ring his death-shriek in your ears! Shelmire, I might tell you of a butchered mother, the lonely farm house, the night assault, the roof in flames. . . . I might paint all this again in the vivid colors of the terrible reality, if I thought your courage needed such wild excitement."

The Americans fought bravely, but they were greatly outnumbered. About eight hundred British soldiers were killed or wounded. About twelve hundred Americans were killed, wounded, or taken prisoner. The Americans lost Philadelphia.

"Sir," Washington wrote in his report to Congress, "I am sorry to inform you, that, in this day's engagement, we have been obliged to leave the enemy masters of the field." He complained of poor advance information on the enemy's number and position. "Notwithstanding the misfortune of the day," he wrote, "I am happy to find the troops in good spirits."

Winter was coming, but Washington wasn't finished. He planned a surprise attack of the British camp in Germantown, Pennsylvania. On October 4, 1777, he divided his men into four columns and sent each on a different road toward the enemy.

The men under the command of General Anthony Wayne went down the main road. They had some early successes and then trapped a British regiment in a large house. Since the British had no hope of escape, Wayne sent a young lieutenant with a white flag to allow the British the opportunity to surrender without harm. But there was a heavy fog that day, and perhaps the British did not see the flag. Whatever the reason, one of them shot from an upper window and killed the lieutenant. After that, Wayne's men were intent on revenge. Their shots tore apart the door, plaster, and bricks of the house. But whenever they charged, they were cut down by British fire. Meanwhile,

*Major General Anthony Wayne's troops on their way to the battle of Germantown, Pennsylvania,
in a disastrous attack against the British stationed in a large house, from a circa 1910 engraving by G. Ulman,
based on a drawing by C. Schuessele*

two other columns of Washington's men, lost in the fog, fired on each other.
The day had started well but ended terribly. Again, Washington's men suffered heavy losses.

Fortunately there was good news farther north. On September 19, 1777,
and again on October 7, in the first and second battles of
Saratoga, New York, also called the battles of Freeman's
Farm, American troops defeated the British. On October 17
British General John Burgoyne surrendered to American

*British General Sir John Burgoyne in 1777 took command of British forces in Canada, led
troops into New York, and took Ticonderoga, but was defeated at Saratoga, from a circa 1875
engraving by Benson J. Lossing.*

General Horatio Gates and agreed to take his troops back to England. They would not return to fight in the Revolution.

The French, who took a keen interest in the fighting, were impressed by the victories at Saratoga. They saw Washington come back after bitter defeat to fight again and again. Now they were convinced the Revolution could succeed. France recognized the independence of the colonies and, in February 1778, signed the Treaty of Alliance that would help lead to America's ultimate victory.

Burgoyne surrenders at Saratoga on October 17, 1777, from a French engraving, date and artist unknown.

16. "Stand Fast, My Boys!"

Washington led his troops to their 1777–1778 winter quarters at Valley Forge, Pennsylvania, a wooded area about twenty miles from Philadelphia. It was a sad march. Although it was bitterly cold, many of the men had no coats or shoes. There was little waiting for them when they reached Valley Forge, not even a village to house them, so Washington's troops set about building one.

The men were divided into groups of twelve. Each group was to build its own fourteen-by-sixteen-foot log cabin. To keep out the cold, the logs were coated on the inside with clay and mud. "They appear to me like a family of beavers," a visitor wrote of them, "every one busy: some carrying logs, others

Washington at Valley Forge, Pennsylvania, 1777–1778, from a circa 1893 drawing by Allegra Eggleston, based on a painting by Charles Willson Peale

mud, and the rest plastering them together." They built a city of almost one thousand cabins.

The men now had places to live, but little to wear. They borrowed clothes when they had to go outside on guard duty. Even the officers shared their clothes and joked that while General Washington met with many officers, he met with only one uniform.

There was not enough straw for the floors of the cabins, so many men slept on the cold, wet dirt. Those men who had no blankets slept by the fire.

Valley Forge lay in the middle of a fertile agricultural region, rich in wheat and cattle. What was missing were Patriots willing to give or sell what they had put away for the winter to the American army. All Washington could use to pay for food was Continental paper money and the farmers preferred English gold, so instead of selling to their own countrymen they brought their produce to Philadelphia and sold it to the British. One American officer assigned to buy provisions found such resistance that he approached local farmers dressed in a British uniform.

The conditions were dire. General J. M. Varnum wrote that his men had been two days without bread. General Jedediah Huntingdon wrote that his men were ready to fight. "Fighting," he wrote, "was far preferable to starving." Hundreds of the army's horses starved to death. As the winter wore on, there were the remains of so many horses lying about that Washington worried they would spread disease.

By the end of the winter, conditions improved when food arrived from New England. Also, with the coming of spring, the men found fruits and plants to eat.

After the war, there were many stories told and paintings done of Washington praying at Valley Forge. While there is no evidence he did, after the Revolution he spoke of his gratitude "for the interposition of Providence"

Washington in his office at Valley Forge, from a circa 1900 engraving by J. Hellawsh

and "the protection of Almighty God." Surely, for a man who spoke of God's protection, the suffering of his men was a cause for prayer.

On February 10, Martha Washington joined her husband. She was a great comfort to him and his men. At least twice a week she held a reception for the officers. She visited sick soldiers and, every day but Sunday, she knitted socks and patched torn clothes. When she had the cloth for it, she even made shirts for the men.

On February 23, Baron Friedrich Wilhelm von Steuben arrived in camp. A former soldier in the Prussian army, and once on the staff of King Frederick the Great of Prussia, von Steuben was shocked at the condition of the half-naked, hungry troops and their weapons. Von Steuben didn't speak any English, nonetheless, he taught the men discipline and drilled them in the use of their guns until they could load and fire them with their eyes closed. He taught them to obey ten commands, just enough to ensure an able fighting force.

Von Steuben was often impatient with the troops. When the men failed at some drill, he cursed them in French and German and then told his aide to curse them in English. But despite his short temper, the men loved him. His

Washington and von Steuben walk among the troops at Valley Forge, from a circa 1890 illustration by Howard Pyle.

dinner table was always crowded. "Poor fellows," he said of regular soldiers who ate with him, "they have field officers' stomachs, without their pay or rations." He sold his personal items to pay for one dinner, and after the surrender at Yorktown, sold his horse so that he could give a dinner for the defeated British officers.

Good news reached Congress on May 2, 1778. Messengers arrived from France with two treaties, one that recognized the independence of the United States, another that pledged its help in the Revolution. On May 6, at Valley Forge, Washington and his men celebrated. The army was assembled. There were prayers, a parade, and shouts of "Long live the King of France . . . Huzza for the American States . . . Long Live General Washington!"

On June 18 news of the enemy reached Washington. The British, now under the command of General Henry Clinton, who succeeded General William Howe as commander in chief, had crossed the Delaware River and were on their way through New Jersey. They traveled slowly with a supply train twelve miles long. On Saturday, June 27, the Redcoats camped on high ground near Monmouth Courthouse. The next morning Washington sent General Charles Lee to attack the enemy. But Lee delayed—he had no plan. When he thought the British were about to attack, he ordered a retreat.

Washington rode toward the battlefield and met American troops running from battle. He hurried to the front and confronted General Lee. Washington hated profanity, but there are reports that he cursed at Lee "till the leaves shook on the trees."

General Henry Clinton, who succeeded Howe as British commander in chief in 1778, took Charleston and the southern Continental army in 1780, from a circa 1875 engraving by Benson J. Lossing.

Washington rebuking General Charles Lee, who was retreating from the battle of Monmouth, New Jersey, from a circa 1900 engraving, artist unknown

"Go to the rear, you cowardly poltroon!" Washington shouted.

Washington rallied his men. Well trained by von Steuben, they obeyed orders. In just a few minutes they formed lines and held off the British.

All the men suffered on that terribly hot day, reported at over one hundred degrees. More than one hundred British and American troops died from the heat. As Washington directed his troops, the horse he was on collapsed and died. He quickly mounted another and called out to his troops, "Stand fast, my boys!"

According to a popular story, Mary Hayes, nicknamed Molly, was with her husband at the battle of Monmouth. Molly grabbed a pitcher, filled it with water from a nearby spring, and brought it to the thirsty men. "Molly," soldiers called to her. "Molly! Pitcher!"

Mary "Molly Pitcher" Hayes, heroine at the battle of Monmouth, fires a cannon at the British, from a circa 1910 engraving by J. Rogers, based on a painting by D. M. Carter.

Battleground at Monmouth, New Jersey, from a circa 1900 engraving, artist unknown

When Molly's husband collapsed from heatstroke, she gave him a drink, tied a wet rag around his head, dragged him into some shade, and then took over his position loading and firing a cannon. The next day she was still covered with dirt and blood when she met Washington, who made her a sergeant. After that, Mary Hayes, or "Molly Pitcher" as many people remember her, dressed in a soldier's coat and hat and worked as a servant at Washington's headquarters.

The morning after the battle of Monmouth, Washington prepared to continue the fight, but the enemy was gone. Clinton had let his men rest for a few hours and then, at ten o'clock at night, he led them to ships waiting at nearby Sandy Hook, where they set sail for New York.

The Continental army did not defeat the Redcoats at Monmouth, but when it was over, it was the Redcoats who snuck off in the middle of the night, abandoning their hold on Philadelphia, the capital of the new nation. Washington and his rebel army had proven themselves the equal of the well-trained, well-armed enemy.

The battle of Monmouth was the last major battle of the Revolution in the north.

17. "Whom Can We Trust Now?"

In 1778, when the French sided with America, what began as a revolution became a much wider conflict. The next year Spain allied itself with France against England, and in 1780 the Dutch, in a dispute over commerce and shipping, declared war on England. By then, much of the Western world was at war with the British Empire.

In mid-July 1778, French Admiral Charles Hector d'Estaing arrived in Delaware Bay with four thousand French soldiers on eighteen ships. At first d'Estaing planned to capture Newport, Rhode Island, for the Patriots, but bad weather ruined those plans. In November he sailed south to guard the French West Indies from possible British attack.

Washington moved his troops to New York's Westchester County, and they settled in small camps on both sides of the Hudson River. Winter 1778–1779 quarters were in Middlebrook, New Jersey. It was a quiet time, but one of despair for Washington.

Gouverneur Morris of New York, a member of Congress (1777–1780) and Washington's minister to France (1792–1794), from a reprint of a circa 1850 wood engraving by Lossing and Barritt, based on a drawing by Benson J. Lossing

"Can we carry on the war much longer?" he wrote to Gouverneur Morris of New York, a member of the Continental Congress. Washington, who couldn't supply his army, wrote, "A rat in the shape of a horse is not to be bought at this time for less than £200." He complained about the cost of saddles, boots, shoes, flour, hay, and beef; and with prices going up, he couldn't pay his soldiers a living wage.

In December 1778 he wrote to Benjamin Harrison, a Virginia member of the Congress, "Our affairs are in a more distressed, ruinous, and deplorable condition than they have been in since the commencement of the War. . . . The common interests of America are mouldering and sinking into irretrievable (if a remedy is not soon applied) ruin. . . . I am alarmed and wish to see my Countrymen roused."

For five weeks, beginning in late December 1778, Washington met in Philadelphia with members of the Continental Congress. They talked about plans for the coming military campaigns. The army could strike enemy posts along the coast or those in upstate New York, or it could just defend itself against British attack.

American troops were tired. Supplies were low and money was short. Washington and Congress decided that the Continental army would wait and let the enemy pick the next battles.

Washington's troops guarded the Hudson River, an important water link between the eastern and middle states. Meanwhile, the British changed their strategy and moved their battles south, where the people were more loyal to the king. On December 29, 1778, they captured the port of Savannah, Georgia.

During the spring and early summer of 1779, British General Clinton sent his men on destructive raids. On June 1 they took the New York posts at Stony Point and Verplanck's Point along the Hudson. In early July his men burned stores and wharfs in New Haven, Norwalk, and Fairfield, Connecticut. Clinton hoped these attacks would draw Washington into battle. But Washington wouldn't move. He knew that with the British soldiers so far from home and their base of supplies, and with other battles in Europe for them to fight, time was on the side of the Continental army.

On July 15, Washington sent General Anthony Wayne with twelve hundred troops to retake Stony Point. Wayne and his men marched quietly at night and waded through the river. At midnight they reached the fort and broke through the wooden wall with axes, capturing the fort.

By the end of July 1779 Washington moved his headquarters to West Point, New York. This began what was mostly a quiet time for Washington, a more social time. "Since our arrival at this happy spot," he wrote in an August 16 dinner invitation to a friend, "we have had a ham, sometimes a shoulder of bacon, to grace the head of the table; a piece of roast beef adorns the foot; and a dish of beans, or greens, almost imperceptible, decorates the centre." He added that

Major General Anthony Wayne of Pennsylvania led the right wing of the October 1777 attack at Germantown, Pennsylvania, and in July 1779 led the forces that captured Stony Point, New York, from a circa 1875 engraving by Benson J. Lossing.

if his cook "has a mind to" there might be beefsteak pies, dishes of crabs, and even an apple pie.

If Washington felt at first inadequate to the position of commander in chief, it seems he grew into the job. During the summer, M. Gerard, the French minister to the United States, met in Philadelphia with a committee of Congress. They discussed how French and American troops could work together. The minister also had many long meetings with Washington. "It is impossible for me briefly to communicate the fund of intelligence which I have derived from him," Gerard wrote home. "I will say now only, that I have formed as high an opinion of the powers of his mind, his moderation, his patriotism, and his virtues."

Though the French sent much-needed supplies, the Americans still needed money. By fall 1780, many American soldiers hadn't been paid for months, and those who were paid found that it wasn't enough to support their families. Congress was afraid a federal tax would turn people against them, but borrowing money was also not a solution, because by 1779 the new nation had almost no credit. Printing more money would not help because Continental paper money was almost worthless. A suit and hat had cost Patriot Samuel Adams two thousand Continental dollars. In Philadelphia two handkerchiefs cost $60, a fork cost $37, and a frying pan cost $125.

Continental money, from a circa 1875 engraving by Benson J. Lossing

At the beginning of the war, Robert Morris, a Pennsylvania representative at the Continental Congress, raised money for the Continental army. Morris enlisted the help of Haym

Salomon, who had fought a losing battle for the independence of his native Poland. In 1772 Salomon came to New York, became a merchant and banker, and soon an American Patriot. In 1780 Morris sent a messenger to Salomon, who was, at the time, in synagogue, Congregation Mikve Israel, observing Yom Kippur, a day of the fasting and prayer. "I have exhausted even my personal sources of aid," Morris wrote. "I must beg of you to act immediately with whatever resources you have to satisfy our distress." Salomon appealed to others in the synagogue and raised money to pay the troops, which was delivered at sundown when the holy day was done. Together, Morris and Salomon, often using their own money, helped finance the Revolution.

London-born Esther De Berdt also raised money for the troops. In May 1770 she married Joseph Reed, an American working in England, and came to America with him in October 1770. By 1775 her husband was George Washington's military secretary. During the Revolution, Esther Reed formed an organization of thirty-nine women who went door-to-door collecting money in support of Washington's troops. They collected more than 300,000 Continental dollars in all. Reed planned to distribute the money among the soldiers, but Washington wouldn't let her. He feared they would use it to gamble or buy liquor, so instead she spent the money on linen, which she and her friends used to make shirts for the soldiers.

Washington spent the difficult winter of 1779–1780 in Morristown, New Jersey, where there was so little food that he wrote, "The Soldiers eat every kind of horse food but Hay." On January 3, 1780, there was a blizzard that left at least four feet of snow, destroyed the troops' tents, and closed the roads.

That winter also marked the beginning of the downfall of one of Washington's "most valued commanders." In December General Benedict

Benedict Arnold of Connecticut, American general and traitor, from a circa 1900 engraving, artist unknown

Arnold was found guilty of using his military position for personal profit. Washington gave him a mild scolding but promised him new opportunities of "regaining the esteem of your country." Instead, Benedict Arnold marked himself as an American traitor.

Arnold was hot-tempered, so perhaps his treason was revenge for being rebuked by his commander. Or perhaps his wife, Peggy Shippen, the daughter of a leading Tory, led him to treachery. Whatever the cause, in May 1779 he began a secret correspondence with British Major John André and joined a plot to deliver West Point to the British.

In September 1780 André put on civilian clothes, took the name of John Anderson, and made his way through American troops, heading toward West Point, which was commanded by Arnold. Three card-playing American soldiers stopped André, planning to rob him. They took him into the bushes and undressed him in search of money. Instead, they found papers hidden in his boots that proved he was a spy. The soldiers brought André to their commanding officer.

John André, early a talented artist and poet, later the British military officer who conspired with American traitor General Benedict Arnold, from a circa 1885 drawing by H. Rosa

"Whom can we trust now?" Washington asked, when he learned of Benedict Arnold's treason.

The British started rumors that there were more spies among the American officers. Washington sent secret agents to New York to investigate and found there was no truth to them.

Washington appointed a board of officers to try André. They found him guilty of spying and sentenced him to death. On October 2, 1780, André was hanged before an assembly of American soldiers. His last words were, "I pray you to bear me witness that I met my fate like a brave man."

Benedict Arnold escaped to a British ship. He continued to fight in the Revolution, but now he served in the king's army. "What would the Americans do with me if they should catch me?" he once asked an American prisoner. In 1777 Arnold had been wounded while fighting *for* America. "They would cut off and bury with military honors your leg that was wounded in Saratoga," the prisoner answered, "and hang the rest of you."

Benedict Arnold was never caught. He died in London in 1801.

18. "Posterity Will Huzza for Us"

British troops led by General Henry Clinton had moved south. On April 9, 1780, they entered Charleston, South Carolina. Ten days later General Lord Cornwallis arrived there with more men. The Americans were surrounded. Shortly past midnight on May 12, General Benjamin Lincoln surrendered. Almost the entire southern Continental army, some fifty-five thousand Patriot troops, were taken as prisoners, along with Patriot guns, ammunition, and ships.

The harbor at Charleston, South Carolina, in 1780, from a circa 1850 engraving based on a drawing by Leitch

The battle of Camden, South Carolina, an American defeat, August 16, 1780, from an engraving, date and artist unknown, based on a painting by Alonzo Chappel

In June General Clinton left Cornwallis in charge of the southern army and went to New York. In August Cornwallis led an attack against some three thousand American troops camped near Camden, South Carolina under the command of General Horatio Gates, the hero of Saratoga. The Americans ate an unsettling dinner of bread, beef, molasses, mush, and dumplings and, by morning of the sixteenth, when the British attacked, many were sick from the food.

The British shouted, fired their guns, then charged with their bayonets. Some of the Americans, the regular troops, stood their ground. But the inexperienced state militia panicked, threw down their weapons, and ran, with the retreat led by General Horatio Gates, who raced on horseback one hundred eighty miles from Camden, all the way to Hillsborough, North Carolina. This was the second great defeat within just three months for the southern Continental army, but it was the last important British success in the south. Shortly after that, on October 14, 1780, General Nathanael Greene took command of the shattered southern army.

American General Daniel Morgan, originally of New Jersey, most noted for his stunning victory at Cowpens, South Carolina, January 17, 1781, from a circa 1900 engraving, artist unknown

On October 7, 1780, at Kings Mountain in South Carolina, a troop of American frontiersmen soundly defeated Major Patrick Ferguson and about fifteen hundred Redcoats. Three months later, on January 17, 1781, at Hannah's Cowpens in South Carolina, General Daniel Morgan trapped British forces led by the infamous General Banastre Tarleton, nicknamed Bloody Ban because in a previous battle, his men brutally killed surrendering American soldiers. More than nine hundred Redcoats were killed or captured at Cowpens. Then, on March 15, 1781, at the battle of Guilford Courthouse in North Carolina, both sides suffered terrible losses—four hundred Americans and six hundred British.

The war was not going well for the British. It was time to reassess their strategy.

"One maxim appears to me to be absolutely necessary for the safe and honourable conduct of this war," General Lord Cornwallis wrote in a May 16, 1781, letter to British commander in chief General Henry Clinton, "that we should have as few posts as possible, and that wherever the King's troops are, they should be in respectable force." In the same letter he wrote, "I shall take the liberty of repeating that if offensive war is intended, Virginia appears to me to be the only Province in which it can be carried on."

On April 25, following his own recommendation, Cornwallis and his troops set off for Virginia. They marched through Petersburg, Richmond, and Jamestown, the place of the first English settlement in America. In August they stopped by the York River, in Yorktown.

Soon after Cornwallis had settled, Washington learned that a French naval fleet under the command of Admiral François-Joseph-Paul de Grasse was sailing north from the West Indies, toward Chesapeake Bay. Washington quickly moved his army south, out of New York, toward Virginia and a showdown with British forces.

French naval officer Count François-Joseph-Paul de Grasse, whose more than twenty ships in Chesapeake Bay blocked a British retreat, helping ensure victory for the Continental army in the battle of Yorktown, Virginia, from a circa 1875 engraving by Benson J. Lossing

On September 2 Washington's troops passed through Philadelphia. The two-mile-long line began with officers and their staff, servants, and baggage. Behind them were soldiers in their ragged uniforms who marched to the beat of fifes and drums. Then came the supply wagons, and some soldiers' wives and children. Women watched from open windows, cheered, and threw flowers to the soldiers. The next day the French, in their handsome uniforms, marched through, and again, people cheered.

On September 5 a battle in the Atlantic Ocean, in water just beyond Chesapeake Bay, effectively won the Revolution for the United States. British Admiral Thomas Graves led a fleet of nineteen warships toward the bay. In the distance his men saw what at first looked like pine trees,

The French engaged the British in the sea just beyond Chesapeake Bay, September 5, 1781,
from an 1881 engraving by J. O. Davidson.

but really were the masts of French warships under the command of Admiral de Grasse. Aboard them was a huge fighting force that sailed out to the enemy and fired at the masts and sails of the British ships. Within a short time, the decks of the British ships were a mix of broken timber and blood.

When de Grasse returned to Chesapeake Bay, he found Admiral de Barras waiting there with eight more French warships that had sailed from Newport, Rhode Island.

French military officer Jean-Baptiste-Donatien de Vimeur, Comte de Rochambeau, who came to
the United States in 1780 and assisted Washington in the capture of Yorktown, Virginia, from a
circa 1850 wood engraving by Lossing and Barritt, based on a drawing by Benson J. Lossing

The French controlled the bay. There would be no escape by sea for Cornwallis and his troops. Soon, Washington and General Jean-Baptiste-Donatien de Vimeur, Comte de Rochambeau, would lead American and French troops and surround them on land.

Late at night on September 9, Washington arrived at Mount Vernon. He hadn't been home for six years and four months, not since he left to attend the Second Continental Congress. He looked older now and tired. Martha was surprised, but delighted, to see him. For the first time Washington saw her four grandchildren, his step-grandchildren, who had been born while he was away. The next morning Washington's many slaves came to the main house to welcome him back.

On September 11 there was a great feast for Washington, his officers, and his neighbors. On the twelfth he was off again. His stepson, Jacky Custis, went with him as an aide.

American troops were already at Yorktown under the command of General Marquis de Lafayette. Cornwallis made a great strategic mistake and didn't attack this relatively weak force in early September. He lost the chance to escape the trap Washington was setting for him.

By September 28, some sixteen thousand American and French troops had gathered in a semicircle around Yorktown. The Americans were on one side in three divisions under the command of Generals Lincoln, Lafayette, and von Steuben. The French were on the other side under Rochambeau. They were ready to take on Cornwallis and the seven thousand men under his command.

That night Washington slept under a mulberry tree with the tree's roots as his pillow. He stayed there with his men until October 6 when, at night, American troops moved closer, to within six hundred yards of the British line. They dug trenches, dragged cannons, and prepared to fight. On the

Governor of Virginia Thomas Nelson's Yorktown house, used as headquarters for Cornwallis in 1781, from a circa 1900 engraving, artist unknown

afternoon of October 9, "General Washington put the match to the first gun," according to a soldier who was there, and "a furious discharge of cannon and mortars immediately followed."

Lafayette asked Virginia Governor Thomas Nelson where to aim their guns, and Nelson pointed to a large house on a hill as the likely headquarters of Cornwallis—it was *his* own house. "Fire upon it," he said. "Never spare a particle of my property so long as it affords a shelter to the enemies of my country."

At first Cornwallis stayed in the house of Nelson's father. He left when his cook, while carrying a soup tureen, was killed by cannon fire. Cornwallis moved to Nelson's house, but cannon fire chased him off. At last he moved into a cave by the river.

American and French cannons fired on the British for several days and the British fired back. "The bomb shells," according to an observer, "incessantly crossing each other's path in the air." During the day, the observer saw

The cave by the Yorktown River where Cornwallis hid during the Patriot shelling of British strongholds at Yorktown, from a circa 1850 wood engraving by Lossing and Barritt, based on a drawing by Benson J. Lossing

the black balls fly. At night "they appear like a fiery meteor with a blazing tail." Some shells overshot the town and made huge splashes as they fell in the water.

Dr. James Thatcher, an army surgeon, wrote in his journal, "During the assault, the British kept up an incessant firing of cannon and musketry from their whole line." Washington dismounted, stood in the line of fire, and watched. When one of his aides suggested he step back, he refused. As always, he set an example for his men, whom he expected to be courageous in battle.

By October 16 Cornwallis was desperate. He tried to escape with his army across the York River, but a storm forced him to give up the plan. By the next day he knew he had lost. Shortly after nine in the morning, a single soldier stood on the British side and beat a drum. Then a British officer stood and held up a white handkerchief.

On October 19, 1781, Cornwallis signed the articles of surrender.

"This is to us a most glorious day, but to the English, one of bitter chagrin and disappointment," Dr. James Thatcher wrote in his journal. "Being on horseback, I anticipate a full share of satisfaction in viewing the various movements in the interesting scene."

That afternoon, two parallel lines were set, each more than a mile long, the Americans in one line and their allies, the French, in the other. Washington instructed his men not to insult the British with shouts of victory. "It is sufficient for us that we witness their humiliation. Posterity will huzza for us."

At two o'clock the British troops came out. They marched to an open field where they put down their guns. As they walked through the lines of American and French troops, their drummers beat to the tune of an old English nursery rhyme:

If ponies rode men and if grass ate the cows
And cats should be chased into holes by the mouse . . .
If summer were spring and the other way 'round
Then all the world would be upside down.

Truly, it was a world turned upside down. A ragtag army with their ally, the French, had defeated the mightiest armed force of the time.

After the surrender, Washington, Rochambeau, and Cornwallis dined together. Washington held up his glass and made a toast to "the king of France." Rochambeau toasted "the United States." Cornwallis toasted "the king," to which Washington added, "of England—confine him there."

When Lord North, the English prime minister, heard news of the surrender at Yorktown, he paced back and forth, spread out his arms, and cried out, "Oh, God! It is all over!" When the people of London learned of the

The British surrender at Yorktown, October 19, 1781, from a 1905 reprint of an earlier drawing, artist unknown.

surrender, a weeklong riot broke out that only ended when British soldiers fired on their own people.

There were four English commanders in chief during the Revolution: Generals Thomas Gage, William Howe, Henry Clinton, and, beginning in May 1782, Guy Carleton, until 1783, when the Treaty of Paris officially ended the war. The Americans only had one: General George Washington.

Washington led farmers and tradesmen who had enlisted for just a few months at a time, some without muskets or gunpowder, against a well-trained,

Cornwallis **TAKEN!**

Newport, October 25, 1781

YESTERDAY Afternoon arrived in this Harbour Capt. Lovett, of the Schooner Adventure, from York River, in Chesapeak Bay, (which he left the 20th instant) and brought us the glorious News of the Surrender of Lord Cornwallis and his Army Prisoners of War to the allied Army, under the Command of our illustrious General; and the French Fleet, under the Command of His Excellency the Count de Grasse ... By this glorious Conquest, NINE THOUSAND of the Enemy, including Seamen, fell into our Hands, with an immense Quantity of Warlike Stores, a forty-gun Ship, a Frigate, an armed Vessel, and about one hundred Sail of Transports.

well-armed British army supported by a mighty navy. Many of his men could not form a proper column or follow simple orders. Many of the American people, an estimated one third, did not support the Revolution. And at times, the inefficient new government of the United States did not fully support him. But Washington held the army together.

Washington gained his men's confidence, respect, and even love. His men followed him barefoot through the snow at Trenton. They wintered with him at Valley Forge, without proper clothes, food, or firewood. Surely, they fought not only for independence, but also for Washington.

The Revolution was fought from Canada to Georgia, and Washington continually adapted his plans to suit the terrain. He knew how costly it was for the British to have an army so far from home, that time was on his side. His continued willingness to retreat, to save his men, and to pick his battles led to final victory.

19. "I Here Offer My Commission"

Washington's stepson, Jacky Custis, who had accompanied him to Yorktown as an aide, was already sick with "camp fever," dysentery, when the fighting began. He knew he was dying. When the battle was over, he witnessed the surrender. Then he was taken thirty miles away to Eltham, Virginia, where Washington's friend Dr. Craik looked after him.

Jacky Custis was twenty-eight years old with four young children. On November 5, when he died, George and Martha Washington and Custis's wife, Nelly, were by his bedside. Washington hugged Martha and Nelly and said, "From this moment I adopt his two youngest children as my own." Those two children were George Washington Parke Custis, who later wrote a biography of his adopted father, and Eleanor Parke Custis.

Washington's stepson, Jacky Custis, from a circa 1870 engraving by Lossing and Barritt, based on a drawing by Benson J. Lossing

Washington was greatly affected by the death of his stepson. In the notes of a 1787 book, *Travels in North America,* by the Frenchman the Marquis de Chastellux, the translator, John Kent, wrote, "I had the pleasure of passing a day or two with Mrs. Washington at the General's house in Virginia where she appeared to me to be one of the best women in the world, and beloved by all about her. . . . The family were then in mourning for Mr. Custis. . . . The General was uncommonly affected at his death, insomuch that many of his friends imagined they perceived some change in his equanimity of temper."

Washington went from his stepson's deathbed at Eltham to Mount Vernon and then to Fredericksburg, where his mother lived, to a ball held to celebrate the victory at Yorktown. Many French officers were eager to see

Washington's mother. George Washington Parke Custis wrote in his biography of Washington that the French expected "glitter and show which would have been attached to the parents of the great in the countries of the old world." They were surprised when Mrs. Mary Washington entered the room "dressed in the very plain yet becoming garb worn by the Virginia lady of the old time . . . and at an early hour, wishing the company much enjoyment of their pleasures,

Washington escorts his mother to a ball celebrating the Patriot victory at Yorktown, from a circa 1890 illustration by Howard Pyle.

observed, that it was high time for old folks to be in bed, and retired, leaning, as before, on the arm of her son."

Next, Washington went to Philadelphia to meet with members of the Continental Congress. There was a feeling among them and others that the Revolution was won. But General Clinton and many British troops were still in America. Washington knew the Revolution wouldn't be over until a treaty was signed. Congress agreed. It promised Washington troops and money, and with that, in April 1782, Washington rejoined his army in Newburgh, New York.

In May 1782, while Washington was at Newburgh, he received a seven-page letter from one of his men, Colonel Lewis Nicola, who proposed the new nation be ruled by a king. "In that case," he wrote, the same abilities that led us "to victory and glory . . . would be most likely to conduct and direct us in the smoother paths of peace." He wanted Washington to be the first king of the United States, King George I.

Washington's headquarters at Newburgh, New York, 1782, from a circa 1893 drawing by Allegra Eggleston

Americans of the 1780s were accustomed to monarchy, so the sentiments expressed in the letter should not have been surprising. Even the cry "Long live the king!" was not abandoned during the Revolution. American Patriots simply changed it to "Long live Washington!" What was remarkable was Washington's response, that he could look beyond his own glory to the needs of the nation.

Washington was sure Nicola wrote his letter on behalf of many of his fellow soldiers. He replied that the letter gave him "painful sensations." He questioned what he did to give Nicola such an idea. To make him king, Washington wrote, would be "the greatest mischief that can befall my country . . . banish these thoughts from your mind, and never communicate, as from yourself or any one else, a sentiment of the like nature."

When Nicola received Washington's response, he wrote a letter of apology, and another, and another—three letters in three days. Clearly, he understood Washington's aversion to introducing the monarchy to the new nation.

On March 23, 1783, a ship arrived with a more welcome letter. It was from the Marquis de Lafayette, who had returned to France. He wrote that in January a peace treaty had been signed in Paris—the Revolution was over. On April 17 Washington received official notice of the peace from Congress. Two days later, on April 19, exactly eight years from the day that the first shots of the Revolution were fired in Lexington, Massachusetts, the proclamation of the peace was read to the troops with orders from Washington that the chaplains "will render thanks to Almighty God for all His mercies."

"Huzza! Huzza!" the men shouted. Following that they sang out, "No king, but God! No king, but God!" At night there were fireworks. While his men celebrated, Washington left for Ringwood, New Jersey, to arrange for an exchange of prisoners with the British.

The war was won. It was time for Washington to retire to Mount Vernon.

Washington says good-bye to his officers at Fraunces Tavern, New York City, December 4, 1783, from an 1895 reprint of an earlier drawing, artist unknown.

On December 4, 1783, Washington's officers gathered in Fraunces Tavern in New York City to say good-bye to their commander. Shortly after noon, he walked in, filled a glass with wine and said, "With a heart full of love and gratitude, I now take leave of you." He drank the wine and then, one by one, as the officers reached out to shake his hand, Washington embraced them. When it was time to leave, the men followed Washington quietly and teary-eyed until he boarded a flatboat that would take him to Paulus Hook, the first stop on his way to Annapolis, Maryland. Washington turned and waved his hat to his men, a silent farewell.

People in every town and village he passed through came out to greet and cheer for Washington. There were speeches and toasts made in his honor, a hint at the great outpouring of affection he would receive five and a half years later, on his way to taking the oath of office as the nation's first president.

In 1775 Washington had refused a salary as commander of the army. He asked only that he be reimbursed for his expenses. Now, on his way to Annapolis, he stopped in Philadelphia, met with the Comptroller of the Treasury, and submitted his expense accounts, including what he paid on his own for meals at his headquarters for his officers, bodyguards, and servants, and the cost of housekeepers, blacksmiths, and spies. The total was more than fifty thousand dollars.

Two pages from Washington's expense book

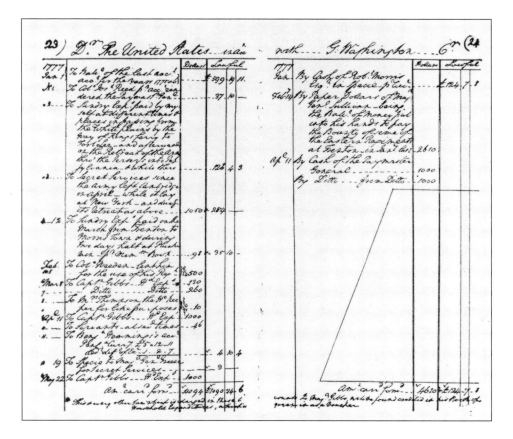

Washington resigns his position as commander of the army in the Hall of Congress, Annapolis, Maryland, December 23, 1783, from a circa 1910 engraving based on the painting by John Trumbull.

At noon on December 23, 1783, George Washington entered the Hall of Congress. The hall and gallery were crowded. Thomas Mifflin of Pennsylvania, the new president of Congress, welcomed Washington.

"Having now finished the work assigned me," Washington told Congress, "I retire from the great theater of action. . . . I here offer my commission, and take my leave of all the employments of public life."

The next morning, Washington left Annapolis. Later that same day, Christmas Eve, he arrived at his beloved Mount Vernon. "I feel myself eased of a load of public care," he wrote in a letter to Governor George Clinton of New York. "I hope to spend the remainder of my days in cultivating the affections of good men and in the practice of the domestic virtues."

Washington Reacts to the Peace
from his writings

Letter to Elias Boudinot
President of Congress
March 30, 1783

Your Excellency will permit me, with the most lively sensations of gratitude and pleasure, to return you my warmest Thanks for the Communication you have been pleased to make to me and the Army, of the glorious News of a General Peace; an Event, which cannot fail to diffuse a general Joy throughout the United States: but to none of their Citizens a greater Share, than to the Officers and Soldiers, who now compose the Army. It is impossible for me to express the Effusion of Joy, with which I beg your Excellency, to accept a Return of my sincerest Congratulations on this happiest of Events.

Letter to Major General
Nathanael Greene
March 31, 1783

You will give the highest Credit to my sincerity, when I beg you to accept my warmest Congratulations on this glorious and happy Event, an Event which crowns all our Labors and will sweeten the Toils which we have experienced in the Course of Eight Years distressing War. The Army here, universally participate in the general Joy which this Event has diffused.... It remains for the States to be Wise, and to establish their Independence on that Basis of inviolable efficacious Union, and firm Confederation, which may prevent their being made the Sport of European Policy; may Heaven give them Wisdom to adopt the Measures still necessary for this important Purpose.

Letter to Alexander Hamilton
March 31, 1783

I rejoice most exceedingly that there is an end to our Warfare, and that such a field is opening to our view as will, with wisdom to direct the cultivation of it, make us a great, a respectable, and happy People.... No man in the United States is, or can be more deeply impressed with the necessity of a reform in our present Confederation than myself.

20. "No Longer a Public Man"

In 1783, when Washington went home, he felt, he wrote in a letter to Henry Knox, as a weary traveler carrying a heavy burden must feel when a long journey is done. "Strange as it may seem," he added, "I was no longer a public man."

"I have become a private citizen on the banks of the Potomac," Washington wrote to Lafayette. "I have not only retired from all public employments, but I am retiring within myself. . . . I will move gently down the stream of time until I sleep with my fathers."

The winter of his return was cold and quiet. Snow and ice blocked the roads. Washington couldn't even travel to Fredericksburg to visit his mother. With

The garden house at Mount Vernon, Washington's Virginia estate, from a circa 1870 engraving by Lossing and Barritt, based on a drawing by Benson J. Lossing

spring, the pace of his life quickened. Washington spent much of his time farming. He studied books and began a system of crop rotation. He planted on the same fields at different times wheat, corn, potatoes, oats, and grass. He even drew a map with each field numbered and the crops to be planted for the next several years.

There were five farms on his Mount Vernon estate, and Washington named them Mansion House Farm, River Farm, Union Farm, Muddy Hole Farm, and Dogue Run Farm. Each farm had an overseer to manage it who reported to Washington every Saturday afternoon. The reports described the work of each slave, what crops had been planted or picked, and news of the livestock.

In September 1784 Washington made a 680-mile tour on horseback to the lands he owned beyond the Allegheny Mountains. He traveled with his

A map of Washington's farms, from a map by G. W. Boynton, based on one by Washington

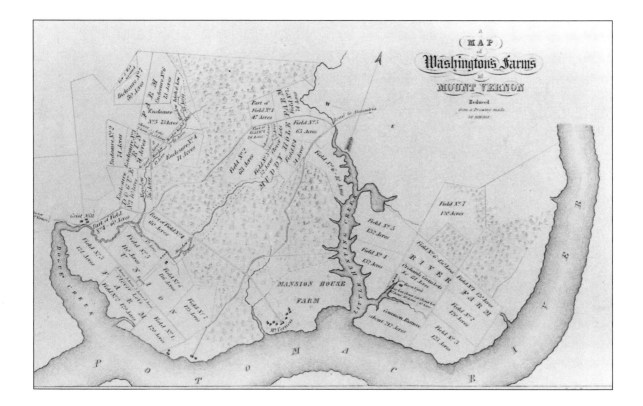

nephew Bushrod Washington, two friends, and three servants. They took the same route Washington had taken when he accompanied General Braddock in the French and Indian War. Washington visited Braddock's grave and thought back, no doubt, to July 14, 1755, when he led a quiet funeral service for the fallen general. Much had changed since 1755, when Washington's public career was just beginning. Now he felt it had come to its end, to a quiet time on his beloved Mount Vernon.

Washington did more than farm on his estate—he also ran a wheat-grinding mill and, in 1786, boasted that the flour made at his mill was "equal, I believe, in quality to any made in this country." Washington kept a wood-burner busy making charcoal for the big house. He had looms, too, on which six slaves made hundreds of yards of cloth each year. There was a blacksmith shop that did whatever work was needed for Washington's farms and also work that came from the outside. He had teams of carpenters and gardeners, a brick maker, a mason, a cooper (barrel maker), and a shoemaker.

Gifts from the king of Spain and the Marquis de Lafayette started a new enterprise for Washington: breeding mules, great work animals that are the offspring of a donkey and a horse. In 1786 the king sent Washington a large, gray, sluggish male donkey, which he named Royal Gift. Lafayette sent a ferocious, black one from Malta, which Washington named Knight of Malta. With them Washington bred some of the finest mules in America.

At Mount Vernon Washington was a man of steady habits. He got up each morning before sunrise and went to his study, where he read and answered letters until breakfast. Then he ate, rode

Washington's inkstand, from a circa 1870 engraving by Lossing and Barritt, based on a drawing by Benson J. Lossing

Banquet hall at Mount Vernon, from a circa 1893 drawing by Allegra Eggleston

to his farms, checked on his crops, and gave orders to his overseers. By three o'clock he had dinner with his family and guests. His habit was to allow five minutes for latecomers to dinner, and then to begin. "Gentlemen," he told tardy guests, "we are too punctual for you." He ate heartily, especially fish, which he particularly enjoyed. Dessert would often be baked apples or berries in cream or milk. After dinner, he often snacked on nuts while he talked with his guests. By ten, he was in bed for the night.

Washington's retirement from public life revolved around business, riding, entertaining visitors, and family. One night's dinner talk gives some insight into how Washington conducted his business.

Henry Lee, the captain of Lee's Legion, an active cavalry troop in the Continental army, was a constant visitor. One evening Washington asked to buy two carriage horses. "I have a fine pair," Lee said, "but you cannot get them . . .

because you will never pay more than half price for anything, and I must have full price for my horses." With that, Martha Washington laughed, and according to a letter Lee's son wrote, Mrs. Washington had a pet parrot perched next to her that laughed, too.

Henry Lee of Virginia, a cavalry commander in the Revolutionary War, a frequent visitor at Mount Vernon, and the son of Mary Bland, who is thought to be the "Low Land Beauty" Washington wrote of in his diary, from a circa 1870 engraving by Lossing and Barritt, based on a drawing by Benson J. Lossing

Washington was well-known to be careful in all his business dealings. According to one story, while Washington was away, the walls of a room in Mount Vernon were plastered and the plasterer paid. When Washington returned he measured the walls and found the charge too expensive for the work done, too much by fifteen shillings, not a large sum. Nonetheless, he collected the money, not from the worker who had died, but from his widow's second husband who had advertised his willingness to settle his wife's debts.

Washington was just as exacting when it was not to his benefit. While he traveled, he stayed with his servant in the same inn. After one visit, the innkeeper charged ninepence less for the servant. Washington explained that his servant ate as much as he did and insisted on paying the higher amount for them both.

Washington was a sporting man and always enjoyed a good fox hunt, but during the Revolution his hounds were given away. Lafayette and some other French officers sent him some new ones, large, big-mouthed dogs. But these dogs didn't seem interested in chasing, catching, and killing a fox. "Out after breakfast with my hounds, found a fox and ran him," Washington wrote in his diary. He chased it for three hours. "I came home and left the huntsmen with them, who followed in the same manner two hours more." But the dogs didn't catch the fox.

Mrs. Washington didn't like the new dogs and didn't want them near the house. When one was seen carrying off a ham just out of her oven, she insisted Washington get rid of them, which he did.

There was a constant stream of letters and visitors. It wasn't until June 30, 1785, a year and a half after he returned home, that Washington wrote in his diary, "Dined only with Mrs. Washington, which, I believe, is the first instance of it since my retirement from public life."

Elkanah Watson visited in the winter of 1785. "I found him kind," Watson wrote, "agreeably social." Watson had a bad cold and Washington urged him to take something for it. Watson refused. That night, in his room, he had a coughing fit. "The door of my room was gently opened, and, on drawing my bed curtains, I beheld Washington himself, standing at my bedside with a bowl of hot tea in his hand."

Washington spent time with his family, including Jacky's children, the

Washington's tea service, from a circa 1870 engraving by Lossing and Barritt, based on a drawing by Benson J. Lossing

boy and girl he'd adopted after Jacky's death. Lafayette wrote how good he was with them. He wrote of the boy, "A very little gentleman with a feather in his hat, holding fast to one finger of the good General's remarkable hand . . . so large that hand!"

Washington was a celebrity. Wherever he went, people stared. On Sundays they crowded his church to see him. Many artists and sculptors came to Mount Vernon to paint his portrait or create a statue of him. "I am now altogether at their beck," Washington wrote to a friend in 1785, "and sit 'like patience on a monument,' whilst they are delineating the lines on my face."

The sculptors began by making a life mask. "He oiled my features over," Washington later said of Joseph Wright, a sculptor, "and placing me flat upon my back upon a cot, proceeded to daub my face with plaster. Whilst in this ludicrous attitude, Mrs. Washington entered the room, and seeing my face thus overspread with the plaster, involuntarily exclaimed." Washington couldn't help himself. He smiled. The wet plaster shifted, so the mouth of that mask and all the statues made from it show Washington with strangely twisted lips.

French sculptor Jean-Antoine Houdon's 1785 marble statue of Washington, from a circa 1870 engraving by Lossing and Barritt, based on a drawing by Benson J. Lossing

There were also requests from people who wanted to write Washington's biography and historians who wanted to talk to him about the Revolution. Some came to visit Mount Vernon. Others wrote to him. Letters arrived from old soldiers, inventors, and missionaries, as well as from French officers who had served with him. The officers and the king and queen invited him to sail to France and visit. Washington wrote back that he was too old for such a trip.

In many of his letters Washington expressed gratitude for his good health. But in truth, he was often sick. In 1755, while he was Braddock's aide, he had a high fever and headaches. Three years later, just before he married Martha, he was severely ill for several months. Now, in his retirement from public life, his hands had a slight tremor. His eyesight and hearing were poor. From his early twenties, Washington had toothaches. One after another, he had his teeth pulled out and in 1789 started wearing false teeth. The best set, made of hippopotamus tusk, gold, and human teeth, was prepared for him by Dr. John Greenwood, a New York dentist.

Washington had led the nation in the battle for independence, but that victory didn't guarantee a well-functioning government. Each state and Congress issued its own paper money. Each state charged different taxes on imported goods, and no one built or maintained roads between the states. The country was ruled then by the Articles of Confederation, the government that started with a committee from the Second Continental Congress headed by John Dickinson of Pennsylvania. He had proposed a strong central government with little power left for the states, but this was in the midst of the Revolution, and members of Congress refused to replace one strong, distant government with another strong, though not as distant one. What they created was little more than a partnership treaty between the thirteen states.

"I often think of our situation," Washington wrote to John Jay of New

York, "and view it with concern." He wrote to James Warren of Massachusetts that the Confederation "appears to me to be little more than a shadow without substance."

In 1785, representatives of Virginia and Maryland met to talk about rights to rivers the two states shared. The talk soon was about the need for a stronger central government. There were similar talks among leaders throughout the country. Beginning in May 1787, representatives from twelve states, all but Rhode Island, met in Philadelphia for a Constitutional Convention. George Washington was chosen to head the Virginia delegation.

At first, Washington refused to go. Just a few years earlier he had resolved to remain a private citizen, but on May 9 he started out in his carriage toward Philadelphia. He arrived on May 13 and his first stop was a visit with Benjamin Franklin. The warm relationship between the two men reveals a lot about them both. They were the two most loved and famous men in America, but there was no envy between them. In his last letter to Franklin, sent two years later in 1789, Washington wrote, "So long as I retain my memory, you will be recollected with respect, veneration, and affection by your sincere friend." In his last will and testament Franklin wrote, "My fine crabtree walking-stick, with a gold head, curiously wrought in the form of the cap of liberty, I give my friend, and the friend of mankind, General Washington."

Twelve days after Washington's arrival in Philadelphia, on May 25, enough delegates had gathered to begin the sessions. Their first order of business was to elect Washington, by unanimous vote, as president of the convention. They met for four months, through the summer, and the meetings were so secret that windows in some of the rooms were nailed shut.

There were many issues for the delegates to resolve. Chief among them was how to share the power of government among states with large and

Benjamin Franklin, the eldest of the fifty-five delegates, making a point at the Constitutional Convention, Philadelphia, Pennsylvania, 1787, from a circa 1875 engraving by Benson J. Lossing

small populations. The solution was a two-house legislature. An equal number of representatives from each state would make up the Senate. The number of representatives for each state in the House would be based on its population. The next question addressed and its resolution is a shameful reflection of the period—how to count slaves? It was decided that in figuring a state's population for representation in the House, each slave would be counted as only three-fifths of a person.

On September 17, the last day of the convention, Benjamin Franklin looked to where Washington sat. A picture of the sun was painted on the back of the chair. Franklin said he often looked at that sun behind Washington. "I have the happiness to know," he said when the work of the convention was done, "it is a rising and not a setting sun."

But Washington was not so sure. He knew the Constitution needed to be tested.

"It is the production of four months deliberation," he wrote Lafayette on September 18. "It is now a child of fortune, to be fostered by some and buffeted by others. What will be the General opinion on, or reception of it, is not for me to decide, nor shall I say anything for or against it: if it be good I suppose it will work its way good; if bad, it will recoil on the Framers."

The delegates to the Constitutional Convention were successful planters, lawyers, and merchants—well-educated men. While each represented just one state each, in the end, they all thought of the good of the entire country. The Constitution they wrote, with three branches of government, each a check on the others, remains the blueprint of our nation. After more than two centuries, it is easy to appreciate the wisdom of the men who wrote it, but at the time, according to Henry Knox, it was the people's faith in Washington that gave them the courage to try the new government. It was Washington who presided over the Convention, and he was the first to sign the new Constitution.

The thirteen state legislatures called for elections of delegates who then met in state conventions, debated, and voted on accepting the Constitution.

Many of these people, after fighting so hard for their independence, were not prepared to give up some of it. Even the states' leaders were unsure of the new government. Only Delaware, New Jersey, and Georgia passed the Constitution unanimously. In Massachusetts it received just 52.7 percent of the vote and in Washington's own Virginia, 53 percent . On December 8, 1787, Delaware became the first state to ratify the Constitution. On June 25, 1788, by a vote of eighty-nine in favor to seventy-nine against, Washington's Virginia became the tenth.

With the work of the convention finished, Washington looked forward to going home. He wrote in a letter to Alexander Hamilton sentiments similar to those he had written in 1783 to Knox and Lafayette. "I tell you," he wrote, "it is my great and sole desire to live and die in peace and retirement on my own farm." He wrote that he only wanted "the most enviable of all titles, the character of an honest man."

But he would soon gain another title.

On February 4, 1789, as provided in the Constitution, the Electoral College met to choose the first president of the United States. Each member of the College voted for the same man: George Washington of Virginia.

Much of the world's attention was focused on Washington. True, he had managed to lead a ragtag army to victory against a mighty power, but from the age of nineteen he had prepared himself for military, not political, leadership. Now, with little experience in government, he was about to lead a disparate people under an untested Constitution.

21. "Untrodden Ground"

Today, when we elect a new president, that individual immediately rises in stature to fit the new post, but in 1789, it was the office that gained standing from the man who took it.

"I walk," George Washington said when he first took the office of president, "on untrodden ground." He knew he would set an example for every American leader who would follow him, that his policies must make the thirteen states a nation.

During Washington's first week in New York, beginning April 23, while he waited to take the oath of office, he visited with

Washington in 1789, from a circa 1900 engraving, artist unknown, based on the 1790s painting by Edward Savage

every senator and representative in the city. He hoped to have a friendly working relationship with each of them. But once he took the oath, the visits stopped. From the time of his inauguration, he would receive callers by appointment only and met others once a week when he attended general receptions prepared by his wife, the First Lady.

On May 17, 1789, Martha Washington set out with her grandchildren Eleanor Parke Custis and George Washington Parke Custis for New York. She received some of the same fanfare given her husband just one month before—people gathered to see her, bells were tolled, and guns were fired in salute.

Mrs. Washington had to adjust to her new role. When her husband had left to fight in the Revolution, she had stayed mostly at home. Now she would be at his side. It was not what she envisioned for her waning years.

"I had little thought," she wrote in a December 1789 letter, "when the war was finished, that any circumstances could possibly happen, which would call the General into public life again . . . Yet I cannot blame him for having acted according to his ideas of duty in obeying the voice of his country."

What of her new position as First Lady? "With respect to myself, I sometimes think the arrangement is not quite as it ought to have been, that I, who had much rather be at home, should occupy a place, which a great many younger and gayer women would be extremely pleased . . . I am still determined to be cheerful and happy in whatever situation I may be; for I have also learned from experience, that the greater part of our happiness or misery depends on our dispositions, and not on our circumstances."

Washington had to adjust, too. At his first reception, Colonel David Humphreys, Washington's secretary, entered the room and announced, "The President of the United States." Then an embarrassed Washington walked in. "You have taken me once," he later told Humphreys, "but you

Washington's home 1789–1791, the first presidential mansion, at Pearl and Cherry Streets, New York City, from a circa 1890 drawing, artist unknown

shall never take me in a second time." After that, Washington entered the room unannounced.

There were many people who wanted to see Washington. For them, he set aside two hours each week, Tuesday and Friday afternoons between two and three o'clock. Many people came to visit him then, but only men. Women seldom went to business meetings, but they did attend Mrs. Washington's receptions.

For his receptions, Washington wore a black velvet suit with silver knee buckles, black silk stockings, black shoes with silver shoe buckles, yellow gloves, and a dress sword. His hair was powdered and he carried a two-pointed hat edged with black feathers. He went to Mrs. Washington's receptions in a less formal brown suit and without a sword.

Wherever Washington went, people gathered to see him. "I stood," a contemporary wrote, "when the carriage of the President drew up. . . . As Washington alighted and ascended the steps, paused on the platform, he was preceded by two gentlemen bearing large white wands, who kept back the eager crowd that pressed on every side. At that moment I stood so near I might have touched his clothes; but I should as soon have thought of touching an electric battery. I was penetrated with deepest awe. . . . I saw him a hundred times afterward, but never with any other than the same feeling."

Washington's salary was twenty-five thousand dollars with no allowance for expenses. The money spent on receptions and state dinners was his, and Washington, as always, was careful with his money. But his steward, Samuel Fraunces, the father of the housekeeper whose warning in 1776 saved Washington from poisoning, had different ideas of how a president should live.

One morning at breakfast, Fraunces served a nice piece of shad. "It's very early in the season for shad," Washington said. "How much did you pay for it?"

"Two dollars," Fraunces said.

"Two dollars!" Washington said in shock. "I can never encourage such extravagance at my table. Take it away."

Fraunces took the fish away and ate it himself.

Once a week Washington and Fraunces went over the weekly accounts. Fraunces would leave teary-eyed. "He may discharge me," Fraunces would say after these sessions, "but while I have the honor to be his steward, his establishment shall be supplied with the very best the country can afford." Nonetheless, it was Washington who paid for it all.

One of Washington's first acts as president was to appoint his cabinet. He made John Jay of New York chief justice of the Supreme Court. He asked Henry

John Jay of New York, member of the Continental Congress, 1774–1777, and its president in 1778–1779, became chief justice of the United States Supreme Court 1789–1795, from a circa 1900 engraving, artist unknown.

Knox of Massachusetts, who served as secretary of war in the government under the Articles of Confederation, to remain in that post. He chose Alexander Hamilton of New York as secretary of the treasury, Thomas Jefferson of Virginia as secretary of state, and Edmund Randolph of Virginia as attorney general.

John Adams, the vice president, was the other member of Washington's cabinet. The framers of the Constitution undoubtedly expected the vice president to have a major role in the government, but he didn't. Adams had recommended Washington to be commander of the Continental army, but he was not fully supportive of Washington during the Revolution. In 1777, after Washington's victories at Trenton and Princeton, he complained in Congress that some members "idolize an image which their own hands have molten . . . General Washington." Later, perhaps out of envy, Adams wrote in a letter, "'The Father of his Country,' 'The Founder of the American Republic,' 'The Founder of the American Empire,' etc., etc., etc. These Ascriptions belong to no Man; no! Nor to twenty Men; nor to any hundred Men, nor to any thousand Men."

Alexander Hamilton, born in the West Indies and later of New York, Washington's aide during the Revolutionary War and the first secretary of the treasury, from a circa 1900 engraving, artist unknown

Edmund Randolph, governor of Virginia and the nation's first attorney general and second secretary of state, from a circa 1900 engraving, artist unknown

John Adams of Massachusetts, the nation's first vice president and its second president, from a circa 1875 engraving by Benson J. Lossing

Perhaps Adams's feelings soured his relationship with Washington—either that or the poorly defined role of the vice president left him little to do. Whatever the cause, Washington did not work closely with Adams. By the end of Washington's first term, he left Adams out of most important discussions. Washington's treatment of his vice president became a model for future administrations, which is unfortunate in light of the many talented people who have held that office.

The new government faced many problems. There was no money in the treasury, and there was trouble in the west with rebellious American Indians. But the business of America had to wait. On June 13, 1789, President Washington suddenly developed a high fever and pains in his leg. Dr. Samuel Bard examined him. When he was done, Washington asked for an honest report. "I am not afraid to die," he told Bard, "and therefore can bear the worst."

There is no record of Bard's answer, just that he called in his father, John Bard, also a respected doctor. Father and son agreed. There was a tumor in Washington's leg and they needed to operate.

The doctors cut into Washington's leg and found the tumor was larger than they had thought. This was before there were any real painkillers, but Washington was a good patient. "Cut away, deeper, deeper still!" John Bard told his son. "You see how well he bears it!"

The operation was a success. Within five days, Washington's fever was down. But he was bedridden for six weeks and it took more than twelve weeks for him to fully recover.

Washington needed to rest. Straw was spread on the sidewalk outside to dull the sound of people walking by, and a rope was stretched across the street to keep people and their carriages from riding past his house. Perhaps people then were no more law-abiding than those of later generations—the rope was stolen and had to be replaced.

While Washington was still recovering, he received news of his mother's death. She died August 25, 1789, at the age of eighty-two, a widow for forty-six years. "Awful and affecting as the death of a parent is," Washington wrote to his sister, "there is consolation in knowing that Heaven has spared ours to an age beyond which few attain. . . . It is the duty of her relatives to yield due submission to the decrees of the Creator."

In October Washington left New York for a tour of the northeastern states. He traveled through Connecticut, Massachusetts, and New Hampshire. He visited Revolutionary battlegrounds and met with men who had served with him in the war. Later during his first term he made a tour of the southern states, through Maryland, Virginia, North Carolina, South Carolina, and Georgia. He was pleased to see people busy on farms and with their trades.

Washington reported on his travels in a formal speech to members of Congress. He suggested they consider plans to support the army, make provisions for newcomers to the country to become citizens, establish a national currency, and pay off the national debt.

The United States owed more than $50 million to Americans who supplied food, clothing, and weapons to the Continental army and to the governments of France, Holland, and Spain. The states also owed money, some $25 million, for expenses incurred during the Revolution. Representatives of states that owed very little wanted each state to pay its own debts. Those from states that owed a lot wanted the national government to pay it all. Washington felt the debts were incurred in a shared cause, winning the Revolution, so they should be paid by all. In the end, after days of debate, and a close vote in both houses of Congress, the national government agreed to take on the states' debts.

The debate over states' debts reflects the great challenge Washington faced, to make the needs of one state important to them all. "That there is a diversity of interests in the Union, none has denied," he wrote in spring 1790 to a Virginia friend. "That this is the case, also, in every State, is equally certain; and that it even extends to the counties of individual States can be readily proved."

How did Washington plan to resolve these issues? "To constitute a dispute," he wrote in the same letter, "there must be two parties. To understand it well, both parties, and under all the circumstances, must be fully heard; and, to accommodate differences, temper and mutual forbearance are requisite. Common danger brought the States into confederacy, and on their union our safety and importance depend."

Members of Congress also voted to move the capital for ten years to Philadelphia, then to a place along the Potomac River, what is today called Washington, D.C.

Philadelphia was a center of antislavery sentiment, the home of the nation's first abolition society founded in 1774, the Pennsylvania Society for the Promotion and Abolition of Slavery, and the Relief of Free Negroes Unlawfully Held in Bondage. For a time, Benjamin Franklin, who called slavery "an atrocious debasement," was its president. In 1791 Washington moved to Philadelphia with eight of Martha's household slaves, and according to Pennsylvania law, after living in the state for six months a slave

Washington's Philadelphia home 1791–1796 at 190 Market Street, from a circa 1890 drawing, artist unknown

must be set free. Washington acted in Martha's best interests, but against the spirit of justice and what seemed to be his new, enlightened attitude towards slavery, and instructed his secretary to shuttle his slaves back to Virginia before they would be entitled to their freedom.

In December 1791, changes were made to the Constitution. The first ten amendments, the Bill of Rights, which guaranteed personal rights including the rights to freedom of speech and of the press, became law.

Disagreements broke out in Washington's cabinet, a hint of the coming two-party system. Alexander Hamilton and his followers, called Federalists, believed in a strong central government. Thomas Jefferson and his followers, called Republicans, believed more in the abilities of the American people to govern themselves, and wanted power left to the states.

One of their major disagreements concerned Hamilton's proposal for the establishment of a national bank, which would collect taxes, hold government deposits, issue currency, and watch over the country's finances. Jefferson was against it. He questioned whether the Constitution permitted it. He also feared it would help create a moneyed upper class. Washington saw the need for the bank. In February 1791, after the bill establishing it passed in Congress, Washington signed it into law.

There were armed battles, too. The British, who wanted to keep the fur trade for themselves, armed American Indians, who attacked white settlers. Washington sent Brigadier General Josiah Harmer, a veteran of the Revolution, to protect the frontier.

On September 30, 1790, Harmer led a regiment of more than one thousand soldiers north from Fort Washington on the shore of the Ohio River, the future site of Cincinnati. In mid-October, one hundred eighty of his men who were sent ahead were ambushed by hundreds of hidden American Indians armed with British guns and led by the well-known warrior Little Turtle. Most of the soldiers ran. Those who stood their ground were killed. The army took its revenge, burning American Indian villages and ruining their provisions for the winter, and then returned to Fort Washington.

Harmer had failed.

In 1791 Washington sent General Arthur St. Clair on the same mission. "You have your instructions from the Secretary of War," Washington told

General Arthur St. Clair, who was born in Scotland and came to America in 1758, was a brigadier general in the Revolutionary War, a member of the court that in 1780 convicted Major André of treason, and made commander in chief of the United States Army in 1791, from a circa 1875 engraving by Benson J. Lossing.

him. "I had a strict eye to them, and will add but one word—Beware of a surprise! . . . I repeat it—*Beware of a surprise!*"

On November 4, 1791, just after roll call, St. Clair dismissed his troops. There was a jangling of bells and shouts from the woods, and rifle shots. St. Clair's men were attacked, more than five hundred men killed and some two hundred injured.

One night several weeks later, Washington was at dinner with some guests when an officer brought him news of St. Clair's defeat. Washington said nothing. Then, when the guests had gone and Mrs. Washington was in bed, Washington allowed himself to show his anger. "It's all over!" he told his secretary, Tobias Lear. "St. Clair defeated! Routed! The officers nearly all killed . . . too shocking to think of, and a surprise into the bargain! . . . The very thing I guarded him against—O God! O God!" he said and threw up his hands. "He's worse than a murderer!" Washington was quiet for a moment. He sat on the sofa and then quietly told Lear, "This must not go beyond this room," and then added that when St. Clair returned, "I will receive him without displeasure. I will hear him without prejudice."

When St. Clair returned from the west, he visited with Washington, took his hand, and cried. Washington was kind to St. Clair and didn't reproach him. A committee of the House of Representatives cleared St. Clair of any wrongdoing.

St. Clair was succeeded by General Anthony Wayne, known as "Mad Anthony" during the Revolution because of the fierce, determined, almost reckless way he charged into battle.

While General Wayne raised troops, Washington spoke with members of Congress and state legislatures. He told them that there would be no peace with the American Indians without a respect for their rights to life and property. In August 1794, during Washington's second term, Wayne offered to make peace with the American Indians, but they refused to put down their weapons. Wayne and his troops then attacked and defeated them.

During his first term in 1791, Vermont was admitted as the nation's fourteenth state, the first to have a clause in its state charter outlawing slavery. In 1792 Kentucky became the fifteenth state, and in 1796 Tennessee became the sixteenth.

Toward the end of his first term, Washington thought of retiring. He had just passed his sixtieth birthday. He wanted to go home to Mount Vernon, to be a farmer again. He even asked James Madison to prepare a brief announcement of these intentions. A sure indication of Washington's importance to the new government is that both Jefferson and Hamilton, adversaries who agreed on little else, urged him to stay on. "The confidence of the whole Union," Jefferson wrote, "is centered on you." Hamilton also tried to convince Washington to seek reelection and concluded a letter to him on the subject with, "The sentiments I have delivered upon this occasion, I can truly say, proceed exclusively from an anxious concern for the public welfare and an affectionate personal attachment."

Washington put off retirement, and when the Electoral College met, John Adams was reelected vice president with seventy-seven of eighty-seven votes, and George Washington, with all eighty-seven votes, was reelected president. On March 4, 1793, in the senate chamber, he took the oath of office and began his second term.

22. Mrs. Washington's Dearest Wish

Washington's second inauguration, on March 4, 1793, was much simpler than his first. Judge William Cushing of the Supreme Court administered the oath in the senate chamber, witnessed by government officials, foreign ministers, and as many spectators as the room would hold.

Just a few weeks later, disturbing news reached Washington from France. That country was in the midst of a revolution of its own. On January 21, 1793, King Louis XVI, who had helped the United States fight for its independence, was beheaded. On February 1 the new leaders of France declared war on England and Holland.

Secretary of State Thomas Jefferson felt the "tree of liberty" that flourished in the United States was now being planted in Europe. There was a call in America to help the French rebels, but from the very start of his presidency, Washington's intention was to only do what he felt was best for the United States.

In July 1791 Washington wrote to Gouverneur Morris of New York, who was in France, "I trust we shall never so far lose sight of our own interest and happiness." In 1793, when news of war between France and England reached Washington, he wrote to Thomas Jefferson, "It behooves the government of this country to use every means in its power to prevent the citizens thereof from embroiling us with either of those powers." Washington insisted the country stay out of the conflict, and on April 22 signed his Proclamation of Neutrality.

The American people were outraged.

"Ten thousand people," Vice President John Adams wrote, "threatened to drag Washington out of his house, and effect a revolution in the government, or compel it to declare in favor of the French Revolution and against England."

There was a newspaper drawing of Washington that showed him dressed in royal robes on a guillotine, about to be beheaded. "I had rather be in my grave," Washington told his cabinet, "than in my present situation." But Washington was firm. He directed Jefferson to recognize the new French government, but he kept the United States out of war.

French diplomat Edmond-Charles Genet, a literary scholar but a disastrous minister to the United States, from a circa 1900 engraving, artist unknown

In the midst of all this, Edmond-Charles Genet, the new French minister, arrived in America. He saw a bust of King Louis XVI in Washington's house and declared it an "insult to France." When Washington would not support the French Revolution, Genet said he would appeal directly to the American people. He even paid Americans to arm ships and sent them out to pirate the British.

Washington was furious and the French

government recalled Genet. On February 22, 1795, Washington's sixty-third birthday, Baron Jean-Antoine-Joseph Fauchet, the new French minister, came to see Washington. Fauchet wanted Genet arrested and sent home, but Genet knew what awaited him there—the guillotine. Washington, once angry at Genet, was now benevolent and granted him asylum. Genet remained in the United States as a private citizen.

Next, Washington needed to make peace with England. At the end of the Revolution, British soldiers kidnapped African-American slaves and took them to England. The British still held forts west of the Ohio River. They armed American Indians, who raided American ships, stole goods, and took prisoners. Washington sent Supreme Court Chief Justice John Jay to London to end these problems and negotiate a treaty.

Jay did the best he could. Money owed England would be paid, and in exchange the British agreed to give up their western forts and stop raiding American ships. Washington received angry letters from people who felt the United States gave up too much and got too little in return. Washington described the protests as "exaggerated and indecent." He wrote to Hamilton, "The cry against the Treaty is like that against a mad dog."

Washington recommended the Senate ratify the treaty and, after much debate, it did. Soon people appreciated how much it did to help improve trade.

In addition to all this, Washington had to deal with a group of angry, armed Americans, participants in the Whiskey Rebellion.

In March 1791, to raise money to pay off the nation's debt, a tax was set on liquor. In 1794 western farmers who made their own whiskey refused to pay it. Washington sent a force of more than twelve thousand soldiers to enforce the law. Fortunately there was no fight. By the time the troops arrived, the rebels had gone home.

A few roots of America's future fight for its soul can be found in the first

Gilbert Stuart was born in Rhode Island and studied art in Edinburgh, Scotland, and London, England. Upon his return to the United States in 1793, he painted portraits from life of Washington and other important Americans, from a circa 1900 engraving, artist unknown.

Martha Washington, from a portrait by Gilbert Stuart, circa 1790

year of Washington's second term. One was the passage of the Fugitive Slave Law, which empowered slave owners to capture runaways. Later in 1793, Eli Whitney took out a patent on the cotton gin, a device that greatly increased the profitability of growing cotton and thus increased the demand for African-American slaves. Also that year, fears of a slave uprising were heightened when several slaves in Albany, New York, set fires that resulted in an estimated $250,000 in damages. Five slaves—three men and two women—were arrested, charged with arson, and executed.

Two years later, in 1795, near the end of his presidency, Washington first posed for Gilbert Stuart, a loose-talking, heavy-drinking artist who tried to relax Washington with talk of battles and history. It didn't work. At last he said, "You must let me forget that you are General Washington and that I am Stuart the painter." Washington told Stuart he preferred if they would both remember who they were. Stuart's three portraits of Washington show how Washington's ill-fitting false teeth distorted his mouth.

Washington was still a trusted and popular leader but he decided not to seek a third term. And this decision said a lot about his concept of the new form of government, that he did not see it dependent on one man, even if *he* was that man. It also confirmed his sincerity when, in 1782, he wrote Colonel Nicola of the "painful sensations" he felt at the suggestion he become an American monarch. Many people seek power, but few voluntarily relinquish it. His decision set a precedent that was not broken until 1940 by President Franklin D. Roosevelt. Later an amendment was added to the Constitution that limited a president to just two terms.

On September 19, 1796, a farewell address Washington wrote but never gave was printed in a Philadelphia newspaper. In it Washington wrote of the need for the nation to pay its debts. He wanted commercial connections with other nations but "to have with them as little *political* connection as possible." He warned against forming political parties. Then he wrote of his retirement, "that retreat, in which I promise myself to realize, without alloy, the sweet enjoyment of partaking, in the midst of my fellow Citizens, the benign influence of good laws under a free government."

Unlike the first two elections for president, in this third one there was a contest between two political parties. John Adams was the Federalist candidate against Thomas Jefferson for the Republicans. On February 8, 1897, the votes of the Electoral College were opened and counted, and the result was announced by John Adams, who was still vice president. He announced his own election as president with seventy-one votes to sixty-eight for Jefferson, who, as the candidate with the second highest vote, became vice president.

Washington was pleased to be done with public service, to be able to go home as a private citizen. "I have not a wish to mix again in the great world," Washington wrote on March 3 to Henry Knox, "or partake in its politics. . . . The remainder of my life, which in the course of nature cannot be long, will be occupied in rural amusements."

The night before Adams's inauguration, Washington had dinner with Adams, Jefferson, and some foreign ministers and their wives. Washington raised his glass. "Ladies and gentlemen," he said, "this is the last time I shall drink to your health as a public man. I do it with sincerity, wishing you all possible happiness."

The next day, Washington watched as John Adams was sworn in as the nation's second president. After the ceremony, people cheered as Washington walked from the hall. There were tears in his eyes as he waved his hat to the crowd.

Eight years earlier, when Washington first became president, Mrs. Washington wrote in a letter that she had thought when the Revolution was over, "from that moment we should be suffered to grow old together in solitude and tranquility. That was the first and dearest wish of my heart." Now her dearest wish would come true.

Excerpts from Washington's Talk to the Cherokee Nation

(This talk, given in Philadelphia on August 29, 1796, shortly before the end of Washington's second term, shows him to be aware of the problems that expanding settlements brought American Indians, but his solution was surely difficult for an independent people to accept.)

Beloved Cherokees:

Many years have passed since the White people first came to America. In that long space of time many good men have considered how the condition of the Indian natives of the country might be improved; and many attempts have been made to effect it. But, as we see at this day, all these attempts have been nearly fruitless. I also have thought much on this subject, and anxiously wished that the various Indian tribes, as well as their neighbors, the White people, might enjoy in abundance all the good things which make life comfortable and happy. I have considered how this could be done; and have discovered but one path I wish all the Indian nations to walk. From the information received concerning you, my beloved Cherokees, I am inclined to hope that you are prepared to take this path and disposed to pursue it.

Beloved Cherokees,

You now find that the game with which your woods once abounded, are growing scarce, and you know when you cannot meet a deer to kill, that you must remain hungry; you know also when you get no skins by hunting, that the traders will give you neither powder nor clothing; and that without other implements for tilling the ground than the hoe, you will continue to raise only scanty crops of corn. Hence you are sometimes exposed to suffer much from hunger and cold; and as the game are lessening in numbers more and more, these sufferings will increase. And how are you to provide against them? Listen to my words and you will know.

My beloved Cherokees,

Some among you already experience the advantage of keeping cattle and hogs: let all keep them and increase their numbers, and you will have plenty of meat. To these add sheep, and they will give you clothing as well as food. Your lands are good and of great extent. By proper management you can raise livestock not only for your own wants, but to sell to the White people. By using the plow you can vastly increase your crops of corn. You can also grow wheat which makes the best bread as well as other useful grain. To these you will easily add flax and cotton, which you may dispose of to the White people, or have it made up by your own women into clothing for yourselves.... But the cares of the United States are not confined to your single nation. They extend to all the Indians dwelling on their borders....

Beloved Cherokees,

What I have recommended to you I am myself going to do. After a few moons have passed I shall leave this great town and retire to my farm.... When I have retired to my farm I shall hear of you; and it will give me great pleasure to know that you have taken my advice.

23. "I Am Just Going"

It was time for Washington to leave Philadelphia and return to Mount Vernon. He had a house full of furniture and tried to sell some of it to John Adams, but the thrifty new president wasn't interested. Washington did sell

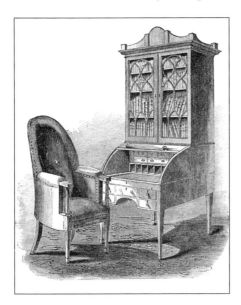

Washington's desk and chair; perhaps the desk is the one he sold to Eliza Powell, from a circa 1870 engraving by Lossing and Barritt, based on a drawing by Benson J. Lossing.

a desk to a friend, Eliza Powell. Luckily, she was discreet. Inside the desk she found some love letters written to Washington by Martha. Powell returned them unopened. Whatever Washington didn't sell, he sent home. His possessions, bedding, folding screens, carpets, plate warmers, fire buckets, and fruit trees filled ninety-seven boxes, forty-three casks, fourteen trunks, and three hampers.

The Washingtons were delighted to go home. As Martha Washington wrote to Lucy Knox, they felt "like children just released from school." Martha had been ill the previous year with malaria and looked forward to resting in her own home, in her own bed. Washington was tired of public life and looked forward to getting back to his farm. They went home with Martha's sixteen-year-old granddaughter Nelly, the girl they'd adopted; Lafayette's sixteen-year-old son, who stayed with them; Washington's secretary Tobias Lear; their many servants; and their parrot, Snipe, and dog, Frisk.

The Washingtons arrived home on March 15, 1797.

There was a lot to be done at Mount Vernon. Washington hired painters, carpenters, brick layers, and glaziers. Then he complained that wherever he went he was disturbed by the sound of hammers and the smell of paint.

Throughout the work, Mount Vernon was busy. It was an open house with lots of visitors. Martha Washington liked to chat with them, and while she talked, she knitted. Both Washingtons busied themselves with letter writing, and their letters reveal how old they felt. "Our dancing days are no more," George Washington wrote in response to his nephew's wedding invitation, and when his sister Betty Washington Lewis died, he wrote to her son, "The melancholy of your writing has filled me with inexpressible concern." And then, perhaps thinking of himself, he added, "The debt of nature however, sooner or later, must be paid by us all."

Washington stayed mostly at home until mid-1798 when a crisis induced him to go to Philadelphia to organize a new army.

The French ordered their warships to stop American boats and "detain them for examination," disrupting American trade. President Adams sent

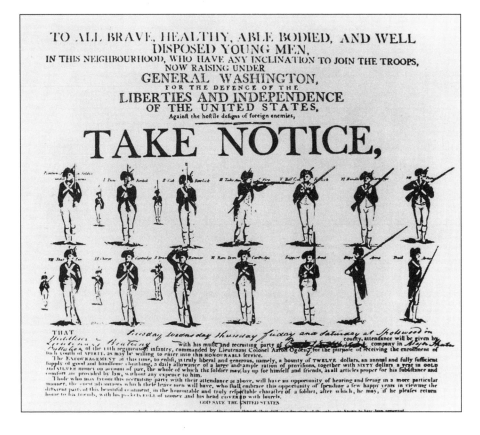

A 1798 recruiting poster circulated at the time of the threatened war with France.

three ministers to France, where they met with three agents. These agents demanded a bribe of $250,000 and a loan to the French government of $10 million. Without that, they said, there would be no negotiations. The American ministers refused to pay and were told to leave the country. In their report, they referred to the three French agents as X, Y, and Z, so this became known as the XYZ Affair. When news of it reached the American people, they were outraged. "Millions for defense," became the rallying cry, "but not one cent for tribute."

Adams and Congress ordered that troops be recruited for the army and navy. They appointed sixty-six-year-old Washington as commander of American forces. At Washington's urging, Alexander Hamilton was appointed his second in command.

The country was ready for war.

There were some minor skirmishes on the sea, but in the end there was no French invasion, so Washington went home. The whole business was settled in 1800, after Washington's death, when the French agreed to no longer stop American ships.

While Washington was busy with farming and soldiering, his nephew Lawrence Lewis and the step-granddaughter he adopted, Nelly Custis, fell in love. They married on Friday, February 22, 1799, Washington's sixty-seventh birthday. The young couple made their home on a section of his Mount Vernon estate.

Sometime after the wedding, according to a letter said to be written by Martha, George Washington had a dream that told him he would soon die. On July 9, 1799, he wrote his last will and testament.

Washington's step-granddaughter Nelly Custis, from a circa 1870 engraving by Lossing and Barritt, based on a drawing by Benson J. Lossing

"I, George Washington, of Mount Vernon, a citizen of the United States, and lately President of the same," he began the handwritten, twenty-eight-page document, "do make, ordain, and declare this instrument, which is written with my own hand, and every page thereof subscribed with my name, to be my last WILL and TESTAMENT, revoking all others."

Facsimiles.
March 12th 1744/5
Geo Washington

Beginning this Eleventh Day of November 1749
Washington

I am Sir, Yr. Most Obed. Hble Serv.
Fort Loudoun
10th Septr. 1757
G Washington

Yr. Most affect Brother,
G Washington
New York 29th of April 1776

Mount Vernon
December 10th
G Washington
1799

Copies of Washington's autographs at ages thirteen,
seventeen, twenty-five, forty-four, and sixty-seven, the last
written just four days before he died

His last wishes surely reveal his real values. He wanted needy, able children of coming generations to be offered the education he always regretted he never had. He left "four thousand dollars, or in other words, twenty of the shares which I hold in the Bank of Alexandria, toward the support of a free school, established at and annexed to, the said Academy for the purpose of educating such orphan children, or the children of such other poor and indigent persons, as are unable to accomplish it with their own means, and who, in the judgement of the trustees of the said seminary, are best entitled to benefit of this donation."

Washington added, "It has always been a source of serious regret," that Americans went abroad for their education and there might learn to appreciate "principles unfriendly to republican government," and encouraged the "establishment of a University in a central part of the United States, to which the youths of fortune and talents from all parts thereof may be sent for the completion of their education."

He left shares of stock he held for the establishment of a university in the new capital, the District of Columbia, and other shares of stock for Liberty Hall Academy in Rockbridge, Virginia.

He wrote in his will of the "vast advantages which the community would derive from the extension of its inland navigation" and left $10,000 for extending the navigation of the James River and £5,000 sterling for the opening of navigation of the Potomac River.

Washington directed that all his debts, "of which there are but few," and none very large, "be punctually and speedily paid." Then, "to my dearly beloved wife" he left the use of his whole estate, except "such parts thereof as are specially disposed of hereafter." Among those parts were his papers, which he left to his nephew Bushrod Washington; the gold-headed cane he inherited from Benjamin Franklin, which he left to his brother Charles

Washington; and a desk and chair, which he left to his friend Dr. Craik. But it is the second item in his will that is perhaps the most interesting. In it he gave instructions on what would be done with his slaves.

"Upon the decease of my wife," he wrote, "it is my will and desire that all the slaves whom I hold in my own right shall receive their freedom." He directed that those too old, too young, or disabled to take care of themselves "be comfortably clothed and fed by my heirs." Those too young to go out on their own and without parents to care for them should "be taught to read and write, and to be brought up to some useful occupation." Washington had instructions on those who remained slaves. "I do hereby forbid," he wrote, "the sale or transportation out of said Commonwealth [Virginia]." He directed "that this clause respecting slaves, and every part thereof, be religiously fulfilled . . . without evasion, neglect, or delay." He did, however, allow a slight wait, "until the crops which may then be on the ground are harvested." When Washington died before Martha, the terms of his will became known. Instead of waiting for Martha to die, all but one of the slaves was set free on January 1, 1801. That one man, Elish, served Martha until she died. Through the remainder of the summer of 1799 and the fall that followed, Washington kept his full schedule of letter writing and making the rounds on his estate. Then, according to an 1840 biography, in early December, he walked with an unidentified nephew and showed him all the changes he planned to make. Among them he wanted the family vault (burial place) to be rebuilt. "'I intend to place it there,'" his nephew later quoted, "pointing to the spot." And he planned that to be the first change he made. "After all," Washington said, "I may require it before the rest."

The nephew left with a friend and Washington wished them a pleasant journey. "It was a bright frosty morning, he had taken his usual ride, and the clear healthy flush on his cheek, and his sprightly manner, brought the remark from both of us that we had never seen the general look so well. . . . A few days afterwards, being on my way home in company with others, while we were conversing about Washington, I saw a servant rapidly riding toward us. On his near approach, I recognized him as belonging to Mount Vernon. He rode up—his countenance told the story—he handed me a letter. Washington was dead!"

In April 1743 Augustine Washington had ridden for several hours in the rain, come home soaked, and died a short while later. On Thursday morning, December 12, 1799, his son George rode in the rain and two days later met the same fate.

In the morning, at about ten o'clock Washington rode out on an overcast day. At one, it started to snow, which changed to hail, and then to a cold rain. Washington continued his ride. He returned home after three o'clock, soaked, but did not change from his wet clothes. He signed some letters, but told his secretary Tobias Lear that the weather, which was not too bad for him to ride in, was now too bad to send a servant out to mail the letters.

By the next morning the snow was three inches deep and Washington stayed at home. His throat was sore and he had a slight cold, but still, in the afternoon when the weather cleared, he went out. That night after his return, when Lear suggested he take something to ease the discomfort in his throat, Washington said, "You know I never take anything for a cold. Let it go as it came."

But the cold wouldn't go. By the middle of the night Washington had trouble breathing. He woke up Martha but wouldn't allow her to call any of the servants. By morning, Washington could hardly talk. A drink of molasses, vinegar, and butter was made to soothe his throat, but he couldn't swallow it.

Rawlins, overseer of one of his farms, came with a knife and cut Washington to make him bleed, a common remedy of the time. "More! More!" Washington said, but after half a pint was taken, Mrs. Washington had Rawlins stop. Washington's friend Dr. Craik and two other doctors came. They tried various remedies. They even bled Washington again. Nothing helped.

"I find I am going," he told Lear. "My breath cannot last long."

The death of Washington, with his wife, servants, and doctors at his side, from a circa 1900 engraving, artist unknown

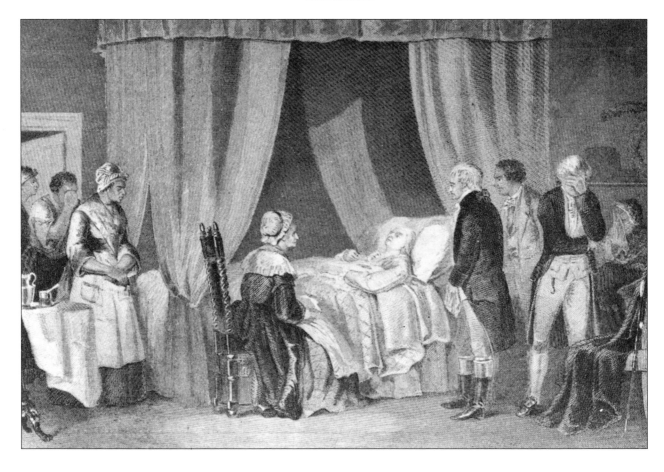

"I told him," Lear wrote later, "I hoped he was not so near the end. He observed, smiling, that he certainly was, and that, as it was the debt which we all must pay, he looked to the event with perfect resignation."

"Doctor," Washington told Dr. Craik later that afternoon, "I die hard, but I am not afraid to go." A few hours later he said, "I am just going. Have me decently buried."

Sometime between ten and eleven o'clock at night, Washington died, "without a struggle or a sigh," Lear wrote.

Mrs. Washington, who sat by his bed, asked, "Is he gone?" When she was told he was, she said, "'Tis well. All is over now. I shall soon follow him."

George Washington died on Saturday night, December 14, 1799. He was sixty-seven years old. Martha Washington died almost two and a half years later, on May 22, 1802, at the age of seventy.

The inscription on the back of these silhouettes from 1799,
presumably done by Washington's step-granddaughter Nelly
shortly before his death, tells their story: "The within are profiles
of General and Mrs. Washington taken from their shadows on a
wall. They are as perfect likenesses as profiles can give."

American Mercury
Thursday December 26, 1799

Published by Elisha Babcock
Vol. XVI

Hartford
no. 808

ALEXANDRIA, Dec. 16.

It is our painful duty to announce to our country and the world the death

OF GENERAL
GEORGE WASHINGTON

This mournful event occurred last Saturday evening, about 11 o'clock. On the preceding night he was attacked with a violent inflamation of the throat, which in less than twenty hours put a period to his life.

Extract of a letter from Alexandria, dated 15th December 1799.

Alas! Our WASHINGTON, our Brave, our Virtuous and our Wise Commander in Chief, is no more!! He was carried off by the quinzy last evening, about 11 o'clock. He rose yesterday morning as usual, but finding himself indisposed, returned to his bed again, and sent for medical aid; but alas! though three able physicians, to wit, Craik, Dick and Brown, from Port Tobacco, arrived at Mount Vernon between the hours of one and three in the evening, they could not save him. As a mark of respect to him, all business will be suspended here tomorrow; and it will stand recorded forever hereafter as a day of mourning.

"Far as the stars
   which gild the vault of
   night
"Unnumber'd pour
   effulgence on the fight
"So Chiefs and enamors
   in crowds abound,
"But rare as comets
   Washingtons are found."

HARTFORD, December 26.
ON SATURDAY THE 14TH INSTANT DIED SUDDENLY AT HIS SEAT IN VIRGINIA
GEN. GEORGE WASHINGTON
COMMANDER IN CHIEF

Of the Armies of the United States of America

MATURE IN YEARS, COVERED WITH GLORY, AND RICH IN THE AFFECTION OF THE AMERICAN PEOPLE

When men of common character are swept from the theater of life, they die without the tribute of public notice or concern, as they had lived without a claim to public esteem. When personages of more exalted worth are summoned from the scenes of sublunary existence, their death calls forth a burst of general regret, and invigorates the flame of Public gratitude. In obedience to the wishes and to the voice of their country, the orator, the poet and the historian combine to do justice to the virtues of their character, while the labours of the painter, the sculptor, and the statuary, in perpetuating their likeness, do homage to their memory.

But, when, in compliance with heaven's high mandate, the hero of the age lies numbered with the dead; When the reverend sage, the August statesman, the father of his country has resigned his breath, When the idol of an empire, the envy and admiration of distant nations, and the brightest ornament of human nature; When WASHINGTON, is no more, let a sense of general loss be testified by the badges of general mourning; but let not the voice of eulogy be heard, lest the weakness of talents, and the deficiency of language, do injustice to the lustre and fame of the deceased.

Mount Vernon
December 15, 1799
Sir,

It is with inexpressible grief, that I have to announce to you the death of the great and good General Washington. He died last evening between 10 and 11 o'clock, after a short illness of about twenty four hours. His disorder was an inflammatory sore-throat, which proceeded from a cold, of which he made but little complaint on Friday. On Saturday morning about three o'clock he became ill. Doctor Dick, attended him in the morning, and Dr. Craik of Alexandria, and Dr. Brown, of Port Tobacco, were soon after called in. Every medical assistance was offered, but without the desired effect. His last scene corresponded with the whole tenor of his life. Not a groan nor a complaint escaped him, in extreme distress. With perfect resignation and a full possession of his reason, he closed his well spent life.

I have the honor to be &c.

TOBIAS LEAR

Epilogue: "Our Washington Is No More!"

The news of Washington's death was first heard in nearby Alexandria. The city's bells started to toll and the soft ringing did not stop for four days and nights. On Monday morning, December 16, the shops were closed and the people of Alexandria all wore black.

News traveled slowly in 1799. The news of Washington's death first reached Congress on Wednesday, December 18.

"Mr. Speaker," John Marshall, who was then a member of Congress and later chief justice of the Supreme Court, said, "Information has just been received that our illustrious fellow-citizen, the Commander in Chief of the American Armies, and the late President of the United States, is no more." Marshall spoke softly. "After receiving information of this national calamity, so heavy and so afflicting, the House of Representatives can be ill fitted for public business. I move you, therefore, they adjourn."

The motion carried. The House adjourned until the next morning.

The next day, Thursday, December 19, Marshall rose again in Congress.

Engraving based on a portrait of Washington by Alonzo Chappel

He was clearly grief-stricken. In a low, sad voice he said, "The melancholy event which was yesterday announced with doubt, has been rendered but too certain. Our Washington is no more! The hero, the sage, the patriot of America—the man on whom in times of danger every eye was turned and all our hopes were placed, lives now only in his great actions, and in the hearts of an affectionate and afflicted people."

Members of the House resolved to wear black and to drape the Speaker's chair in black. They sent condolences to President John Adams.

Adams wrote to the House "on the melancholy and afflicting event," and called Washington "the most illustrious and beloved personage which this country ever produced."

Members of the Senate sent a note to Adams, too. "Permit us, sir," they wrote, "to mingle our tears with yours; on this occasion it is manly to weep. . . . Our country mourns her father. . . . With patriotic pride we review the life of our Washington, and compare him with those of other countries who have been preeminent in fame. Ancient and modern names diminish before him."

"His example is now complete," Adams replied, "and it will teach wisdom and virtue to magistrates, citizens and men, not only in the present age, but in future generations, as long as our history shall be read."

Beginning at eleven o'clock on Wednesday, December 18, people began to gather at Mount Vernon for Washington's funeral. The ceremony was fixed for noon, but it was delayed until the military honor guard arrived. Meanwhile, the body of Washington in its coffin was on the grand porch where he so often sat and entertained guests.

Sometime after three, the funeral procession began. With it, in a salute to the fallen hero, guns were fired from a boat anchored in the Potomac River.

Washington's horse, with his saddle, holsters, and gun, was led riderless by two men dressed in black. After Washington's death, no one was ever allowed to ride that horse. A minister walked beside the coffin and read the words of the church. He finished with, "As it was in the beginning, is now, and ever shall be, world without end, Amen." When the procession reached the family vault, the Reverend Thomas Davis led the funeral service and made a short speech. The soldiers fired their guns three times followed by eleven cannon shots.

The death of Washington had been quick and unexpected. At first, Mrs. Washington had trouble dealing with it, but her religious beliefs gave her comfort. Soon her general cheerfulness returned.

President and Mrs. Adams and many other leading citizens of the nation visited Mount Vernon to console Mrs. Washington. Letters of condolence came from throughout the country and Europe.

When news of Washington's death reached France, all its flags were flown at half-mast. "Washington is dead," Napoléon, that nation's new young leader, declared. "This great man fought against tyranny. He established the liberty of his country. His memory will always be dear to the French people."

Napoléon ordered that black cloth be hung for ten days along with all the nation's flags.

Even the British mourned Washington's death. When the news reached the admiral of the British fleet, he had his ship's flag lowered to half-mast. The sixty other British ships in the water followed his example.

Of the founding fathers of the United States, Washington was a giant among giants. His influence on the nation he helped create is still felt today. While the Constitution outlined our system of government, it was Washington more than anyone else who showed that it could work. How he managed the office of president was a model for all those who followed him. But with it all, there was a modesty about him, a feeling he had that he was no more a patriot than thousands of others were, that he did not deserve great praise.

A 1789 incident clearly shows his attitude toward public service. Washington was on his New England tour and stopped in Ipswich, Massachusetts. Mr. Cleaveland, a local minister, first took off his hat and stepped forward. "Put on your hat, Parson," Washington told him, "and I will shake hands with you."

"I cannot wear my hat in your presence," Cleaveland said, "when I think of what you have done for this country."

"You did as much as I," Washington said. "You did what you could and I've done no more."

Washington did a great deal and is rightfully revered for it all. At his death, John Marshall asked that congress pass a resolution to properly honor "the memory of the man first in war, first in peace, and first in the hearts of his fellow-citizens."

Washington's Words

"The General is sorry to be informed that the foolish, and wicked practice, of profane cursing and swearing (a Vice heretofore little known in an American Army) is growing into fashion; he hopes the officers will, by example, as well as influence, endeavor to check it . . . it is a vice so mean and low without any temptation, that every man of sense, and character detests and despises it."

—From his August 3, 1776, orders to the troops

"Nothing short of Independence, it appears to me, can possibly do. A Peace, on other terms, would, if I may be allowed the expression, be a Peace of War."

—From an April 21, 1778, letter sent from Valley Forge to John Banister, a Virginia delegate to the Continental Congress

"There is nothing so likely to produce peace as to be well prepared to meet an Enemy."

—From a January 29, 1780, letter sent from his headquarters at Morristown to Elbridge Gerry

"I have always considered marriage as the most interesting event of one's life, the foundation of happiness or misery."

—From a May 23, 1785, letter to Burwell Bassett. Washington's nephew was courting Bassett's daughter.

"In answer to the observation you make on the probability of my election to the Presidency (knowing me as you do) I need only say, that it has no enticing charms, and no fascinating allurements for me."

—From an April 28, 1788, letter to the Marquis de Lafayette

"Nothing but harmony, honesty, industry and frugality are necessary to make us a great and happy people."

"While you are quarreling among yourselves in Europe; while one King is running mad, and others acting as if they were already so . . . we shall continue in tranquility here."

—Both quotes from a January 29, 1789, letter to the Marquis de Lafayette

"It is now no more that toleration is spoken of, as if it was by the indulgence of one class of people, that another enjoyed the exercise of their inherent natural rights. For happily the government of the United States, which gives to bigotry no sanction, to persecution no assistance, requires only that they who live under its protection should demean themselves as good citizens."

—From an August 17, 1790, letter to the Touro Synagogue of Newport, Rhode Island

"True friendship is a plant of slow growth."

"Where there is no occasion for expressing an opinion, it is best to be silent, for there is nothing more certain than that it is at all times more easy to make enemies than friends."

—Both quotes from a November 28, 1796, letter of advice sent to his adopted son (and step-grandson) George Washington Parke Custis

"Against the effect of time and age, no remedy has ever yet been discovered; and like the rest of my fellow mortals, I must (if life is prolonged) submit, and be reconciled, to a gradual decline."

—From an October 5, 1798, letter to Landon Carter, who had sent Washington his thoughts on how to remain in good health

Washington's Generals

Benedict Arnold (1741–1801) was born in Norwich, Connecticut. He enlisted twice in British militia units during the French and Indian War and deserted twice. In May 1775, as a colonel of the Massachusetts militia, and with Ethan Allen, he led the capture of Fort Ticonderoga. He fought at Lake Champlain, Ridgefield, and Saratoga. In 1777 Arnold was disappointed when officers of lower ranks were promoted above him. Washington reprimanded him for using his military position for personal profit. In 1780 he was in command of the military outposts at West Point, New York, and was found to have conspired with British Major John André to turn them over to the enemy; he then fled to the British side. In December 1781 he moved to London, where he remained the rest of his life.

James Clinton (1733–1812) was born in Orange County, New York. He took part in the campaigns in Quebec, was commander of New York's Fort Clinton, and defended the New York frontier against Tory and American Indian raids. He joined Washington at Yorktown. His younger brother George was governor of New York (1777–1795 and 1801–1804) and vice president of the United States (1805–1812). His son DeWitt was governor of New York (1817–1823 and 1825–1828).

Horatio Gates (1728–1806) was born in Maldon, England. He took part in Edward Braddock's disastrous 1755 campaign, which is where he first met Washington. Gates retired from the British army in 1772 and, with the help of Washington, settled in Virginia. In 1775 he joined the Continental army and led its forces to important victories at the battles of Freeman's Farm and Bemis Heights, together referred to as the battles of Saratoga. These successes led to French support of the American cause, which was vital to the ultimate American victory. Gates also led American forces in the terrible defeat three years later at Camden, South Carolina.

Nathanael Greene (1742–1786) was born in Warwick, Rhode Island. He was considered by many to be the army's most capable general. He fought in the battles of Boston, Trenton, Fort Washington, Brandywine Creek, Germantown, and Monmouth. When Benedict Arnold's plot to surrender West Point was discovered, Greene succeeded him there. He was president of the court that tried and convicted Major André. In 1780 he was given command of the southern army. His successes there with a hit-and-run type attack, similar in some ways to what is now called guerrilla fighting, contributed greatly to Patriot victory in the south. After the Revolution, the grateful citizens of Georgia gave him a plantation.

Henry Knox (1750–1806) was born in Boston, Massachusetts. At the outbreak of the Revolution, he was a Boston bookseller and joined the Continental army at Cambridge, during the siege of Boston. The heavy guns he brought from Fort Ticonderoga helped chase British forces out of Boston. He participated in the battles of Bunker Hill, Long Island, Trenton, Princeton, Brandywine Creek, Germantown, Monmouth, and Yorktown as Washington's artillery expert. He later was secretary of war (1785–1794).

Marie-Joseph-Paul-Yves-Roch-Gilbert du Motier, Marquis de Lafayette (1757–1834) was a wealthy French nobleman born in Chavaniac, France. In 1777 he arrived in Philadelphia and volunteered to serve in the Continental army. In July he was made a major general. Two months later he fought bravely at Brandywine Creek, and in 1778 ably led troops at the battle of Monmouth. Lafayette was one of the judges at the court-martial of Major André. In 1781, as a commander of Virginia troops, he helped trap Cornwallis at Yorktown. After the Revolution he returned to France. He was hailed a hero when he returned to visit the United States in 1784 and 1824. He was a strong voice for religious tolerance and the abolition of slavery.

Charles Lee (1731–1782) was born in Dernhall, England. He was so short-tempered and headstrong that American Indians named him Boiling Water. Lee served with Braddock in the disastrous defeat of 1755. While he was in America he married the daughter of a Seneca Indian chief. In 1763 he retired from the British army. Two years later he joined the Polish army and rose to the rank of major general. In 1773 he settled in America. Because of his military experience and dedication to American independence, Congress appointed him a major general in June 1775, third in rank behind Washington and Artemas Ward. He served in Boston (1775–1776) and defended Charleston (June 1776). In 1777 he may have helped the British with information. On June 28, 1778, he retreated from the battle at Monmouth, New Jersey, and was soundly scolded by Washington. This led to his court-martial, a one-year suspension from command, and his retirement from the army.

Benjamin Lincoln (1733–1810) was born in Hingham, Massachusetts. He served at the siege of Boston and the battle of Saratoga and in 1778 was given command of the southern troops but lost it after the defeat at Charleston when he and some 5,500 of his troops were captured. In 1781 he was Washington's deputy at the battle of Yorktown. When Cornwallis surrendered, Washington chose Lincoln to represent the Continental army and accept Cornwallis's sword.

Francis Marion (1732–1795) was born in Winyah, South Carolina. He fought in the battles of Charleston, Savannah, and Eutaw Springs. In May 1780, after the loss of Charleston, he ran off to the swamps with fifty-two of his men and harassed the British. This earned him the nickname Swamp Fox. British Colonel Banastre Tarleton called Marion an "old fox" and said, "The devil himself could not catch him."

Richard Montgomery (1736–1775) was born in Dublin, Ireland. His father was a member of the Irish Parliament. Montgomery first came to America to fight the French in the French and Indian War. He went home in 1765 but returned to America in May 1773, bought a farm in New York, and became a Patriot. Along with General Benedict Arnold, he led the December 31, 1775, doomed attack on Quebec, where he was killed.

Daniel Morgan (1736–1802) was born in Hunterdon County, New Jersey. While he served with Braddock in 1755, he struck a British officer and was given five hundred lashes. Sometimes, during the Revolution, to motivate his men before battle, he lifted his shirt and showed them the scars from that whipping. Morgan took

part with Benedict Arnold in the battle for Quebec and with Horatio Gates in the battles of Saratoga. In 1781 he led Patriot forces to a surprising victory over the British at Cowpens, South Carolina. He was a cousin of Daniel Boone.

Israel Putnam (1718–1790) was born in Salem Village, Massachusetts, and fought in three wars: the French and Indian, Pontiac's, and the Revolutionary. He commanded American troops at the battle of Bunker Hill, where, because his men had limited gunpowder, according to some reports, he told them that when the enemy attacked, "Don't fire until you see the whites of their eyes." He also fought at the battles of Long Island and Princeton. In December 1779 he suffered a stroke and was forced to retire from service.

Philip John Schuyler (1733–1804) was born in Albany, New York. He was a delegate from New York to the Second Continental Congress, which appointed him one of the four generals just under Washington. He prepared for the invasion of Canada, but became sick and had to give up his command. Later, when he returned and lost Fort Ticonderoga to the British, he was court-martialed. The court acquitted him. He was a U.S. senator (1789–1791 and 1797–1798) and the father-in-law of Alexander Hamilton.

Arthur St. Clair (1736–1818) was born in Thurso, Scotland. He came to America in 1755. Soon after the battles of Trenton (December 1776) and Princeton (January 1777), where he led troops, he was made a major general and put in command of Fort Ticonderoga. Five months later he led the evacuation of the fort. St. Clair's actions were questioned. A court-martial found he had no choice but to retreat, that it saved the lives of Patriot soldiers. He wintered with Washington at Valley Forge, fought at Monmouth, and raised troops for the battle of Yorktown. In 1791 more than five hundred of St. Clair's troops were lost in a surprise American Indian attack.

John Stark (1728–1822) was born in Londonderry, New Hampshire. In April 1775, as soon as he heard of the battles of Lexington and Concord, he rode to Cambridge and joined the army. He was chosen by his men to be an officer of the

New Hampshire militia. He was with Washington at the battle of Trenton and was one of the judges at West Point who convicted Major André. He was also at the battles of Bennington and Princeton. In 1781 he was made commander of the northern army.

Baron Friedrich Wilhelm von Steuben (1730–1794) was born in Magdeburg, Prussia. From 1757 to 1763 he was on the staff of King Frederick II of Prussia, also known as Frederick the Great. In February 1778 he reported to Washington at Valley Forge with letters of recommendation from the French minister of war and Benjamin Franklin. He joined Washington's staff, and with the help of Nathanael Greene and Alexander Hamilton, he trained the American troops. After that he wrote a drill book that was used by the U. S. Army for more than thirty years. He commanded one of the three divisions at Yorktown. He retired from the army in 1784 and settled in New York.

Artemas Ward (1727–1800) was born in Shrewsbury, Massachusetts. At the outbreak of the fighting he was commander of the Massachusetts militia and held the army together until Washington arrived at Cambridge to take command. Ward was considered for the post of commander in chief of the army. Instead he was appointed just under Washington and soon resigned from the military. He was later a member of Congress (1791–1795).

Anthony Wayne (1745–1796) was born in Chester County, Pennsylvania. He served with Washington at Valley Forge, where he helped supply the army. His most striking victory was at Stony Point, a British stronghold. While discussing the proposed attack with Washington, Wayne is reported to have said, "General, if you will only plan it, I will storm H--l!" At the battle of Stony Point he was shot in the head. He quickly got up and told his men, "March on! Carry me into the fort, for I will die at the head of my column!" They took Stony Point. Wayne survived and Congress awarded him a gold medal for his bravery. He also fought in the battles of Brandywine Creek, Germantown, Monmouth, and Yorktown. While his men nicknamed him Mad Anthony, he was often patient and his campaigns were well planned.

Washington's Cabinet

George Washington didn't have many meetings with his full cabinet, just five during his first term, but he met with the members individually and read and approved all their official letters.

Vice President
1789-1796

John Adams (1735–1826) was born in Braintree (now called Quincy), Massachusetts. He was active in the protests that led to the Revolution, was a member of the committee that in 1776 drafted the Declaration of Independence, and was one of the American delegates who negotiated the Treaty of Paris that ended the war. In 1775 Adams stood before the Second Continental Congress and said he had "but one gentleman in mind" to lead the Continental army, and proposed Washington. Later Adams was critical of how Washington conducted the war. As vice president, Adams was not at most cabinet meetings, but at times he did advise Washington. In 1796, after two terms as vice president, Adams was elected president. He felt the best way to keep the United States neutral in foreign affairs was to make it strong, so he increased the size of the army and armed American merchant ships. Adams appointed a commission to negotiate with the French, who were attacking American ships; but in 1798, when three French representatives demanded a bribe, it was refused. This became known as the XYZ Affair and led to the slogan: Millions for defense, but not one cent for tribute.

Secretary of State
1789-1793

Thomas Jefferson (1743–1826) was born in Shadwell, Virginia. He was the author of the Declaration of Independence, governor of Virginia during the Revolution, and later United States minister to France. As secretary of state his differences with Secretary of the Treasury Alexander Hamilton led to the formation of the nation's first two political parties, Jefferson's Democrat-Republicans, whose policies favored farmers and wanted less government, and Hamilton's Federalists, who supported merchants and industry and

a strong central government. In 1793, when fighting broke out between France and England, Jefferson wanted Washington to side with France and Hamilton favored England. Washington sided with neither country and in April 1793 issued his Proclamation of Neutrality. Jefferson tired of politics and later that year resigned from office, but he was soon back. In 1796 Jefferson was elected vice president, a Republican in a mostly Federalist administration. In 1800 he was elected president. Jefferson, a Republican, had defeated Adams, a Federalist, in what became known as the Revolution of 1800. Jefferson was reelected in 1804. During his two terms he lowered taxes; declared war on Tripoli, a North African state of pirates; and in 1803 approved the Louisiana Purchase, which doubled the size of the United States. One-time political opponents, Thomas Jefferson and John Adams died on the same day, July 4, 1826, exactly fifty years after the independence of the United States was declared with the document Jefferson wrote.

1794-1795

Edmund Randolph (1753–1813) was born in Williamsburg, Virginia. He was the son of John Randolph, attorney general of colonial Virginia who remained loyal to the king and fled to England at the outbreak of the Revolution, and the nephew of the first president of the Continental Congress, Peyton Randolph. Edmund Randolph was for a short time an aide to General Washington, but he spent most of the Revolution involved in Virginia politics and served as the state's first attorney general. Later, at the Constitutional Convention, it was Randolph who presented the Virginia Plan, sometimes called the Randolph Plan, for a federal government with an executive branch and two houses of Congress, with the representatives for both houses apportioned to each state according to its population. He advocated a strong central government with three "presidents," each from a different section of the country, and outlawing importing slaves. As the first attorney general of the United States, he served mostly as Washington's legal adviser. In 1794 he succeeded Jefferson as secretary of state and supported Washington's efforts to remain neutral in the fighting between France and England. He resigned in 1795 under a cloud of suspected bribery and treason when a letter he wrote to a French minister became public. He returned to Virginia, to the practice of law, and in 1807 successfully represented former vice president Aaron Burr, who was accused of treason.

1795–1800

Timothy Pickering (1745–1829) was born in Salem, Massachusetts. He wrote a soldier training manual and later served as quartermaster general (procurer of supplies) for the Continental army. After the war he moved to Pennsylvania, negotiated peace with various American Indian tribes, and helped outline plans for the slave-free settlement of the Northwest Territory. He served in Washington's cabinet as postmaster general, secretary of war, and finally as secretary of state. He served as secretary of state under Adams, too, until 1800, when he was dismissed over a disagreement on the nation's relations with France. Pickering moved back to Massachusetts, whose people he served first in the United States Senate (1803–1811), where he voiced strong opposition to the Louisiana Purchase, and later as a member of the House of Representatives (1813–1817), where he spoke out against American involvement in the War of 1812.

Secretary of the Treasury

1789–1795

Alexander Hamilton (1755 or 1757–1804) was born in the British West Indies, came to the American colonies in 1772, and the next year entered King's College in New York (now called Columbia University). There he wrote pamphlets that attacked British rule in the colonies. In 1775, just after the firing at Lexington and Concord, Hamilton joined the  Continental army and in 1777 became Washington's aide, secretary, and confidant. He remained in the army until 1781, when he returned to New York to study law. In 1787 he was a delegate from New York to the Constitutional Convention, where he pushed for a strong central government. In 1789 Washington named him the nation's first secretary of the treasury, and in that office Hamilton insisted Congress pay all debts left from the Revolutionary War, including those of individual states, and establish a national bank. He wanted the government to help emerging industry, and the Federalist Party was founded on his ideas. The opposing Democrat-Republican Party was founded by James Madison and Secretary of State Thomas Jefferson, who wanted America to be a nation of landholding farmers, with manufacturing left to Europe. In 1804 political differences with Democrat-Republican Aaron Burr led to a duel. Hamilton had no intention of killing his rival and shot his pistol in the air. Burr shot directly at Hamilton, who died the next day of his wounds.

1795–1800

Oliver Wolcott (1760–1833) was born in Litchfield, Connecticut, the son of a signer of the Declaration of Independence of the same name. Wolcott served only briefly in the Continental army. In 1789 he was named auditor of the Treasury, the government's largest department, and forged a close working relationship with Alexander Hamilton. In 1791 Hamilton made him the Treasury's comptroller; and in 1795, when Hamilton resigned, Wolcott was named secretary, a post he held through what remained of Washington's second term and most of John Adams's administration. He was elected governor of Connecticut for ten consecutive one-year terms beginning in 1818.

Secretary of War
1789–1794

Henry Knox (1750–1806) was born in Boston, Massachusetts. At the outbreak of the Revolutionary War, he owned Boston's "London Book Store." During the Revolution he was Washington's chief of artillery (see "Washington's Generals"). He first served as secretary of war in 1785, while the nation was governed by the Articles of Confederation. During his term as secretary he unsuccessfully urged Congress to establish an army of all men between the ages of eighteen and sixty and organize it into three units—advanced corps, main corps, and reserved corps. In 1794 he left office, moved to Thomaston, Maine, and speculated unsuccessfully in land.

1795

Timothy Pickering, *see* Secretary of State

1796–1800

James McHenry (1753–1816) was born in Ireland; he came to the American colonies in 1771 and lived in Philadelphia. He studied medicine and served in the Continental army as a surgeon. In 1778 he reported to Valley Forge and soon earned the respect of Washington, who called him a "Man of Letters" and appointed him his private secretary. In 1781, after the battle of Yorktown, McHenry left the army and moved to Baltimore, Maryland, where he was elected to five one-year terms in the Maryland state senate and in 1787 represented Maryland at the Constitutional Convention. When Washington became president, he often asked McHenry's advice on the appointments of federal officials in Maryland. In January 1796 Washington appointed him secretary of war, a post he held until 1800, through much of John Adams's administration. McHenry reorganized the army to make it more efficient, and he established arsenals. His close relationship with

Alexander Hamilton, an enemy of President Adams, proved his undoing, and in 1800 he resigned and retired to his estate near Baltimore.

Attorney General
1789-1794
Edmund Randolph, *see* Secretary of State

1794-1795
William Bradford (1755–1795) was born in Philadelphia, Pennsylvania, the great-grand-son of an earlier William Bradford, the first printer in Pennsylvania and New York, and the son of the printer and leading member of the Sons of Liberty who was also named William Bradford. The Bradford who was to become Washington's second attorney general volunteered in 1776 as a private in the Pennsylvania militia and later joined the Continental army, where he rose to the rank of lieutenant colonel. From 1780 until 1791 he served as attorney general of Pennsylvania, and for three years after that as a judge on the state's supreme court. As Washington's attorney general, he helped settle the Whiskey Rebellion. Bradford died in office.

1795-1801
Charles Lee (1758–1815), not to be confused with Charles "Boiling Water" Lee (*see* Washington's Generals), was born in Prince William County, Virginia. He was the younger brother of planter and Patriot Henry Lee, the legendary cavalry officer of the Revolution known as Light-Horse Harry who fathered Confederate General Robert E. Lee. Charles Lee, a naval officer during the Revolution, began practicing law in Virginia in 1781. In 1789 Washington appointed him customs collector in Alexandria, and in 1795 attorney general. Lee remained in that office until 1801, through the John Adams administration, and was responsible for the enforcement of the Alien and Sedition Acts, a series of three acts passed by Congress in 1798 that allowed the president to imprison and deport foreigners. In 1801 Lee returned to private law practice and in 1803 unsuccessfully represented William Marbury in the landmark case *Marbury* v. *Madison,* the first time the Supreme Court declared a federal law to be unconstitutional.

Postmaster General
1789-1791

Samuel Osgood (1748–1813) was born in Andover, Massachusetts. He was a successful merchant and an aide to General Artemas Ward at the outbreak of the Revolution. In 1785 he moved to New York City. In April 1789, when Washington came to New York to be inaugurated as the nation's first president, he stayed in Osgood's home. Soon after that, Washington appointed him postmaster general, but his term was brief. In 1791, when the federal government moved to Philadelphia, Osgood chose to remain in New York and resigned the post.

1791-1795

Timothy Pickering, *see* Secretary of State

1795-1801

Joseph Habersham (1751–1815) was born in Savannah, Georgia, the son of James Habersham, a successful businessman and acting governor of Georgia in the early 1770s. Until his death in 1775, James remained loyal to the king, but his son Joseph was a revolutionary, a member of the first patriotic committee of Georgia. In 1775 Joseph Habersham led a successful raid of a British arsenal and in 1776 arrested James Wright, the royal governor of Georgia and his father's friend. The postal department expanded greatly during his term, which extended through the John Adams administration, with the number of post offices increasing from 75 to 903. From 1802–1815, he served as the head of the Savannah branch of the Bank of the United States.

George Washington Time Line

1732	Born between Popes Creek and Bridges Creek, Virginia, February 22 (February 11, Old Style).
1735	Family moves forty miles up the Potomac River to the 2,500-acre farm later named Mount Vernon.
1739	House burns down and family moves again, this time to a plantation along the Rappahannock River later known as Ferry Farm.
1743	Augustine Washington, George's father, dies, April 12.
1748	Surveys western land belonging to Lord Fairfax.
1751	Appointed as major in Virginia militia. Sails to Barbados with his half brother Lawrence, September.
1752	Lawrence Washington dies, July 26.
1753	Leaves Williamsburg for the Ohio Valley, October 31. Meets with French commandant Legardeur de St. Pierre, December 12.
1754	On his way to Fort Duquesne, battles French, killing ten, including Lieutenant Jumonville, the French commander, May 28.
1755	Appointment as aide-de-camp to General Braddock is announced, May 10. Battle of Monongahela, July 9. General Braddock dies, July 13.
1759	Marries Martha Dandridge Custis, January 6.
1760	King George II dies. King George III begins his reign.
1765	Stamp Act, a tax on printed matter sold in the colonies, passes Parliament.
1767	Townshend Acts tax items imported into the American colonies, including lead, glass, paints, paper, and tea.
1770	Boston Massacre, March 5.
1773	Stepdaughter Martha Parke Custis dies, July 19. Boston Tea Party, December 16.

1774		Intolerable Acts.
		The First Continental Congress begins its sessions in Philadelphia, September 5. Washington represents Virginia.
1775		First battles of the Revolution at Lexington and Concord, Massachusetts, April 19.
		The Second Continental Congress begins its sessions, May 10. Washington represents Virginia.
		Elected commander in chief of the Continental army, June 15.
		Takes command of the army at Cambridge, Massachusetts, July 3.
1776		British evacuate Boston, March 17.
		The Declaration of Independence approved by Congress, July 4.
		Crosses the Delaware River and takes Trenton, December 26.
1777		Arrives at Valley Forge, Pennsylvania, December 17.
1778		Meets Baron von Steuben, Valley Forge, February 23.
		The treaties with France are ratified by Congress, May 2.
		Battle of Monmouth, June 28.
		Settles in Middlebrook, New Jersey, for the winter.
1780		Benedict Arnold found guilty of treason. He escapes. His British partner, Major John André, executed, October 2.
1781		Battle of Yorktown, Cornwallis surrenders, October 19.
		Stepson, John Custis, dies, November 5.
1783		Treaty of Paris ending the Revolution is signed, September 3.
		Retires as commander of Continental army, December 23.
1786		Shays' Rebellion, a tax revolt, shows the need for a strong central government.
1787		Elected president of the Philadelphia Convention (Constitutional Convention), May 25.
1788		United States Constitution becomes the basis of the new government when New Hampshire's state assembly becomes the ninth to ratify it, June 21, 1788.
1789		Takes oath as first president of the United States, New York City, April 30.

	Mother, Mary Washington, dies at the age of eighty-two, August 25.
	Tours the northeastern states, October.
1791	Tours southern states, March.
	Bill of Rights ratified, December 15.
1792	Reelected president, December 5.
1793	Takes oath for second term as president, March 4.
1794	Puts down Whiskey Rebellion, September through October.
1796	Makes final report and farewell address to the American people, published September 19.
1797	Retires to Mount Vernon after John Adams is inaugurated as second president, March 4.
1798	Again named commander of the United States Army, July.
1799	Dies at Mount Vernon, December 14.

Important Battles
of the American Revolution

Lexington and Concord, Massachusetts April 19, 1775	700 British soldiers march to Concord to destroy Patriot stores of arms and ammunition.
Fort Ticonderoga, New York May 10, 1775	A quick, bloodless victory for Ethan Allen and his Green Mountain Boys and Benedict Arnold.
Bunker Hill, Massachusetts June 17, 1775	British General Howe forces Patriots to retreat from Boston area.
Quebec, Canada December 31, 1775	American troops led by Benedict Arnold fail to capture Quebec.
Moore's Creek Bridge, North Carolina February 27, 1776	American Patriots under the command of colonels Caswell and Lillington defeat troops loyal to the king.
Long Island, New York August 27, 1776	British troops led by Howe force Washington-led troops to retreat.
Harlem Heights, New York September 16, 1776	Americans send a larger British force into retreat.
White Plains, New York October 28, 1776	British troops led by General Howe force American troops led by Washington to retreat.

Fort Washington,
New York
November 16, 1776

General Howe captures this fort that overlooks the Hudson River. More than 2,600 American troops taken prisoner.

Fort Lee,
New Jersey
November 18, 1776

General Cornwallis captures this fort that overlooks the Hudson River from the New Jersey side.

Trenton,
New Jersey
December 26, 1776

Washington led this successful attack on Hessian troops, German soldiers who were paid to fight for the British.

Princeton,
New Jersey
January 3, 1777

Washington takes British troops by surprise. This and the battle of Trenton encourage American Patriots.

Bennington,
Vermont
August 16, 1777

American forces led by Colonel John Stark defeat the British and take weapons and supplies.

Brandywine Creek,
Pennsylvania
September 11, 1777

Washington-led troops retreat. Howe and his men go on to occupy Philadelphia.

Bemis Heights, First Battle
(Freeman's Farm)
Saratoga, New York
September 19, 1777

American General Horatio Gates defeats British forces under the command of Major General John Burgoyne.

Germantown, Pennsylvania
October 4, 1777

Heavy fog turned this battle, well planned by Washington, into a Patriot defeat.

Bemis Heights, Second Battle
(Freeman's Farm)
Saratoga, New York
October 7, 1777

Burgoyne and his troops attack again (*see* Bemis Heights, First Battle). General Benedict Arnold's strong leadership leads to a Patriot victory. On October 17, Burgoyne surrenders. This victory convinces the French to support the Continental army.

Monmouth, New Jersey
June 28, 1778

Patriots led by Washington hold their ground. There is no clear victor in this, the last major battle of the Revolution in the northern section of the United States.

Savannah, Georgia December 29, 1778	British capture this important southern port.
Naval battle, east coast of England September 23, 1779	John Paul Jones on the American ship the *Bonhomme Richard* leads American forces in this stunning victory over superior British forces. Jones defied the British when he was asked to surrender. "I have not yet begun to fight!" was his memorable answer.
Camden, South Carolina August 16, 1780	Patriots led by General Horatio Gates suffer heavy losses.
Cowpens, South Carolina January 17, 1781	Daniel Morgan led Patriot troops in this remarkable victory.
Guilford Courthouse, North Carolina March 15, 1781	Though American troops are forced to retreat, the British suffer heavy casualties.
Chesapeake Bay September 5, 1781	French Admiral de Grasse defeats the British in this sea battle just outside Chesapeake Bay. This closed off any escape by boat for Cornwallis and his troops at Yorktown.
Yorktown, Virginia October 6–19, 1781	The British, led by Cornwallis, surrender to Washington's men after this, the last major battle of the Revolution.

Source Notes

Among my many sources were biographies of Washington by very distinguished Americans including Dr. Jared Sparks (1789–1866), a history professor at Harvard University for ten years and for three years (1849–1852) president of the university. It was Sparks who edited Washington's early letters, corrected misspellings, and made changes that probably destroyed some of the force of the young soldier's words. Another of my sources was a Washington biography by John Marshall (1755–1835), a participant at the battles of Brandywine Creek, Germantown, and Monmouth; a friend of Washington; and later chief justice of the Supreme Court. His five-volume *Life of Washington* was first published in 1805, just a few years after Washington died. I also worked with a biography by President Woodrow Wilson (1856–1924) written while he was a university professor and a two-volume biography by Wilson's nemesis, Senator Henry Cabot Lodge of Massachusetts (1850–1924). Among the other texts I used were the multivolume biographies written by Washington Irving (1783–1859), Rupert Hughes (1876–1956, an uncle of reclusive billionaire Howard Hughes), Pulitzer Prize–winning Douglas Southall Freeman (1886–1953), and James Thomas Flexner (1908–2003). I also made liberal use of the many books and engravings of historian, editor, and artist Benson J. Lossing (1813–1891). Washington biographers Irving and Lossing had their own connection. When I recently visited Sunnyside, Washington Irving's New York home, I was told by the tour guide that in his study Irving entertained many of the distinguished people of his time, including Benson J. Lossing.

Washington Irving

Preface

The Franklin quote, "like Joshua of old . . . ," is from Ratcliffe (p. 355). Adams's quote, "the most illustrious . . ." is from a speech before the House of Representatives just after Washington died, which I found in McGroarty (p. 17). Another assessment, only slightly less glowing, came from Supreme Court Chief Justice John Marshall, who knew Washington and wrote of him, "His person and whole deportment exhibited an unaffected and indescribable dignity. . . . More solid than brilliant, judgement rather than genius constituted the prominent feature of his character. . . . If his military course does not abound with splendid achievements, it exhibits a series of judicious measures adapted to circumstances, which probably saved his country . . . the lessons of experience were never lost, his errors, if he committed any, were quickly repaired" (Marshall, pp. 376–377).

Chapter One

"Most of his baggage was packed," Flexner (p. 214) wrote of Washington as the retired commander waited for official notice of his election. He wrote, too, that while Washington waited, he "stared disconsolately down his long curving driveway."

Charles Thomson (1729–1824), secretary of Congress, who delivered Senator Langdon's note, was born in Ireland and came to the American colonies in 1741. He lived in Philadelphia, was a classical scholar and a friend of Franklin, and worked for the interests of American Indians, who so trusted him that the Delaware tribe named him "One Who Speaks the Truth." His wife, Hannah Harrison, was the aunt of William Harrison, America's ninth president. The description of his April 14, 1789, visit to Mount Vernon is from the Lossing book *The Home of Washington* (pp. 206–208). According to Lossing, the others at the Washington table that afternoon were Tobias Lear, Washington's secretary; Colonel David Humphreys, once a military aide and then working on a biography of Washington; and "Two or three guests."

Throughout the Revolution, Henry Knox (1750–1806) served alongside Washington. He directed Washington's well-known crossing of the Delaware and commanded the artillery at the battle at Yorktown. In December 1783, when Washington resigned as commander in chief of the army, Knox replaced him. In March 1785, in the government under the Articles of Confederation, Knox was made secretary of war and kept that post in Washington's first cabinet. I found the Knox "Superfine American broadcloth" letter in Fitzpatrick's *The Writings of George Washington* (vol. 30, pp. 218–219).

It was Senator William Maclay (1737–1804) of Pennsylvania who described Washington's appearance in 1789 as wanting "filling up." I found the description in Ford's biography of Washington (p. 40) and the text of the toast to Washington in Alexandria and his response in Lossing's *Home of Washington* (p. 211) and McGroarty (pp. 1–3).

In Philadelphia, Washington spent the night at the home of Robert Morris (1734–1806), a signer of the Declaration of Independence and senator from Pennsylvania who was for a time thought to be the country's richest man. He was criticized for his handling of public funds, investigated, and cleared in 1779 by a congressional committee. By 1798, after some financial reversals, he was taken to debtors' prison in Philadelphia. He was released in 1801 and lived the rest of his life on the charity of his friends.

Woodrow Wilson wrote of Washington's welcome to New York, "His fears foreboded scenes the opposite of these, when he should have shown himself unable to fulfil the hopes which were the burden of all the present joy" (p. 269). The excerpt from Washington's diary "the decorations of the ships . . ." appears in Randall (p. 447) and Irving (vol. 2, p. 254). Randall added that as president, "he worried that his long-fought public reputation would be tarnished." Of his inexperience in politics Randall wrote, "He had no political experience beyond a brief stint as a congressman and fifteen years of inattention to the office of Virginia burgess."

It was Harrison Gray Otis of Massachusetts (1765–1848), a member of Congress (1797–1801), who wrote of the canopy that seemed to shake from the shouts of the crowd. "No one," he wrote many years later, "can describe the silent tearful ecstacy which pervaded the myriads who witnessed that scene." I found this in Freeman (vol. 6, p. 193).

Descriptions of the Washington inauguration and the fact that he placed his hand on an open Bible appear in many books, and in Lossing's *Home of Washington* (p. 216) I found that "Washington laid his hand upon the page containing the fiftieth chapter of Genesis opposite to which were two engravings representing *The Blessing of Zebulon*, the other *The Prophecy of Issacher*." There was a full week between the time Washington arrived in New York and his inauguration, so it is unlikely that Washington found the page at random, and while Lossing did not make the connection between Washington's unease at the office he was about to assume and Joseph's response to his brothers, a reading of Washington's diary entries, and the chapter in Genesis, made it clear. There are various reports that when Washington entered the room there was a frantic search for a Bible for the ceremony, but not according to Irving (vol. 4, p. 255) or Freeman (vol. 6, p. 191).

Washington's religious practices have been speculated on for generations with early historians invested in him being a devout man and later ones not so inclined. "It should be observed," Jared Sparks wrote in his 1839 biography (p. 519), "that in his first military campaigns he was careful to have religious service regularly performed in camp." He also wrote (p. 521), "I shall here insert a letter on this subject, written to me by a lady who lived twenty years in Washington's family." The lady was Eleanor "Nelly" Custis Lewis, the granddaughter of Martha, who in 1799 married Washington's nephew. She wrote of Washington, "No one in church attended to the services with more reverential respect." More recently James Thomas Flexner wrote in his 1969 biography *Washington: The Indispensable Man* (p. 216) that Washington was a deist, "Although not believing in the doctrine of the churches, he was convinced that a divine force, impossible to define ruled the universe." Willard Sterne Randall wrote in his 1997 biography (p. 256), "He was not a deeply religious man." After he left his mother's household, "he may never have taken Anglican communion again, yet he went to church frequently." He was charitable, too, according to Randall, with gifts to his church and the needy.

Chapter Two

According to Randall (p. 10), Lawrence Washington married Amphilis Twigden, a "wealthy and unusually literate young widow." Reports vary on the number of children they had, from six (Randall, p. 10) to fourteen (Kirkland, p. 12). Reports vary, too, as to the true name of his wife. According to Hughes, he married Amphilis Roades, not Twigden (p. 8), "believed to have been the daughter of one of the servants of Sir Edmund Verney."

I found the information on the Reverend Lawrence Washington in Hughes (vol. 1, pp. 7–10), Woodward (pp. 12–13), and Randall (pp. 9–10); and of John Washington, the *Sea Horse,* and Anne Pope and her father in Freeman (vol. 1, pp. 15–18) and Randall (pp. 11–12). Two of John Washington's siblings also came to America, his sister Martha and brother Lawrence.

It was not unusual in Washington's time for one parent to die young and the widow or widower to remarry. His father Augustine's first wife, Jane Butler, was the daughter of Mary and her fourth husband, Caleb (Freeman, vol. 1, p. 34). The first three had died and when Jane Butler was about ten, Caleb died and Mary married for the fifth time. Augustine's second wife, George Washington's mother, was the daughter of Joseph Ball, a sixty-year-old widower, and his wife, the twice-widowed Mary Johnson. Joseph died a few years later, and Mary Johnson married again, a fourth time. The information on the parents of Mary Ball Washington is from Randall (pp. 15–16) and Hughes (vol. 1, pp. 12–14).

Historians differ on the dates of Augustine's marriage to Jane Butler and her death. I chose as my source the well-regarded Irving biography (vol. 1, p. 11). Also, in many texts, only two of their children are remembered, Lawrence and Augustine, perhaps because the others, Butler and Jane, died young.

The fantastic lightning story is from Randall (p. 16), Lossing's *Mary and Martha* (p. 61), Kirkland (p. 33), and Paulding (vol. 1, p. 22).

The "old style" and "new style" calendar discrepancy is explained in many places. I based my explanation on the ones found in Hughes (vol. 1, p. 17) and *Harper's* (vol. 2, p. 22). I found Washington's diary entry on his 1799 birthday celebration in Twohig (p. 422). Eleven days later, on February 22, on his newly recognized birthday (see chapter 23), his nephew and adopted daughter married at Mount Vernon. This was either a coincidence or Washington recognized both birthdays.

Chapter Three

In the 1730s, the people in Washington's Virginia, according to Woodrow Wilson (p. 5), seemed like opinionated elder Englishmen, except they were living on the American frontier.

The 1729 letter about the importance of tobacco to Virginia and Maryland was written to Lord Baltimore by Charles Calvert II (1699–1751), who spent almost his entire life in England, across the ocean from the city named for him and his family. I found an excerpt from the letter in the Gutheim book about the Potomac (p. 72).

The description of Washington's birthplace is from Barton (p. 21), Woodward (p. 21), and Kirkland (pp. 16–18); of the fire is from Lossing's *Mary and Martha* (p. 28); and of some of the furnishings are from Freeman (vol. 1, pp. 95–109), with the assumption that since Mary Washington rescued the family furnishings from the first house, those in Washington's second home, described by Freeman, were present in the first.

I found the letters between Washington and Richard Henry Lee in Lossing's *Home of Washington* (pp. 37–38). Lossing wrote, "They were sent to me a few years ago by a son of Richard Henry Lee." Lee (1732–1794) was born in Westmoreland County, Virginia, and was just one month older than Washington. He served with Washington in the House of Burgesses and represented Virginia in the various Continental Congresses. In June 1776 he proposed the resolution that colonies be "free and independent." In 1784 he was president of the Congress and from 1789 to 1792 he served as a United States senator from Virginia.

While it is undoubtedly odd to write so extensively in a serious biography about a fictionalized one, Weems's book, published soon after Washington's death, has had great influence on the Washington image. Abraham Lincoln, as quoted in Cunliffe (p. xxii), wrote that "away back in my childhood, my earliest days of being able to read, I got hold of a small book . . . Weem's (sic) *Life of Washington*."

Weems's claims that he knew Washington are true as proved by a March 3, 1787, entry in Washington's diary: "The Revd. Mr. Weems . . . came here yesterday" (Twohig, p. 313).

The image we have of George Washington was shaped, in part, by Mason Locke Weems (1759–1825). The cherry tree and cabbage tree stories are the most famous ones, but there are others. Among them was that when there was a fight in school, his classmates would "hunt for George," who would mediate. "Soon as his verdict was heard, the party favoured would begin to crow, and then all hands would return to play again." Weems wrote, too, of Washington the athlete. "At jumping with a long pole, or heaving heavy weights, for his years he hardly had an equal, and as to running, the swift-footed Achilles could scarcely have matched his speed." He wrote of Mary Washington's dream that young George saved her house from fire. Of his death, Weems wrote, "Myriads of mighty angels hastened forth, with golden harps, to welcome the honoured stranger." I found the information on Weems in the introduction to the Belknap Press edition of Weems's *Life of Washington*.

Washington's siblings, as listed in Hughes (vol. 1, p. 13) were Betty (1733–1797), Samuel (1734–1781), John Augustine (1736–1787), Charles (1738–1799), and Mildred (1739–1740).

The details of Augustine Washington's death are from Lossing's book *Mary and Martha* (p. 31). Many years after Augustine Washington's death, George Washington Parke Custis (1781–1857) wrote that on his deathbed Augustine thanked God that he never hit a man in anger for if he had, he was sure he would have killed him and "his blood at this awful moment would have lain heavily on my soul." Custis was the grandson of Martha Washington and later, at the death of his father, the adopted son of George Washington (from Freeman, vol. 1, p. 72, footnote).

Chapter Four

The information about Mr. Williams and the example of Washington's precise calculations are from Woodward (p. 24). Lawrence Washington of Choptank was the cousin who wrote about Mary Washington. I found the letter in Taylor (p. 69). "She awed me in the midst of her kindness," he wrote, "and even now, when time has whitened my locks and I am the grandfather of a second generation, I could not behold that majestic woman without feelings it is impossible to describe."

The description of Mary Ball Washington having hair "like unto flax" and cheeks "like May blossoms" is from Woodward (p. 15), who quotes a "contemporary of Mary Ball, whose name has been lost in the desert of anonymity."

The details of Mary Washington's pleas for butter and assistance from the Virginia Assembly are from Bellamy (pp. 19–25) and Emery (pp. 29–32).

The information on the War of Jenkins's Ear is from Woodward (pp. 30–32), Lossing's *Home of Washington* (pp. 39–42), and Whipple (pp. 38–41).

I found Joseph Ball's letter in Hughes (vol. 1, p. 35) and Freeman (vol. 1, pp. 198–199). In colonial times it seems the sea enticed many boys. Benjamin Franklin wrote in his autobiography that his father feared if he did not find an agreeable trade for him, "I should break away and get to sea."

Washington's journal entries are from *The Diaries of George Washington* (pp. 6–23).

The letter from Lord Thomas Fairfax to Mary Washington appears in Hughes (vol. 1, pp. 37–38). In it Fairfax likened women to spiders: "May the Lord help him [George], and deliver him from their nets." Lord Fairfax (1691–1781), the sixth Baron of Cameron, was educated at Oxford, and was middle-aged when he quit England and came to Virginia, but he remained loyal to the king. In 1781, according to *Harper's* (vol. 3, pp. 305–306), at the age of ninety, when he heard news of Washington's victory at Yorktown, he called for his servant to carry him to his bed, "for I am sure," Fairfax said, "it is time for me to die." He died on December 12, 1781, less than two months after Cornwallis surrendered.

Chapter Five

I found in Ford (pp. 61 and 84) the fact that the maxim on young men was in *The Young Man's Companion*, a book Washington studied as a youth, and Washington's 1749 letter about his "Low Land Beauty" in Fitzpatrick's *Writings of Washington* (vol. 1, pp. 15–16).

The quotes from Washington's letters to Sally Fairfax are from Randall (pp. 53 and 165–167), and the notes on the ladies from Washington's diaries are from Ford (p. 109). The information about Ann Carrol and Mary McDaniel is from court records detailed in Hughes (vol. 1, pp. 56–57) and Woodward (p. 42).

I found that Mary Philipse engaged Washington's heart in Ford (p. 90), and that "She was too much like his mother" in Randall (p. 154). Two years later Philipse married Roger Morris (1717–1794). During the Revolution, Morris remained loyal to King George III and his land was confiscated by the Continental army. After the Revolution, Roger and Mary retired to England.

I found that Washington loved to dance yet compared it to war in Hughes (vol. 1, p. 190).

Washington's journal entries of his 1751 trip to Barbados show some inventive spelling, often different spellings of the same words. He wrote *breese* and *Breeze*, *sale* and *sail*, *Dalphin* and *Dolphin*, and *Chooner* and *Schooner*. Excerpts of his entries appear in Hughes (vol. 1, pp. 58–60), Whipple (pp. 87–90), and Andrist (vol. 1, p. 27). My information on Lawrence Washington's illness is from Irving (vol. 1, pp. 39–42). The details of Lawrence Washington's will are from Hughes (vol. 1, p. 64).

Chapter Six

Dinwiddie and Washington's half brothers, Lawrence and Augustine, had personal interests in the Ohio Valley. They were among twenty partners in the Ohio Company with a grant from the king of England for 500,000 acres in the valley.

The British sent orders to Lieutenant Governor Dinwiddie of Virginia to build two forts by the Ohio River. Along with the orders, they sent thirty small cannons and eighty barrels of gunpowder to defend the forts.

Dinwiddie's note, "Sir, the lands . . . your peaceable departure," appears in Whipple

(p. 100), that French commander St. Pierre was courteous in Sparks (p. 26), and his reply to Dinwiddie in Irving (vol. 1, p. 60). Entries of Washington's journal are in Twohig (p. 30), Whipple (vol. 1, p. 100), and Sparks (p. 30). I found excerpts from the Gist journal in Sparks (pp. 28–30).

"Here, indeed," Lodge wrote of the nature of Washington as revealed in his journals (vol. 1, pp. 66–68), "is the man of action and of real silence, a character to be much admired and wondered at in these or any other days."

Chapter Seven

I found excerpts of the text of Dinwiddie's orders to Washington and their correspondence in Hughes (vol. 1, pp. 99–102). The description of Washington's first battle appears in Headley's *Illustrated Life of Washington* (pp. 42–50) and Seelye (pp. 46–49). Seelye (p. 49) noted that, years later, Washington was asked if he ever wrote that he was charmed by the sound of gunfire. "If I did," he replied, "it must have been when I was very young."

I found that Jumonville and Villiers were brothers in Randall (p. 102).

The French later claimed Jumonville was in the Ohio Valley on a peaceful mission.

The description of the battle at Fort Necessity is from Freeman (vol. 1, pp. 403–406). The quote from Chief Tanacharison, "The French . . . on the meadow," is from Hughes (vol. 1, pp. 159–160) and Lodge (vol. 1, p. 74), who found it in a 1759 book by Charles Thomson, later secretary of Congress, the same man who, in 1789, brought Washington news of his election as the first president of the United States.

Participants in the French and Indian War

Fort Necessity was in present-day Fayette County, Pennsylvania. Also in the terms of surrender of the fort were the conditions that the captured French prisoners would be returned and that the English would not build a fort "in this place or from here to the summit of the mountains for one year." I found this information in Lossing's *Outline History* (p. 132) and Randall (pp. 94–106).

At the time of Washington's first battles in the Ohio Valley, there were four weekly newspapers in Boston, each with an average circulation of about six hundred copies. But the readership of the newspapers was much wider than sales would indicate. Many newspapers sold well beyond the city, and each copy was passed from one reader to another. Many people went to their local tavern to borrow a newspaper and read the latest news. All in all, the flattering reports on Washington were widely read. This view and the summary of newspaper reports of Washington's first battles are from Frank E. Dunkle's essay "Beginning a Legend: George Washington in the Boston Newspapers, 1754–1758," found in Rozell (pp. 171–185).

Robert Orme was the Braddock aide who wrote to Washington that the general "would be very glad of your company." I found his letter and Washington's reply in Hughes (vol. 1, pp. 199–200).

General Edward Braddock (1695–1755), the son of Edward and Mary, was born in London. Just before he came to Virginia, he served as governor of Gibraltar. Despite his very talented cooks, according to Seelye (p. 61), Braddock complained he had nothing fresh to eat. Benjamin Franklin heard his complaints and sent each officer a package of cheese, butter, wine, chocolate, coffee, tea, biscuits, rice, raisins, mustard, sugar, pepper, vinegar, and meats. "A report has long been current in Pennsylvania," Sparks wrote (p. 66, footnote), "that Braddock was shot by one of his own men, founded on the declaration of a provincial soldier, who was in the action." Sparks does not write whether, according to the report, the shooting was intentional or not.

Braddock's encounter with Franklin and the quote, "May indeed . . . an impression," are from Franklin's autobiography (pp. 222–241). Information for my description of Braddock's defeat is from Irving (vol. 1, pp. 109–126).

I found Washington's July 18, 1755, letter to his brother John Augustine "Jack" Washington about his rumored death in Fitzpatrick's *Writings of Washington* (vol. 1, pp. 152–153). Washington also wrote of the battle. "We have been most scandalously beaten by a trifling body of men, but fatigue and want of time will prevent me from giving you any of the details, until I have the happiness of seeing you at Mount Vernon, which I now most ardently wish for. . . . Pray give my compliments to all my friends." Washington also wrote to his mother (Hughes, vol. 1, pp. 268–269), "The Virginia troops . . . showed a good deal of bravery, and were nearly all killed. . . . The dastardly behavior of those they called regulars exposed all others, that were ordered to do their duty, to almost certain death . . . they ran as sheep pursued by dogs, and it was impossible to rally them."

"It is a sensible . . . rash conduct" is from excerpts from Joseph Ball's letter to Washington as they appear in Woodward (p. 79).

Many years after Braddock's defeat, Washington was near the Ohio River again and an old American Indian chief and some of his tribe came to visit. The chief said he was at the battle and shot at Washington many times. Others did, too, but when no one could hit him the chief was convinced Washington was guarded by the Great Spirit. The meeting with the American Indian chief was reported by Dr. James Craik, a friend of Washington who was at the battle and was with him fifteen years later when he met the chief who came to honor "God's favorite." I found this in Sparks (p. 66).

Chapter Eight

Along with Washington's proposals for frontier safety, he sent, according to Hughes (vol. I, p. 302–303), the scalp of a French officer, Monsieur Douville, and asked that the soldiers who killed the officer be given a reward. The irony of it is that Douville wanted peace. The man who killed him found papers on Douville directing him to do all he could to protect the settlers from harm.

In Virginia, a reward of £10 was offered for every adult male American Indian scalp. It was later raised to £15.

The information on Washington's experiences on the frontier is from Randall (pp. 147–163), Seelye (pp. 72–75), and Hughes (vol. I, pp. 301–342).

It was Dr. James Craik who bled Washington, and he did it three times.

General John Forbes (1710–1759) was trained as a physician but left medicine to become a soldier. He commanded eight thousand men against the abandoned Fort Duquesne. He died in Philadelphia (*Harper's*, vol. 3, pp. 401–402).

I found the testimonial speech on Washington's 1758 retirement from the military, "You took us . . . affable a companion," in Thayer (pp. 245–247).

Chapter Nine

Governor William Shirley (1693–1771) was born and trained as a lawyer in England. He came to Boston in 1734 and was appointed governor in 1741. In 1755 he was appointed commander of the British forces in America (*Harper's,* vol. 8, p. 178).

According to Hughes (vol. 1, pp. 297–298), when Washington met Shirley, he spoke first of the governor's son who had been Braddock's aide and was killed at the battle of Monongahela. Washington had "many a tale to tell of the death of young Shirley. He got inside the old man's heart, no doubt." The quote "In case it should happen . . . take the command" is from Hughes (vol. 1, p. 298).

The story of the wager is from Seelye (p. 76). The woman who made the bet was Mrs. Morris, perhaps the wife of Lewis Morris, a New Yorker and later a signer of the Declaration of Independence.

Mercer's description of Washington, "His head . . . composed and dignified," is from Ford (pp. 38–39).

Martha Dandridge Custis was less than five feet tall, almost a foot and a half shorter than Washington. In her first marriage, she had given birth four times but only two children survived. When she met Washington she was plump, no longer the petite young woman who had married Daniel Parke Custis. I found that she was hot-tempered and stubborn in Ford (pp. 93–94). I found a description of her appearance and skills in Engle (pp. 212–213). According to Engle, after her first husband's death, she inherited a vast estate including a house in Williamsburg called, for obvious reasons, Six-Chimney House, and about $500,000, which probably made her the richest woman in 1750s Virginia.

I found that Washington stayed much longer than he had originally intended at the home of his friend Major Chamberlayne in Lodge (vol. 1, p. 98) and Bishop's remark, "Twas strange . . . punctual men," in Lossing's *Home of Washington* (p. 63). According to Hughes (vol. 1, p. 447), Lossing was a friend of the Custis family, and while he wrote of Washington's first meeting Martha Custis, he had before him "a piece of Mrs. Washington's wedding dress and a piece of her white satin ribbon."

Washington's letter to Sally Fairfax, "I confess . . . how impossible this is," according to Randall (p. 179), "surfaced only after historians and biographers overlooked it for two centuries." At first it was considered a hoax, but in 1958, after some examination, it was found to be authentic. The excerpt in Randall reveals Washington resigned to "a destiny" that did not include Sally Fairfax. I based much of my assessment of his feelings on this letter.

The Reverend David Mossom had performed Martha Dandridge's wedding to Daniel Parke Custis ten years earlier. While most historians write that the wedding was held in the bride's home, there are some, including Lodge (vol. 1, p. 98), who write it was in Mossom's church. According to Hughes, Mossom was not an inspiring preacher, with just seven or eight very old congregants at most services. The Reverend Mossom preached to them from a written text and did not look up from the paper. The details of the wedding are from Hughes (vol. 1, pp. 445–456), Lodge (vol. 1, pp. 98–99), and Randall (pp. 191–192). Years after Washington's marriage to Martha, John Adams asked, "Would Washington have ever been commander of the revolutionary army or president of the United States if he had not married the rich widow of Mr. Custis?" Surely he could have. His wife's inheritance helped Washington, but in 1758 he was already a famous military leader, and that is what led to him being selected as commander of the Continental army. His success in the Revolution led to him being elected president.

Mary Washington's letter to her brother Joseph Ball in London, "There was no end . . . in the army," dated July 26, 1759, was quoted in Hughes (vol. 1, p. 454). "It is well to rejoice when the mood is on, for it may not come again," Hughes wrote, indicating the irony of Mary Washington's belief that with his marriage, her son had given up his military ambitions.

Chapter Ten

I found reference to the letters from Washington's farm managers concerning the clothes and blankets for his slaves in Ferling (p. 68). Other details of Washington as master, employer, and farmer are found in Ford (pp. 140–159) and Hughes (vol. 2, pp. 79–88). The Washington quotes on Betty Davis are from Schwartz (p. 185).

The story of Washington's first appearance as a member of the House of Burgesses is from Irving (vol. 1, p. 188).

Washington drew his map at a meeting of the Pohick church where he was a vestryman. He was also a vestryman of a church in Alexandria. While Washington went to church often, his wife was more religious. Each day after breakfast she spent an hour in private prayer and meditation. I found this and details of the meeting at the Pohick church in Thayer (pp. 286–288) and in Headley's *Illustrated Life of Washington* (pp. 94–95).

The boxing matches in Washington's era were particularly violent. Fighters tried to gouge out each other's eyes. I found details of Washington's time in Williamsburg in Hughes (vol. 2 , pp. 35–48), the details of Washington's correspondence with the Reverend Boucher in Seelye (p. 98) and Randall (pp. 228–230), and the details of Patsy's death in Randall (p. 250) and Hughes (vol. 2, pp. 159–166).

Ona Judge was Martha's household slave, and at the end of Washington's second term, while others packed for their return to Virginia, she prepared for her escape. One evening in May or June 1796, while the Washingtons were eating dinner, she quietly walked out. She hid for a while with friends and then sailed to Portsmouth, New Hampshire. Soon after that, Washington learned her whereabouts and, for more than two years, was intent on bringing her back. She never returned to Mount Vernon and died a free woman in 1848. The information on Ona Judge is from Wiecek (pp. 319–334) and www.seacoastnh.com/blackhistory/ona.html.

Soon after they married, Martha wrote to her sister of her hope to have a child with George, even her belief that it would be a girl. I read of Jacky's disease and that Martha had measles in Randall (pp. 393 and 196), and of George Washington's mumps in Randall (pp. 224–225). The letter to George Augustine Washington is from Fitzpatrick's *Writings of Washington* (vol. 29, p. 29). Excerpts from Washington's writings in "Washington's Changing Attitude toward Slavery" are from Fitzpatrick's *Writings of Washington*.

Chapter Eleven

Kings George I and George II seldom attended cabinet meetings. They couldn't understand what was being said and, for the most part, left the ruling of England to their miniters. King George II died when he fell in his closet (Parton, vol. 1, p. 417). I found that King George I spoke no English and that his son, George II, spoke only broken English in Hayes (vol. 1, p. 455).

George III (1738–1820) married Charlotte Sophia in 1761. They had fifteen children. In 1810 Amelia, their youngest daughter, died and George III had a breakdown. In 1811 his son

George IV took over his duties, so while he lived sixty years from the time he first took the throne, George III's reign lasted just slightly more than fifty years. Parton (vol. 1, p. 417) wrote of the sevenfold increase in England's expenditures. I found that King George III was in confinement at the time the Stamp Act was passed in Hughes (vol. 2, p. 664).

Chief Pontiac (1720–1769) fought alongside the French in the defeat of General Braddock in 1755. I found his message from the Great Spirit in *Harper's* (vol. 7, p. 253).

According to Reich (pp. 156–157), in 1771 one third of all English trade was with the American colonies and 65 percent of that was clothes and cloth.

In 1764, even before the Revenue Act, there was a tax on molasses. In 1733 the tax was set at six pence per gallon but went mostly uncollected. In 1764 the tax was lowered to three pence in the hope that the lower tax would actually be collected. In 1766 it was lowered to one pence per gallon (Martin, p. 109).

Woodrow Wilson wrote that Washington took no part in the Stamp Act debate in the House of Burgesses (p. 133). Washington's letter to Francis Dandridge is in Fitzpatrick's *Writings of Washington* (vol. 2, pp. 425–427).

According to Headley's *Illustrated Life of Washington* (pp. 107–108), there were five hundred men on horseback, each holding a wooden club, who surrounded the Connecticut agent. In Pennsylvania the agent, John Hughes, and some friends, including Deborah Franklin, Benjamin Franklin's wife, stood outside his home with guns. Hughes wrote to Franklin, who was in England at the time as a representative of Pennsylvania, "We are all yet in the land of the living and our property safe, Thank God." The information on the attacks on Oliver's and Hutchinson's homes is from Martin (pp. 113–114) and Irving (vol. 1, pp. 205–206).

The nine colonies represented at the Stamp Act Congress were Massachusetts, Rhode Island, Connecticut, New York, New Jersey, Pennsylvania, Delaware, Maryland, and South Carolina. In a bit of irony, the chairman of the Stamp Act Congress was Timothy Ruggles of Massachusetts. He and Robert Ogden of New Jersey were two of the almost thirty delegates not to sign the Declaration of Rights. During the Revolution Ruggles and Ogden remained loyal to King George III (*Harper's*, vol. 8, p. 349).

I found excerpts from Washington's "repeal of the Stamp Act letter" in Sparks (p. 107) and Irving (vol. 1, p. 208). Washington's letter to George Mason and Mason's reply were both dated April 5, 1769 (Hughes, vol. 2, pp. 180–181).

In 1768, British goods worth £2,157,218 were sold in the northern colonies. In 1769 sales fell to £1,336,122, a drop of 38 percent (Hughes, vol. 2, p. 185).

Josiah Quincy worked with John Adams to defend the British soldiers tried for shooting Crispus Attucks and other American Patriots at what later became known as the Boston Massacre. I found his statement at the December 16, 1773, meeting and the description of the Boston Tea Party from George Hewes, a participant, in Commager (pp. 2–5).

In his letter to Fairfax, Washington's statement of Great Britain's tyranny was in the form of a rhetorical question. I found excerpts from this letter and Washington's statement at the August 1 meeting in Lodge (vol. 1, pp. 123–124). Franklin's and other colonists' reactions to the Boston Tea Party and the "Boston ought to be knocked about" quote are from Hughes (vol. 2, pp. 196–197).

Details of the May 1774 meetings in Williamsburg, Washington's meals with Lord Dunmore, and the meeting with Washington's Fairfax County neighbors are from Irving (vol. 1, pp. 232–235) and Hughes (vol. 2, pp. 201–215). The quote "Whilst we are . . . just ourselves" is from Hughes (vol. 2, p. 211). General Gage's "The Americans . . . English are lambs," is from Irving (vol. 1, p. 234). And "There is no . . . accomplish this end" is also from Irving (vol. 1, p. 238). "I will raise . . . Boston," is from Hughes (vol. 2, p. 215).

Chapter Twelve

I found in *Harper's* (vol. 3, p. 158) that it was the Reverend Jacob Duché (1737–1798), who opened Congress with a reading from the thirty-fifth Psalm and that as "A descendent of a Huguenot, he naturally loved freedom." He was a Patriot until 1777 when the British occupied Philadelphia. Then he became pessimistic about the prospects for independence, changed his loyalties, and in a letter urged Washington to do the same. Members of the Continental Congress saw the letter and Duché fled to England. In 1790 he returned to Philadelphia, where he died.

On September 5, when the Congress opened, there were representatives from just eleven of the colonies. Georgia was not represented and the three delegates from North Carolina arrived later, on September 14. I found different reports on the actual number of delegates, fifty-one, fifty-four, and fifty-six. I found Adams's "Here is a . . . conduct" and the fact that the meetings opened with the reading of the thirty-fifth Psalm in Irving (vol. 1, p. 242).

Patrick Henry's assessment of Washington's role at the First Continental Congress, and that the Virginia representatives left together for Philadelphia on horseback from Washington's home, are from Lodge (vol. 1, pp. 125–127). In Hughes (vol. 2, p. 221), Henry is quoted somewhat differently: "Col. Washington, who has no pretensions to eloquence, is a man of more solid judgement and information than any man on that floor." While the words are not exactly the same, the sentiment is.

Woodward (p. 266) wrote of the secret session at which some delegates, including Pendleton, spoke against naming Washington commander in chief of the Continental army.

Robert Mackenzie was later wounded while fighting for the British at Bunker Hill. I found Washington's letter to him, "That the people . . . North America," in Fitzpatrick's *Writings of Washington* (vol. 3, pp. 244–247) and Hughes (vol. 2, p. 224), and his letter to Mrs. Washington, "My greatest . . . her spirits," and to Jacky Custis, quoted near the end of the chapter, "I am new . . . to avoid it," are from the same source (pp. 293–295 and pp. 295–296).

Patrick Henry (1736–1799) worked at various jobs, including as an innkeeper. Then, after studying law for six weeks, he became a lawyer and in 1765 a member of the House of Burgesses, where he was a leader of the Patriots who sought independence from Great Britain. In 1776 he became the first governor of Virginia, and in 1795 Washington's secretary of state. I found his "Give me Liberty" speech in *Harper's* (vol. 4, pp. 370–380); excerpts from Washington's letter to his English friend, "Americans will fight . . . sad alternative," in Sparks (p. 125 and p. 127); and excerpts from his "I shall . . . if needful" letter to his brother in Hughes (vol. 2, p. 228).

The testimony of American soldiers at Lexington, Massachusetts, John Robinson's "I being . . . were shot dead," and John Parker's "I immediately . . . from us," on April 19, 1775, are from the May 17, 1775, issue of the *Pennsylvania Gazette*.

Lewis's fight with American Indian forces was along the Ohio River at Point Pleasant. The discussion on the appointment of Washington as commander in chief of the Continental army is from Hughes (vol. 2, pp. 235–239) and Irving (vol. 1, pp. 272–275), and the correspondence between Adams and his wife and Washington and his wife and stepson is in Hughes (vol. 2, pp. 246–250). When Hancock, who wanted the post of commander in chief, saw it would go to Washington, Adams wrote, "I never remarked a more sudden and striking change. . . . Mortification and resentment were expressed as forcibly as his face could exhibit them."

I found excerpts from John Adam's letter to his friend, "There is something . . . his country," in Irving (vol. 1, p. 275) and Hughes (vol. 2, p. 248). Washington's response to his appointment, "Though I am truly . . . honored with" and "I do not . . . profit from it" are from Irving (vol. 1, p. 275).

The details of the battle of Bunker Hill are from Martin (p. 143) and Paulding (vol. 1, pp. 149–152), and Washington's reaction is from Hughes (vol. 2, p. 256).

Chapter Thirteen
My sources for descriptions of the conditions of the army were Ferling (pp. 123–127), Hancock (pp. 190–192), Wilson (pp. 179–181), Whipple (p. 226), Freeman (vol. 3, pp. 483–485), and Flexner's *George Washington in the American Revolution* (pp. 29–32).

Washington's headquarters in Cambridge was a large, beautiful house, later the home of the poet Henry Wadsworth Longfellow.

General William Howe (1729–1814) was, according to *Harper's* (vol. 4, p. 436), an uncle of King George III. In May 1775 he arrived in Boston with added troops for General Gage. When Gage was recalled to England, Howe became commander of the British forces. In July 1777 his older brother, Admiral Richard Howe (1725–1799), came to America and joined the fight against the Continental army.

I found excerpts from Rev. Emerson's letter, "There is . . . officers and soldiers" in Kirkland (p. 237) and "Search the volumes . . . entered the ranks" (p. 245).

I found in Hughes (vol. 2, p. 331) that Martha Washington had not been out of Virginia until her 1775 trip to Cambridge to visit her husband. The friend to whom she wrote her December 30 letter, "Every person seems to be cheerful and happy here . . . ," was Miss Ramsay (Hughes, vol. 2, p. 333), perhaps a relation of William Ramsay, the founder of Alexandria, Virginia. It was a cheerful, gossipy letter, no doubt reflective, of Martha

Washington's nature, but full of the spelling mistakes common in her correspondence. "Your Friends Mr Harrison & Henly," she wrote in that letter, "are boath very well, and I think they are fatter than they were when they came to the Camp. . . . The girls rest satisfied on Mr Harrisons account for he seems two fond of his Country to give his heart to any but one of his Virginia Friends, thare are but Two Young Laides in Cambridge, and a very great number of Gentlemen so you may gess how much is made of them—but neither of them is pritty I think." I found details of her visit and what was left by the British when they evacuated Boston in Hughes (vol. 2, pp. 327–336 and 374).

Among the parties Martha gave in Cambridge was one to celebrate the Washingtons' wedding anniversary (Whipple, part 1, p. 237).

Washington wrote, "Search the volumes . . . to this time," to Joseph Reed (1741–1785), who was born in Trenton, New Jersey, was a delegate to the Second Continental Congress, and went with Washington to Cambridge as his secretary. Surely Reed must have been away from the camp in January 1776 when the letter was written. I found excerpts from it, that Mrs. Washington knitted while she entertained in Cambridge and that wooden dummies stood guard while the British evacuated Boston in Norton (pp. 164–165, 159, and 172).

Washington had Thomas Paine's *Common Sense* read to his troops in December 1776.

The details of Knowlton's attack on the guardhouse and the comedy "The Blockade of Boston," Washington's February 16 orders, and the British officer's March 3 letter are from Irving (vol. 1, pp. 409–410, 413, 414).

The story of Washington and Mrs. Edwards's granddaughter is from Wilson (p. 185) and Taylor (p. 193).

Chapter Fourteen

I found the statement of Dr. William Eustis, "Their design was . . . the best man on earth: General Washington," in Hughes (vol. 2, p. 392). In the same source were "He appealed . . . a confident look," and Washington's statement "The unhappy . . . all others" (pp. 401–402) and "those who . . . indisputable rights" (p. 424).

The details of the plot to assassinate Washington are from Hughes (vol. 2, pp. 392–399) and Irving (vol. 1, pp. 450–453). Dr. Eustis's eyewitness report of the execution is from Hughes (vol. 2, pp. 400–401). According to Hughes, the fault in the plan was that too many people were in on it. He wrote that earlier, a waiter in a tavern saw notes being passed around and lots of whispering. He hid in a closet, and what he overheard led to the arrest of one of the plotters. That the housekeeper was loyal to Washington is from Seelye (pp. 139–140), which seems likely since the housekeeper was never tried for the crime.

The pedestal from the King George III statue was first used as a tombstone for a British officer. I found in Lossing's *Field Book* (vol. 2, pp. 595–596) that it was later used as a doorstop at the Jersey City home of the Van Voorst family.

I found the details of the peace overture in Marshall (pp. 48–50), Hughes (vol. 2, pp. 422–424), Norton (pp. 177–180), and Everett (pp. 117–118).

Nathan Hale (1755–1776) was born in Coventry, Connecticut. He graduated Yale in 1773 and taught at Union Grammar School in New London, Connecticut, until after the battles of Lexington and Concord, when he joined the militia. He took part in the siege of Boston. The hangman was William Cunningham, whose cruelty was well known. After the Revolution he claimed he had killed two thousand prisoners, some by starving them, others by poisoning their food. I found information on Hale in Lossing's *The Two Spies* (pp. 3–34).

No one knew who started the fire in New York City. It spread quickly and there were too few buckets and too little water to fight it. Women and children ran from one house to the next, but there seemed to be no escape. The fire destroyed about one fourth of the city.

I found Washington's cry, "Good God . . . this day," in Kirkland (p. 283). Washington's letter to his brother John Augustine, "You can scare . . . pretty well up," is in Fitzpatrick's *Writings of Washington* (vol. 6, pp. 396–399).

Chapter Fifteen

The description of the battle of Trenton and Washington's reaction are from Sparks (pp. 195–204). "The effect of this victory," according to Sparks, "was like sudden life to the dead . . . and wherever over the land the name of Washington was uttered, tears fell like rain drops, and blessings innumerable were invoked on his head." I found that Lieutenant James Monroe was injured in Brookhiser (p. 29), and the dialog between Washington and the citizen who pointed the way to the enemy, "I don't

Hessian flag taken at Trenton

know . . . you, sir," in Norton (p. 213) and Irving (vol. 2, p. 99). I found Washington's state-ment, "This is a glorious day for our country," in Hughes (vol. 2, p. 598).

It was British General William Erskine, according to *Harper's* (vol. 7, pp. 295–296), who told Cornwallis the sounds in the distance were cannon fire and that Washington had out-maneuvered them. According to Irving (vol. 2, p. 113), it was also Erskine who urged Cornwallis to attack on January 2 before Washington would have had the chance to escape. The statement by Cornwallis, that he would "bag the old fox," is from Irving (vol. 2, p. 113). Fitzgerald's "Thank God . . . is safe" and Washington's "Bring up . . . our own" are from Irving (vol. 2, p. 117). Erskine's "To arms . . . out-generaled us" is from Hughes (vol. 3, p. 30).

Marie-Joseph-Paul-Yves-Roch-Gilbert du Motier, Marquis de Lafayette (1757–1834) was just twenty when he arrived at Valley Forge, a wealthy, inexperienced volunteer. He participated in many battles, including the ones at Monmouth, New Jersey, and Yorktown, Virginia. His energy and enthusiastic support of the Revolution made him an effective officer and a lifelong friend of Washington.

Tadeusz (Thaddeus) Andrzei Bonawentura Kosciusko (1746–1817) planned the building of fortifications key in the battles at Saratoga. After the 1783 Treaty of Paris, he returned to Poland and fought there against the Russians. He returned to the United States in 1797 and was given back pay and some land in Ohio for his service in the Revolution. A true believer in liberty, Kosciusko used the money to buy slaves and set them free [Dupuy (pp. 414–415)].

Count Kazimierz (Casimir) Pulaski (1747–1779) fought in the battles of Brandywine Creek and Germantown and died from injuries inflicted during the siege of Savannah, Georgia. Information on his contribution to the Revolution is from *Harper's* (vol. 7, p. 330).

Baron Johann de Kalb (1721–1780) sailed to America with Lafayette in 1777, wintered with Washington at Valley Forge, and fought at Camden, South Carolina, where he was killed [*Harper's* (vol. 5, p. 201)].

Baron Friedrich Wilhelm von Steuben (1730–1794) trained American troops in the strict Prussian manner. Troops responded to him, perhaps, because under his severe manner was a soft heart. There are many stories of his acts of kindness. According to one, he was once traveling from New York to Virginia when he heard a small African-American child crying because he had been taken from his parents and sold to a southern slaveholder. Steuben quickly "bought" the child from his slaveholder and returned him to his parents. This and the information of Steuben in chapter 16 are from Headley's *Washington and His Generals* (vol. 1, pp 206–220).

I found excerpts of Lafayette's correspondence, "The moment I heard of America . . ." in Hughes (vol. 3, p. 144).

Washington and many of his officers listened to the Reverend Jacob Trent's September 10, 1777, charge to the troops, "Soldier! . . . wild excitement." I found it quoted in Norton (pp. 230–231).

I found Washington's report to Congress after the battle at Brandywine Creek and the description of the disastrous battle at Germantown in Whipple (pp. 335–336 and 338–343).

Chapter Sixteen

The description of building the cabins at Valley Forge is from Headley's *Illustrated Life of Washington* (pp. 299–303) and Whipple (part 2, pp. 23–25), and the men suffering in the cold from Seelye (pp. 230–231). In February 1778, according to Woodward (p. 295), 4,000 of the 9,000 men with Washington at Valley Forge had no shoes or coats.

There are many stories of Washington praying at Valley Forge. In Hughes (vol. 3, p. 282) there is even a story that when an officer interrupted him at his prayers, Washington turned, shot at the soldier, and then returned to his devotions. Hughes did not report whether the soldier was injured. Washington's statements of gratitude to God for "the patronage of Heaven" in the Revolution is from his statement to Congress after the Revolution, when he resigned his commission as commander in chief of the Continental army, as quoted in Wilson (pp. 226–227).

The stories of von Steuben's good nature and "Poor fellows . . . or rations" are from Headley's *Washington and His Generals* (vol. 1, pp. 206–220, the quote on p. 218).

It was General Scott, according to Seelye (p. 249) and Lawson (p. 127), who reported that Washington swore till the leaves shook. I found that Washington called Lee a "cowardly poltroon" (coward) in Thayer (p. 388).

The story of the freckle-faced Irish woman Mary Hayes, also known as Molly Pitcher, is found in many places, including Seelye (pp. 247–248) and Hughes (vol. 3, pp. 378–379). Hughes writes of two traditions, one that "Molly Pitcher" was made a sergeant and given a gold piece by Washington, the other that she was made a lieutenant and given half-pay for life.

Chapter Seventeen

I found Washington's notes to Gouverneur Morris and Harrison in Hughes (vol. 3, pp. 430 and 436–437) and Sparks (pp. 286–287).

The Washington letter about his sumptuous dinners was written to the surgeon general, Dr. Cochoran. In the playful letter Washington wrote that his cook "has had the sagacity to discover that apples will make pies." It took the Weems-invented cherry tree story to connect him with cherry pies. I found the "Since our arrival . . . the centre" letter in Sparks (pp. 302–303).

I found French Minister Gerard's comments on Washington, "It is impossible . . . virtues," in Everett (pp. 142–143).

The details of the dire financial straits of Washington's army are from Woodward (pp. 362–364) in a chapter titled "Worthless Money," and information on the contributions of Robert Morris and Haym Salomon is in *Harper's* (vol. 6, pp. 293–294) and Milgrim (pp. 63–76). The information on Esther De Berdt Reed is from Garraty (vol. 18, pp. 263–264).

A gift from a French officer

I found Washington's "Whom can we trust now?" in Lossing's *Two Spies* (p. 96). That there were rumors started by the British of more American spies is from Sparks (pp. 317–318). Major John André's quote is from Seelye (p. 282). I found Arnold's question, "What would . . . catch me?" and the American prisoner's answer, "They would . . . of you," in *Harper's* (vol. 1, p. 219).

Chapter Eighteen

The details of Washington's short visit to Mount Vernon in September 1781 are from Hughes (vol. 3, pp. 650–651).

At Camden, South Carolina, 2,400 British troops routed 2,400 Americans (Daniel, p. 173).

The Cornwallis letter is from Commager (p. 1202), and so are the Thatcher diary entries (pp. 1233 and 1241).

Estimates of the number of Allied troops at Yorktown vary widely, from 16,000 in *Harper's* (vol. 10, p. 477) and Seelye (p. 299) to 31,000 in Hughes (vol. 3, p. 659). The eyewitness quotes are from Irving (vol. 4, pp. 168–170). Nelson's quote is from Seelye (p. 304). Washington's words on not insulting the British are from Seelye (p. 306) and Whipple (vol. 2, p. 129). The quote "The most delightful music to us all" is from Dos Passos (p. 1).

Flag taken at Yorktown

The losses due to fighting at Yorktown were: 156 British soldiers killed, 326 injured, and 70 missing, according to Fleming's *Beat the Last Drum* (p. 334). An estimated 90 American and French soldiers were killed, 293 injured. Many more were in hospitals because of disease, an estimated 2,000 British and 1,500 American and French. Hundreds died from smallpox and were left in the streets. Horses died from starvation and were thrown into the river.

Rochambeau's and Cornwallis's toasts and Washington's response, "Confine him there," are from Hughes (vol. 3, p. 679) and Whipple (vol. 2, p. 133).

Five days after the surrender at Yorktown, General Clinton entered Chesapeake Bay with many troops. He had hoped to join the battle, but he was too late. The last great battle of the Revolution was over.

Chapter Nineteen

The account of the death scene of Jacky Custis and the description of Mary Washington at the Fredericksburg ball are from Whipple (vol. 2, pp. 140–142), who quotes, "glitter and show . . . her son," from *Recollections of Washington* by George Washington Parke Custis, the young child adopted that day by Washington.

Washington's adopted daughter, Eleanor Parke Custis, later married Washington's nephew, Lawrence Lewis, the son of Washington's sister Betty (*see* chapter 23).

I found the quote from John Kent on Washington's reaction to the death of Jacky Custis, "I had . . . of temper," in Hughes (vol. 3, p. 684).

Lewis Nicola was a seasoned officer and had once commanded an American fort. I found in Irving that Washington felt sure Nicola wrote as a representative of many fellow soldiers (vol. 4, p. 187).

Washington's orders to thank God for the peace and details of the celebration on April 19, 1783, are from Whipple (vol. 2, pp. 157–158).

On August 26, Washington stood before Congress. "To you, sir," Elias Boudinot of New Jersey, the president of Congress, said, "peculiar praise is due. Your services have been essential in acquiring and establishing the freedom and independence of your country." Members of Congress voted to have a bronze statue made of Washington sitting on a horse with the inscription: "The United States in Congress assembled, ordered this statue to be erected in the year of our Lord 1783, in honor of George Washington, the illustrious commander in chief of the armies of the United States of America during the war, which vindicated and secured their liberty, sovereignty, and independence." It was to be made, according to Sparks, by "the best artist in Europe," but "the intention of this resolve was not fulfilled." (pp. 367–368).

Details of Washington's farewell to his officers are from Sparks (p. 372) and Irving (vol. 4, pp. 210–211).

The total of Washington's expense account in Irving (vol. 4, p. 211) is listed as about £14,500. In *Harper's* (vol. 10, p. 222) it is listed as $64,315. In Lossing's *Field Book of the Revolution* (vol. 2, p. 634) it is listed as $74,485. Randall (p. 404) listed it as $414,000. Randall (p. 403) estimated that if Washington had taken a salary, his pay for the eight years of the Revolution would have totaled $48,000, which he estimated in his book to be worth about 1.5 million 1997 dollars.

The description of Washington's December 1783 appearance before Congress and his letter to Clinton are from Irving (vol. 4, pp. 212–213).

Chapter Twenty

I found Washington's letter to Henry Knox on his retirement, "Strange . . . public man," in Fitzpatrick's *Writings of Washington* (vol. 27, pp. 339–341). I found Washington's letters to Lafayette from which I excerpted "I have become . . . my fathers" in Irving (vol. 4 pp. 214–215).

More than 1,300 yards of cloth were made on Washington's estate in 1768. I did not find an exact measurement of the cloth made for 1783–1789, the years of his retirement from public life.

I read of Washington's timely eating habits and that he told guests, "Gentlemen, we are too punctual for you," in Ford (p. 171). Washington's eating habits are from Kirkland (pp. 416–417).

Wilson (pp. 228–229) quotes Washington's mother as saying in 1781, when she heard her son was in Fredericksburg, "Go and tell George to come here instantly." Wilson (p. 239) wrote about Washington "and the little toddling boy" and of Lafayette's description of the boy holding fast to Washington's finger.

The description of the many businesses Washington ran from his Mount Vernon estate are from Flexner's *George Washington and the New Nation* (pp. 40–41) and Ford (pp. 120–123). The description of his farming methods is from Sparks (pp. 386–388). According to Lossing's *Home of Washington* (pp. 189–190), the male donkeys each arrived with some females. According to Lossing, at Washington's death, a wagon team of four of Washington's mules was sold for $800. Details of his western trip are from Randall (p. 418).

The story of the French dogs and Mrs. Washington's ham is from Whipple (vol. 2, pp. 190–191), Lossing's *Home of Washington* (pp. 183–184), and Seelye (pp. 319–320). The reports on his exacting attitude in financial dealings are from Lodge (vol. 2, pp. 346–349).

Information on the many letters sent to Washington is from Lodge (vol. 2, p. 3).

Henry Lee (1756–1818) was said to be the son of the "Low Land Beauty" Washington wrote about in his youth. On December 26, 1799, Lee gave a moving eulogy for Washington before both houses of Congress. The story of his refusal to sell Washington his horses is from Irving (vol. 4, pp. 232–233), who quotes a letter from Lee's son.

Washington's tea set

The story of Elkanah Watson's visit was reported in a book Watson wrote, *Men and Times of the Revolution*. I found it quoted in Flexner's *George Washington and the New Nation* (p. 25). Elkanah Watson's notes on his visit to Mount Vernon are from Irving (vol. 4, pp. 229–230). Watson was a stranger to Washington. He came to Mount Vernon, a sort of hotel on the Potomac, with a letter of introduction from two of Washington's friends.

Reports on Washington's health and false teeth are from Woodward (pp. 389–390) and Flexner's *George Washington and the New Nation* (p. 204).

According to the Articles of Confederation, Congress had the power to tax, make peace and war, conduct foreign relations, mediate between states, print and borrow money, manage affairs between states and American Indians, and have an army and navy. But, according to Article II, "Each state retains its sovereignty, freedom and independence, and every Power, Jurisdiction and right, which is not by this confederation expressly delegated to the United States in Congress assembled." This and other information on the Articles of Confederation are from Freidel (pp. 96–98).

Excerpts from Washington's letters to John Jay and James Warren are from Lossing's *Home of Washington* (p. 193) and Irving (vol. 4, pp. 237–238). The incident of the lost notes and letter to Lafayette are from Irving (vol. 4, pp. 244–246).

I found in Lodge (vol. 2, p. 259) that Washington's first stop in Philadelphia was to visit Franklin, in Parton (vol. 2, p. 605) Washington's last letter to Franklin, "So long . . . sincere friend," and also in Parton (vol. 2, pp. 591–592) the wording of Franklin's last will, "My fine . . . General Washington."

The proceedings at the Constitutional Convention were secret, and Irving (vol. 4, pp. 244–245) relates that according to Leigh Pierce, a delegate from Georgia, Washington stood at the end of one day's business and said, "Gentlemen, I am sorry to find that some one member of this body has been so neglectful of the secrets of the convention as to drop in the State House a copy of the proceedings; which, by accident was picked up and delivered to me this morning. I must entreat gentlemen to be more careful lest our transactions get into the newspapers and disturb the public repose by premature speculations." Washington threw the papers on the table and said, "Let him who owns it take it." Then he took his hat and walked out. Leigh Pierce was missing his notes and at first worried that the ones Washington had thrown down were his, but he looked at them and saw they were not in his handwriting. He went to his room and found his notes in the pocket of a coat he had worn earlier. According to Pierce, no one stepped forward and claimed the notes.

According to Martin (p. 195), three state legislatures, those in Delaware, New Jersey, and Georgia, voted unanimously to accept the Constitution. The votes to ratify were close in Massachusetts (187–168), New Hampshire (57–47), Virginia (89–79), New York (30–27), and Rhode Island (34–32). On May 29, 1790, more than a year after Washington became president, Rhode Island became the last of the original thirteen states to ratify.

"In the midst of hurry, and in the moment of departure from the City," Washington began his September 18, 1787, letter to Lafayette, "I address this letter to you. The principal, indeed the only design of it, is to fulfil the promise I made, that I would send to you the proceedings of the Federal convention, as soon as the business was closed." The entire letter is in Fitzpatrick's *Writings of Washington* (vol. 29, pp. 276–277).

Washington's letter to Hamilton is in Fitzpatrick's *Writings of Washington* (vol. 30, pp. 65–67).

Chapter Twenty-one

I found Washington's assessment of his new role, "I walk untrodden ground," and the importance of Washington's precedent-setting role as the first president in the biography written of him by Woodrow Wilson (pp. 273–275), who wrote it before he entered politics and became the twenty-eighth president, and from Irving (vol. 4, p. 259). Mrs. Washington's letter was written to a Mrs. Warren, dated December 26, 1789. I found "I had . . . his country . . . our circumstances" in Sparks (pp. 422–424). I found Washington's reaction at his first formal reception as president in Irving (vol. 4, p. 266).

"I was penetrated with deepest awe" was written by a Philadelphia citizen who saw Washington come to the Hall of Congress in that city during his second administration. The writer followed Washington into the hall and wrote, "Lobbies, gallery, all were wrapped in deepest attention. And the souls of the entire assemblage seemed peering from their eyes as the noble figure deliberately and unaffectedly advanced up the broad aisle of the hall. . . . No house of worship was ever more profoundly still than that large and crowded chamber." I found this moving description of the effect Washington had on his contemporaries in Whipple (vol. 2, pp. 270–271).

Washington's steward, Samuel Fraunces, was a well-known New York City tavern owner. He was from the West Indies and was known as Black Sam. The story of the too-expensive fish and description of Washington's dress at formal receptions are from Seelye (pp. 330–333).

According to Flexner (*George Washington and the New Nation*, p. 195), Washington set aside two hours each week for visitors. I found in Headley's *Illustrated Life of Washington* (p. 437) that Washington set aside only one hour, Tuesday afternoons at three o'clock, for visitors. According to Lossing's *Home of Washington* (p. 225), the Tuesday afternoon sessions "were very numerously attended, but by gentlemen only."

The information on the relationship between Washington and Adams is from Flexner (*George Washington and the New Nation*, pp. 213–214). "Before the end of the first term," Flexner wrote, "the Vice Presidency was established in the backwater from which it has never emerged." I found Adams's complaint before Congress, that its members idolized Washington, in Bellamy (p. 291). Adams wrote his "Father of his Country" letter to Benjamin Waterhouse of Rhode Island, a doctor and member of the first faculty of Harvard Medical School. I found the same excerpt in Hughes (vol. 3, p. 251) and Bellamy (p. 290). Washington Irving (vol. 3, p. 316, citing Jared Sparks's *Life of Gouverneur Morris*, p. 460) wrote that Adams "considered the post of Vice-President beneath his talents. 'My country,' writes he, 'has in its wisdom, contrived for me the most insignificant office that ever the invention of man contrived or his imagination conceived.'"

The description of Washington's surgery, the efforts to keep the street outside his house quiet, and Washington's statement, "I am not afraid to die," are from Wilson (pp. 277–278), Kirkland (pp. 442–443), and Irving (vol. 4, pp. 271–272), respectively.

Washington's letter on the importance of compromise between representatives of different states, "That there . . . importance depend," was to a Dr. Stuart, and I found it in Irving (vol. 4, pp. 293–294).

In his letter to his sister, Washington wrote that he hoped his mother "is translated to a happier place." This letter is from Fitzpatrick's *Writings of Washington* (vol. 30, pp. 398-403). The information on the length of Washington's recovery is from Sparks (pp. 414-415).

I found information on Washington's efforts to evade the Pennsylvania law that granted freedom to slaves who lived in the state for six months in Wiencek (pp. 315-317) and at http://ushistory.org/presidentshouse/slaves. I found that Franklin called slavery "an attrocious abasement" in Parton (vol. 2, p. 604).

The information on Harmer's and St. Clair's disastrous encounters are from Irving (vol. 4, pp. 305–307 and 318–324), including that Washington's parting words were "Beware of a surprise!" (vol. 4, p. 323) and his reaction to the rant, "It's all over . . . without predjudice" (vol. 4, pp. 323–324).

I found that St. Clair cried when he met with Washington in Seelye (p. 342).

According to Headley's *Washington and His Generals* (vol. 1, p. 221), the name Mad Anthony was first given to General Wayne "by a witless fellow in the camp who used always to take a circuit when he came near Wayne, and shaking his head, muttered to himself, 'Mad Anthony! Mad Anthony!'" The name fit, so the troops took it on.

Flexner, in *Washington, The Indispensable Man* (pp. 253–254), wrote that Washington spoke with lawmakers about justice in dealing with the American Indians, that "the frontier would always be aflame if the murder of an Indian were not considered the same as the murder of a white man."

According to *Harper's* (vol. 10, p. 251), almost all the American Indians killed by Wayne's troops in the August 1794 battle had British weapons.

I found excerpts from Jefferson's and Hamilton's letters urging Washington to seek reelection in Irving (vol. 4, pp. 332 and 336–337).

The Electoral College vote for vice president was John Adams, 77; George Clinton, 5; Thomas Jefferson, 4; and Aaron Burr, 1 (Flexner, *George Washington and the New Nation*, p. 383).

Chapter Twenty-two

I found excerpts from Washington's letters to Morris, "I trust . . . happiness," and Jefferson, "It behooves . . . those powers," in Lodge (vol. 2, pp. 139 and 144). The Adams quote, "Ten thousand . . . against England," is from Whipple (vol. 2, p. 277). Washington's "I'd rather be in my grave" is from Seelye (pp. 346–347).

Information on Genet is from *Harper's* (vol. 4, pp. 42–44) and Flexner's *Washington, The Indispensable Man* (pp. 286–302). In Philadelphia church bells rang and cannons were fired to welcome him. Genet married twice, first to the daughter of Governor George Clinton of New York, then to the daughter of Samuel Osgood of Massachusetts, once the postmaster general of the United States.

John Jay (1745–1829) of New York was a delegate to the First Continental Congress, the main author of the first constitution of the state of New York, the first chief justice of the Supreme Court, and from 1795 to 1801 governor of New York. During his term as governor, slavery in that state was abolished. My information on John Jay and the treaty he negotiated with England is from many sources, especially *Harper's* (vol. 5, pp. 125–128).

The description of the Jay Treaty and the reaction to it is from Wilson (pp. 304–306).

The information on Washington and Stuart, including Stuart's "You must let me forget . . . the painter," is from Flexner's *George Washington: Anguish and Farewell* (pp. 309–317).

Washington's farewell message was published in the September 19, 1796, issue of the Philadelphia newspaper *American Daily Advertiser*. I found it in Andrist (vol. 2, pp. 372–374).

The information on the election of 1796 is from Graff (p. 25).

Washington's letter to Knox, "I have . . . rural amusements," and his toast, "Ladies and gentlemen . . . happiness," at the March 3 dinner are from Irving (vol. 4, pp. 421–422). That Washington had tears in his eyes is from William A. Duer, president of Columbia College, who was there, as recounted in Irving (vol. 4, pp. 422–423).

Mrs. Washington wrote of her "dearest wish" in a December 26, 1789, letter to Mrs. Warren. It is reprinted in a footnote in Sparks (pp. 422–424).

Washington's full 1796 address to the Cherokee nation is in Fitzpatrick's *Writings of Washington* (vol. 35, pp. 193–199).

Chapter Twenty-three

The information on how Washington prepared to go home is from Flexner's *George Washington: Anguish and Farewell* (pp. 337–339) and Randall (p. 496).

Martha Washington's quote that she and her husband felt like "children just released from school" is from Bellamy (p. 380).

The "debt of nature" quote from the condolence letter Washington wrote upon his sister's death is from Fitzpatrick's *Writings of Washington* (vol. 35, pp. 434–435).

Information on the XYZ Affair, including the quote "detain them for examination," is from *Harper's* (vol. 10, p. 462).

My information on the wedding at Mount Vernon on February 22, 1799, is from Irving (vol. 4, p. 442).

I read of Martha's letter that told of Washington's dream foretelling his death in Henriques (p. 10).

Washington's entire last will is found in Sparks (pp. 545–557) and Headley's *Life of Washington* (pp. 517–528). The information on the release of Washington's slaves on January 1, 1801, is from Wiencek (p. 358).

The key of the Bastille, a gift from Lafayette to Washington

"I shall describe the last parting with one of his favorite nephews," Paulding wrote (vol. 2, pp. 195–197), but he did not identify the nephew. With that Paulding wrote of the nephew's recollection of his last visit with Washington and how he learned of his death.

It is interesting to note that while the weather was not too bad for Washington to go outside riding, he felt it was too bad to send out a servant. This, the quotes, and the scenario of his death are from Irving (vol. 4, pp. 445–450).

Epilogue

Marshall's announcement of Washington's death to Congress, "Mr. Speaker … they adjourn … melancholy … afflicted people," and the correspondence of Congress with

John Marshall

Adams, "Permit us . . . before him," and "His example . . . be read," are from McGroarty (pp. 15–19). The description of Washington's funeral is from Lossing's *Mount Vernon* (pp. 340–343), Norton (pp. 386–390), and Headley's *Illustrated Life of Washington* (p. 465). The minister's words are from Woodward (pp. 459–460).

I found that Mrs. Washington's religious beliefs helped her regain her cheerful nature in Lossing's *Mount Vernon* (p. 349). I found in Headley's *Illustrated Life of Washington* (p. 466) and Norton (p. 391) the responses of Napoléon and the admiral of the British fleet.

Headley wrote of Washington's death in his *Illustrated Life of Washington* (pp. 465–466): "As the sad news slowly traveled over the land, a cry of bitter anguish followed it, for sudden darkness had fallen on the nation, a calamity overtaken it, for which there seemed no remedy and no solace. The people were his children—and they mourned him as orphans."

Washington's 1789 meeting with Mr. Cleaveland and their words, Washington's "Put on . . . done no more" and Cleaveland's "I cannot . . . this country" are from Lodge (vol. 2, p. 354).

John Marshall made his often quoted assessment of Washington, "first in . . . fellow citizens," in a speech to Congress on December 19, 1799, as quoted in Irving (vol. 2, pp. 499–500).

Washington's Words

All are from Fitzpatrick's *Writings of Washington.*

"The General . . . despises it" is from vol. 5, p. 367.

"Nothing short . . . Peace of War" is from vol. 11, p. 289.

"There is . . . meet an Enemy" is from vol. 17, p. 463.

"I have always . . . happiness or misery" is from vol. 28, p. 152.

"Private life . . . can bestow" is from vol. 29, p. 475.

"In answer . . . allurements for me" is from vol. 29, p. 479.

"Nothing but harmony . . . happy people" and "While you are . . . tranquility here" are from vol. 30, pp. 186–187.

"It is now . . . good citizens" is from vol. 31, p. 93, note.

"True friendship . . . slow growth" and "Where there . . . than friends" are from vol. 35, pp. 295–296.

"Against the effect . . . gradual decline" is from vol. 36, p. 484.

Washington's Generals

The Tarleton quote on Marion, "The devil himself could not catch him," is from Dupuy (p. 487).

Washington's Cabinet

Information on the frequency of cabinet meetings and that Washington checked all official letters is from Randall (p. 460). Other information on members of Washington's cabinet is from *American National Biography*.

Selected Bibliography

Alden, John R. *George Washington*. Baton Rouge: Louisiana State University Press, 1984.

Andrist, Ralph K., ed. *George Washington: A Biography in His Own Words*. New York: Newsweek, 1972.

Bancroft, Aaron. *The Life of George Washington*. Boston: Phillips, Sampson, and Company, 1857.

Bellamy, Francis Rufus. *The Private Life of George Washington*. New York: Thomas Y. Crowell, 1951.

Brookhiser, Richard. *Rediscovering George Washington*. New York: The Free Press, 1996.

Brooks, Elbridge S. *The True Story of George Washington*. Boston: Lothrop, Lee, and Shepard, 1895.

Commager, Henry Steele, and Richard B. Morris, eds. *The Spirit of 'Seventy-Six: The Story of the American Revolution as Told by Participants*. New York: Da Capo Press, 1995.

Daniel, Clifton, ed. *Chronicle of America*. Mount Kisco, N.Y.: Chronicle Publications, 1989.

Dos Passos, John. *The Men Who Made the Nation*. New York: Doubleday, 1957.

Dupuy, Trevor N., Curt Johnson, and David L. Bongard. *The Harper Encyclopedia of Military Biography*. Edison, N.J.: Castle, 1992.

Elson, Henry W. *Side Lights on American History*. New York: Macmillan, 1900.

Emery, Noemie. *Washington: A Biography*. New York: G. P. Putnam's Sons, 1976.

Encyclopedia of World Biography. 21 volumes. Detroit: Gale, 1998.

Engle, Paul. *Women in the American Revolution*. Chicago: Follett, 1976.

Everett, Edward. *The Life of George Washington*. Boston: Gould and Lincoln, 1860.

Ferling, John E. *The First of Men: A Life of George Washington*. Knoxville, Tenn.: The University of Tennessee Press, 1988.

Fisher, Leonard Everett. *To Bigotry No Sanction: The Story of the Oldest Synagogue in America*. New York: Holiday House, 1998.

Fitzpatrick, John C. *The Spirit of the Revolution*. Port Washington, N.Y.: Kennikat Press, 1970, reprint of the 1924 edition.

——, ed. *The Diaries of George Washington*. 4 volumes. Boston: Houghton Mifflin, 1925.

——, ed. *The Writings of George Washington from Original Manuscript Sources*. 39 volumes. Washington, D.C.: United States Government Printing Office, 1931–1944.

Fleming, Thomas. *Beat the Last Drum*. New York: St. Martin's Press, 1963.

——. *Benjamin Franklin: A Biography in His Own Words*. New York: Newsweek, 1972.

Flexner, James Thomas. *George Washington and the New Nation*. Boston: Little, Brown, 1969.

——. *George Washington: Anguish and Farewell*. Boston: Little, Brown, 1969.

——. *George Washington in the American Revolution.* Boston: Little, Brown, 1967.

——. *Washington, The Indispensable Man.* Boston: Little, Brown, 1969.

Ford, Paul Leicester. *The True George Washington.* Philadelphia: J. B. Lippincott, 1896.

Franklin, Benjamin. *The Autobiography of Benjamin Franklin.* New York: Walter J. Black, 1941.

Freeman, Douglas Southall. *George Washington.* 6 volumes. New York: Charles Scribner's Sons, 1954.

Freidel, Frank, and Henry N. Drewry. *America, a Modern History of the United States.* Lexington, Mass.: Heath, 1970.

Garraty, John A., and Mark C. Carnes, eds. *American National Biography.* Oxford: Oxford University Press, 1999.

Graff, Henry F., ed. *The Presidents.* New York: Macmillan, 1997.

Gutheim, Frederick. *The Potomac.* New York: Rinehart, 1949.

Hancock, Morris. *Washington's Life and Military Career.* Chicago: Thompson and Thomas, 1900.

Harper's Encyclopedia of United States History. 10 volumes. New York: Harper & Brothers, 1907.

Harrison, Maureen, and Steve Gilbert, eds. *George Washington in His Own Words.* New York: Barnes and Noble, 1997.

Hayes, Carlton J. H. *A Political and Cultural History of Modern Europe.* 2 volumes. New York: Macmillan, 1933.

Headley, J. T. *The Illustrated Life of Washington.* New York: G & F Bill, 1860.

——. *Washington and His Generals.* 2 volumes. New York: A. L. Burt, n. d.

Henriques, Peter R. *The Death of George Washington.* Mount Vernon, Va.: Mount Vernon Ladies Association, 2000.

Hughes, Robert. *George Washington: The Human Being and the Hero.* New York: William Morrow, 1926.

——. *George Washington: The Rebel and the Patriot.* New York: William Morrow, 1927.

——. *George Washington: The Savior of the States.* New York: William Morrow, 1930.

Hyde, Mrs. Anna M. *The American Boy's Life of Washington.* New York: Thomas R. Knox, 1884.

Kaminski, John P., and Jill Adair McCaughan, eds. *A Great and Good Man: George Washington in the Eyes of His Contemporaries.* Madison, Wis.: Madison House, 1989.

Knollenberg, Bernhard. *George Washington: The Virginia Period.* Durham, N.C.: Duke University Press, 1964.

Lawson, Don. *The American Revolution.* New York: Abelard-Schuman, 1974.

Leckie, Robert. *The Wars of America.* New York: Harper & Row, 1968.

Little, Shelby. *George Washington*. Garden City, N.Y.: Halcyon House, 1943.

Lodge, Henry Cabot. *George Washington*. 2 volumes. Boston: Houghton Mifflin, 1889.

Lossing, Benson J. *The Home of Washington*. Hartford, Conn.: A. S. Hale, 1870.

——. *Mary and Martha, the Mother and the Wife of George Washington*. New York: Harper & Brothers, 1886.

——. *Outline History of the United States*. New York: Sheldon and Company, 1879.

Marshall, John. *The Life of George Washington* (the edition written for the use of schools and published after Marshall's death). Philadelphia: James Crissy, 1838.

Martin, James Kirby, Randy Roberts, Steven Mintz, Linda O. McMurry, and James H. Jones. *America and Its People*. New York: HarperCollins, 1989.

McGroarty, William Buckner, ed. *Washington, First in the Hearts of His Countrymen*. Richmond, Va.: Garrett and Massie, 1932.

Milgrim, Shirley. *Haym Salomon: Liberty's Son*. Philadelphia: Jewish Publication Society, 1975.

Norton, John N. *The Life of George Washington, Commander in Chief*. New York: Pudney and Russell, 1860.

Parton, James. *Life and Times of Benjamin Franklin*. 2 volumes. Boston: James R. Osgood, 1864.

Paulding, James K. *A Life of Washington*. 2 volumes. New York: Harper & Brothers, 1840.

Randall, Willard Sterne. *George Washington: A Life*. New York: Henry Holt, 1997.

Raphael, Ray. *A People's History of the American Revolution*. New York: Harper Perennial, 2002.

Ratcliffe, Susan, ed. *People on People*. New York: Oxford University Press, 2001.

Reich, Jerome R. *Colonial America*. Englewood Cliffs, N.J.: Prentice Hall, 1994.

Rozell, Mark J., William D. Pederson, and Frank J. Williams, eds. *George Washington and the Origins of the American Presidency*. Westport, Conn.: Praeger, 2000.

Schwartz, Barry. *George Washington: The Making of an American Symbol*. New York: The Free Press, 1987.

Seelye, Elizabeth Eggleston. *The Story of Washington*. New York: D. Appleton, 1893.

Selby, John. *The Road to Yorktown*. New York: St. Martin's Press, 1976.

Sparks, Jared. *The Life of George Washington*. Boston: Ferdinand Andrews, 1839.

Taylor, Rev. Edward M. *George Washington: The Ideal Patriot*. New York: Eaton and Mains, 1897.

Tebbel, John. *George Washington's America*. New York: E. P. Dutton, 1954.

Thane, Elswyth. *Potomac Squire*. New York: Duell, Sloan, and Pearce, 1963.

Thayer, William. *From the Farm House to the White House: The Life of George Washington*. Chicago: Albert Whitman, 1927.

Twohig, Dorothy. *George Washington's Diaries.* Charlottesville, Va.: University Press of Virginia, 1999.

Weems, Mason L. *The Life of Washington.* Edited by Marcus Cunliffe. Cambridge: Belknap Press of Harvard University Press, 1962.

Whipple, Wayne. *The Story-Life of George Washington.* 2 volumes. Philadelphia: John C. Winston, 1911.

Wiencek, Henry. *An Imperfect God: George Washington, His Slaves and the Creation of America.* New York: Farrar, Straus, and Giroux, 2003.

Wilson, Woodrow. *George Washington.* New York: Harper & Brothers, 1898.

Wister, Owen. *The Seven Ages of Washington.* New York: Garden City Publishing, 1907.

Woodward, W. E. *George Washington: The Image and the Man.* New York: Boni and Liveright, 1926.

Zagarri, Rosemarie, ed. *David Humphreys' "Life of General Washington" with George Washington's "Remarks."* Athens, Ga.: University of Georgia Press, 1991.

Illustration Credits

pp. 6, 7, 9, 13, 20 (top), 21 (top), 31, 39, 43, 44, 45, 52, 54, 71, 99, 103 (bottom), 114 (bottom), 121, 157, 236: Brooks, Elbridge S., *The True Story of George Washington*, pp. 13, 27, 43, 48, 49, 51, 56, 59, 60, 61, 65, 78, 79, 85, 96, 117, 135, 138, 139, 155.

pp. ii, 119, 126, 143, 146 (top), 194, 205: Grafton, John, *The American Revolution, A Picture Sourcebook*, pp. 62, 72, 95, 103, 114, 128, 129.

pp. 1, 4, 17 (top and bottom), 19, 20 (bottom), 22, 33 (top and bottom), 42, 53, 61, 68, 69, 76, 77, 78, 79 (top), 82 (top and bottom), 83 (top), 85, 86, 87, 88, 92, 94, 96, 98, 106, 107, 112, 113 (bottom), 116, 117, 120, 122, 129, 131 (bottom), 133, 136, 140 (top), 144, 148, 151, 173, 176, 177 (top and bottom), 186, 188 (top), 211 (top and center), 212 (all), 213 (all), 214 (top two and bottom), 217, 218, 221 228, 260: *Harper's Encyclopedia of United States History*, vol. 1: pp. 219, 381, 383, 444; vol. 2: pp. 223, 373, 426; vol. 3: pp. 39, 117, 305 (two), 419; vol. 4: pp. 3, 42, 47, 169, 175, 197, 207; vol. 5: pp. 80, 126, 263, 285, 337, 338, 346, 370, 373, 431, 447; vol. 6: pp. 107, 112, 235, 251, 259, 292, 365, 416, 479; vol. 7: pp. 56, 253, 334, 374, 376, 379, 503; vol. 8: pp. 90, 178, 210, 211, 343, 364, 444; vol. 10: pp. 4, 91, 148, 149, 158, 189, 211, 226, 227, 336, 481.

pp. 35, 55, 65, 114 (top): Headley, J. T., *The Illustrated Life of Washington*, pp. 26, 75, 90, 396.

p. 32: Hyde, Anna M., *The American Boy's Life of Washington*, pp. 49, 251.

p. 58: Kirkland, C. M., *Memoirs of Washington*, p. 165.

pp. xiv, 2 (top), 8, 21 (bottom), 24, 29 (top and bottom), 37, 67, 72, 153, 161, 163, 165, 166, 167, 192, 195, 201, 211, 247, 250, 251, 254, 259: Lossing, Benson J., *Home of Washington*, frontispiece, pp. 35, 39, 40, 55, 59, 66, 90, 98, 110, 117, 118, 128, 151, 157, 178, 207, 216, 229, 237, 240, 254, 266, 314, 346, 399.

pp. 47, 79 (bottom), 123 (center), 125 (bottom), 131 (top), 137, 138, 145, 170, 178, 182, 214 (third), 215 (bottom): Lossing, Benson J., *Outline History of the United States*, pp. 130, 133, 154, 169, 189, 193, 195, 202, 204, 225, 232, 246.

pp. 142, 146 (bottom), 149: Lossing, Benson J., *The Pictorial-Field Book of the Revolution*: vol. 1: p. 302, vol. 2: p. 554, vol. 2: p. 321.

p. 140 (bottom): Lossing, Benson J., *Two Spies*, p. 37.

pp. 23, 30, 127, 155, 164: Seelye, Elizabeth Eggleston, *The Story of Washington*, pp. 14, 17, 78, 234, 314, 319.

p. 162: Sparks, Jared, *The Life of George Washington*, p. 386.

pp. 2 (bottom), 34, 38, 41, 49, 63, 64 (top), 83 (bottom), 93, 95, 103 (top), 108, 109, 113 (top), 123 (top and bottom), 125 (top), 132, 158, 159, 188 (bottom), 196, 200, 215 (top and center): Whipple, Wayne, *The Story-Life of George Washington*, vol. 1: pp. 45, 68, 100, 124, 158, 162, 169, 192, 203, 211, 225, 242, 293, 341; vol. 2: frontispiece, pp. 56, 114 (two), 162, 167, 188, 199, 289, 317, 329.

pp. 50, 51, 64 (bottom), 81, 89, 130, 154, 175, 181: Wilson, Woodrow, *George Washington*, pp. 77, 83, 105, 136, 167, 201, 219, 241, 273.

Recommended Websites

http://www.whitehouse.gov/history/presidents/gw1.html

http://www.mountvernon.org/

http://lcweb2.loc.gov/ammem/gwhtml/gwhome.html

http://www.georgewashington.si.edu

http://www.nps.gov/gewa

http://www.gwpapers.virginia.edu

Index

Page numbers in *italics* refer to illustrations.

Adams, John, 8, 12, 89, 95, 112, *178*, 192, 217, 220
    election to presidency of, 189–90
    George Washington and, xiii, 96, 177–78, 186, 206, 216
    as president, 192, 193–95, 206, 207, 216, 218, 219, 221
    as vice-president, 177–78, 184, 186, 216
Adams, Samuel, 70, 95, 138
African Americans, 20, 68, 187, 188
    see also slaves, slavery
Alexandria, Va., 3, 18, 51, 57, 204, 220
Allegheny River, 44, *44*, 45, *45*, 57
Allen, Ethan, 94–95, *95*, 211
Alliance, Treaty of (1778), 126
American colonies, 15, 19–21, 29, 41-42, 103
    boycotting of British goods by, 78–82, 87–88, 90, 98
    independence called for by, 89–90, 90–91, 95, 112–13
    military of, 74, 98, 99; *see also* Continental army;
        Virginia militia
    tobacco industry in, 15, 20–21, 67–68
    see also Revolutionary War; United States
American Indians, xiii, 33, 45, 52, 58, 77, 96, 212, 218
    in battle at Fort Necessity, 47–50
    expanding settlements and, 191
    in mission to Fort Le Boeuf, 43–44
    in "Pontiac's War," 77–78
    U.S. battles with, 178, 182–84, 187, 211, 214
    see also French and Indian War; *names of specific tribes*
American Revolution, *see* Revolutionary War
André, John, 140–41, *140*, *182*, 211, 212, 215
Annapolis, Md., 157, 158–59, *159*
Arnold, Benedict, 94, *140*, 213, 214
    as traitor, 140–41, 211, 212
Articles of Confederation, 168, 177, 219
Attucks, Crispus, 82

Ball, Joseph (uncle), 30-31, 56, 66
Baltimore, George Calvert, Lord, 73
Baltimore, Md., 3–4, 219, 220
Barbados, 39–40, *39*, 41
Beauties of Washington, The (Weems), 24–26
Beaver, 85
Bemis Heights, battle of, 211
Bennington, battle of, 215
Bible, xiv, 8, *8*, 9, 17, *17*, 73, 117

Bill of Rights, 181
Bishop (servant), 63
Bland, Mary, *165*
Bland, Richard, 88
Blockade of Boston, The, 107
Boston, Mass., 80, 90, 91, 96, 102, *108*, 122, 212, 213
    battle of Bunker Hill in, 98–99, *98*, *99*, 100, *103*, 106,
        212, 214
    Redcoats in, 105, 107–9, *109*, 110, 212, 213
Boston Gazette, 45
Boston Harbor, 83–85, 87, 105
Boston Massacre, 82, *82*, 108
Boston Port Bill, 85–87
Boston Tea Party, 83–85, *85*
Bowling Green, N.Y., 113–14, *114*
boycotts, of British goods, 78–82, 87–88, 90, 98
Braddock, Edward, 50–55, *51*, *52*, *54*, *55*, 56, 57, 59, 60, 104,
    115, 163, 168, 211, 212, 213
Brandywine Creek, Pa., battle of, *103*, 123–24, *123*, 212, 215
Bridges Creek, 16, 21
British navy, 28, 29, 30–31, *31*, 78
Brooklyn, N.Y., 115, 116
Bunker Hill, battle of, 98–99, *98*, *99*, 100, *103*, 106, 212, 214
Burgoyne, John, 125–26, *125*, *126*
Burr, Aaron, 217, 218

Cambridge, Mass., George Washington's troops stationed
    in, 103–9, *103*, 212, 214, 215
Camden, S.C., battle of, 143–44, *143*, 211
Canada, 51, 60, 77, 95, *125*, 152, 214
Carpenter's Hall, 89, *89*
Carrol, Ann, 37
Cary, Mary, 36
Cary, Wilson, 36
Cato (Addison), 118
Chamberlayne, Major, 62
Champlain, Lake, 95, 211
Charles I, King of England, 14, 79
Charleston, S.C., 121, 142
    battles at, 121, *131*, 142, *142*, 213
Charlestown, Mass., 107
Cherokee Nation, 191
Chesapeake Bay, Va., battle at, 145–47, *145*, *146*, 152

Christmas Day, battle on, 119–20

Church of England, 14, 17

Civil War, English, 14

Clarke, Major, 39–40

Clinton, DeWitt, 211

Clinton, George, 160, 211

Clinton, Henry, 131, *131*, 133, 137, 142–43, 144, 151, 155

Clinton, James, 211

Common Sense (Paine), 107

Concord, Mass., 91–92, *93*

 battle at, 93–94, *94*, 99, 214, 218

Congress, *see* Continental Congress

Connecticut, 80, *106*, 111, 137, 179, 219

Constitution, U.S., xiii, 9, 207, 208

 changes made to, 181–82, 189

 formation of, 169–72, 177

Constitutional Convention, 169–72, *170*, 217, 218, 219

Continental army, *96*, *122*, *145*, 179, 211, 213, 218, 219, 220

 British driven out of Boston by, 106–9, *109*, 110, 212, 213

 in Cambridge, 103–9, *103*, 212, 214, 215

 foreign volunteers in, *122*, 123, *123*

 George Washington appointed to, 96–97, 100, 177

 George Washington as commander of, xiii, 28, 37, 61, 96–99, *99*, 100, 103–9, *103*, 111, 112–41, 145–52, 153, 155, 172, 177

 George Washington resigns from, 157, *157*, 158–60, *159*

 lack of funds and supplies in, 102–3, 105–6, 115, 118, 127–30, 135–36, 138–40, 152

 as ragtag group of soldiers, 37, 103–5, 109, 120, 150, 172

 of the south, *131*, 142–45, 212, 213

 at Valley Forge, *123*, 127–30, *130*, 152, 214, 215, 219

 see also Revolutionary War; *names of specific battles*

Continental Congress, 111, 112–13, *112*, 116, 124, 130, 136, *136*, 138, 155, 156, 159, 160, 168, *176*, 177, 179–80, 183, 195, 213, 215, 217, 218

 First, 88–90, *88*, *89*

 George Washington's death and, 204–6

 in George Washington's inauguration, 1, 2, 6, 7, 10, 12

 Second, 85, *89*, 94–97, 147, 168, 214, 216

Continental money, 128, 138–39, *138*, 168

Continental navy, *83*

Cornwallis, Charles, 120–22, *120*

 in battle and surrender at Yorktown, 142–43, 144–45, 147–50, *148*, *149*, 152, 212, 213

Cowpens, S.C., battle at, 144, *144*, 214

Craik, Dr., 153, 198, 200, 201, 202, 203

Cromwell, Oliver, 14

crop rotation, 162

Crown Point, N.Y., 95, 107

Custis, Daniel Parke (wife's first husband), 67

Custis, Eleanor "Nelly" Calvert (stepdaughter-in-law), 73, 153

Custis, Eleanor "Nelly" Parke (adopted daughter), 153, 166–67, 174, 193, 195, *195*, *201*

Custis, George Washington Parke (adopted son), 153, 154–55, 166–67, 174

Custis, John "Jacky" Parke (stepson), 66, *72*, 73, 98, 147, 153–54, *153*

Custis, Martha Dandridge, *see* Washington, Martha Dandridge Custis

Custis, Martha "Patsy" Parke (stepdaughter), 66, *72*, 73

Dartmouth, 85

Davis, Betty, 70

Davis, Thomas, 207

Dawes, William, 91

de Barras, Admiral, 146

Declaration of Independence (1776), 112–13, *113*, *116*, 216, 219

Declaration of Rights and Grievances (1765), 80, *81*

de Grasse, François-Joseph-Paul, 145–46, *145*, 152

Delaware, 171, 172

Delaware River, 5, 131

 George Washington's crossing of, 5, 118–20, *119*

Delawares, 77–78

d'Estaing, Charles Hector, 135

Dickinson, John, 95, 168

Dinwiddie, Robert, 42, *42*, 43, *43*, 45, 46, 50, 58

Dorchester Heights, Mass., 108

Dunmore, Lord, 86, *86*

Eleanor, 85

Electoral College, 1, 172, 184, 189

Elizabethtown Point, N.J., 6

Eltham, Va., 153, 154

Erskine, William, 121, 122

Eutaw Springs, battle of, 213

Fairfax, George William, 32, 37

Fairfax, Lord Thomas, 32–35, *32*, *33*, *34*, 42, 116

Fairfax, Sally Cary, 36–37, 64

Fairfax, William, 32

Fairfax County, Va., 87

Fairfield, Conn., 137

Fauchet, Jean-Antoine-Joseph, 187

Fauntleroy, Betsy, 37

Federal Hall, N.Y., 7–8, *7*, *9*, 10

Federalist Party, 181–82, 189, 216–17, 218

Ferguson, Patrick, 144

Ferry Farm, *see* Pine Grove

First Continental Congress, 88–90, *88, 89*

Fitzgerald, Edward, 121

Forbes, John, 59, 60

Fort Clinton, 211

Fort Cumberland, 52, 57, 61

Fort Dinwiddie, 58

Fort Duquesne, 52–53, 57–60

Fort Le Boeuf, 41–45, *42, 44*

Fort Lee, 118

Fort Necessity, 47–50, *50*

Fort Pitt, 59

Fort Ticonderoga, 94–95, *95*, 107, 108, *108, 125*, 211, 212, 214

Fort Washington, 118, 182, 212

France, 19, 42, 102, *136*, 179, 217, 218

    in Chesapeake Bay battle, 145–47, *146, 152*

    Fort Le Boeuf and, 41–45

    and Fort Necessity battle, 46–50

    George Washington's death observed by, 207

    military of, 74, 78, 168

    revolution in, 185–87, 217

    U.S. alliance with, 126, 130, 135, 138, 145–47, 148–49, 150, 152

    XYZ Affair and, 193–95, *194*, 216

    see also French and Indian War

Franklin, Benjamin, 52, *53*, 56, 84, 112, *170*, 215

    as abolitionist, 70, 180

    George Washington and, xiii, 169, 171, 197

Fraunces, Miss, 111, 176

Fraunces, Samuel, 176

Fraunces Tavern, 157, *157*

Frederick II, King of Prussia, 129, 215

Fredricksburg, Va., 2, *2*, 22, *22*, 23, 26, 55, 72, 154, 161

Freeman's Farm, battles of, 125–26, 211

    see also Saratoga, N.Y.

French and Indian War, 19, 46–60, *47*, 76–77, 90, 163, 211, 213, 214

    British taking of Fort Duquesne in, 57–60

    and Fort Necessity battle, 47–50, *50*

    and Monongahela battle, 52–56, *54*

French Revolution, 185–87, 217

Fugitive Slave Law, 188

Gage, Thomas, 87, *87*, 90, 91, 100–101, 151

Gaspee, 83, *83*

Gates, Horatio, 125–26, 143–44, 211, 214

Genet, Edmond-Charles, 186-87, *186*

George II, King of England, 76

George III, King of England, xiii, 9, 76–77, *76*, 86, 90, 106, *114*, 120

    Stamp Act and, 78–79, 80, 81, 113

George IV, King of England, 77

Georgia, 89, 152, 171, 179, 212, 221

Germantown, Pa., battle of, *123*, 124–25, *125, 137*, 212, 215

Gist, Christopher, 43–45, *45*

Graves, Thomas, 145–47

Great Britain, 13–15, 16, 18, 42

    boycotting of goods from, 78–82, 87–88, 90, 98

    colonial prewar confrontations with, 80, 82–88

    colonies' call for independence from, 89–90, 90–91, 95, 112–13

    in French and Indian War, 46–60

    French Revolution and, 185–86

    George Washington's death observed by, 207

    military of, 5, 61, *65*, 74, 77–78, 91, *93*, 98, 103, 116–18, *117*, 156, 212

    see also Redcoats; *names of specific wars and battles*

    navy of, 28, 29, 30–31, *31*, 56, 78, 91

    peace attempt of, 114–15

    in "Pontiac's War," 77–78

    surrender at Yorktown by, *120*, 130, 149–52, *151*, 153, 154

    taxes imposed by, 78–82

    U.S. postwar treaty with, 187

    in War of Jenkins's Ear, 28–29

Greene, Nathanael, 144, 160, 212, 215

Green Mountain Boys, 94–95

    see also Allen, Ethan

Greenway Court, 33, *33*, 36

Gregorian calendar, 18

Gregory XIII, Pope, 18

Grenville, George, 78, *78*

Griffin's Wharf, 83–84

Guilford Courthouse, N.C., battle of, 144

Hale, Nathan, 116–18, *117*

Hall of Congress, 159, *159*

Hamilton, Alexander, 160, 172, 177, *177*, 184, 187, 195, 214, 215, 217, 218, 219, 220

    as Federalist, 181–82, 216–17, 218

Hancock, John, 96

Hardy, Charles, 61–62

Harlem Heights, battle of, 116, 118

Harrison, Benjamin, 88, 136

Harrison, William Henry, 2

Hayes, Mary "Molly Pitcher," 98, 132–33, *132*

Henry, Patrick, 70, 71, 88, 89, 90, 91
    Stamp Act opposed by, 79–80, *79*

Hessian soldiers, 5, 98, 114, *114,* 120

Hewes, George, 84

Hickey, Thomas, 111–12

Hillsborough, N.C., 144

Holland, 179, 185

Houdon, Jean-Antoine, *167*

House of Burgesses, 16, 50, *71, 86*
    Boston Port Bill discussed in, 86–87
    boycotts called for by, 80, 81–82, 87
    George Washington as member of, 71–72, 79–80,
        81–82, 86–87
    Stamp Act discussed in, 79–80, *79*

House of Representatives, U.S., 1, 12, 170, 183, 204, 205, 218

Howe, Richard, 114–15

Howe, William, 102–3, *103,* 107, 108–9, 110, 114, 116–17,
    123, 131, 151

Hudson River, 118, 135, 136, 137

Humphreys, David, 31, 174–75

Huntingdon, Jedediah, 128

Hurons, 77-78

Hutchinson, Thomas, 80, 83, 84

indentured servants, 21, 68

Indian Queen Tavern, 72

Intolerable Acts (1774), 85, 87–88

Ipswich, Mass., 208

Ireland, 14, 102

James River, 197

Jamestown, Va., 145

Jay, John, 168–69, 176, *176,* 187

Jefferson, Thomas, 71, 86, 87, 177, 184, 185, 186, 216–17
    Declaration of Independence written by, 112–13, *113,*
        216
    as Republican, 181–82, 189, 216, 217, 218

Julian calendar, 18

Jumonville, Joseph Coulon de Villiers, Sieur de, 47, 49, *49,* 50

Kentucky, 184

Kinderhook, N.Y., 111

Kings Mountain, S.C., 144

Knox, Henry, 1–2, *1,* 10, 106, 107, *108,* 161, 171, 172, 176–77,
    189, 212, 219

Knox, Lucy, 193

Kosciusko, Thaddeus, 123, *123*

Lafayette, Marquis de, 75, *122,* 123, 147, 148, 156, 161, 163,
    165, 167, 171, 172, 193

Langdon, John, 1–2

Lear, Tobias, 183, 193, 200–201, 202–3

Lee, Charles, 220

Lee, Charles "Boiling Water," 96, *96,* 106, 131–32, *131,*
    212–13

Lee, George, 40

Lee, Henry, 164–65, *165,* 220

Lee, Richard Henry, 23, 88, 112, *112*

Lewis, Andrew, 96

Lewis, Betty Washington (sister), 22, 193

Lewis, Lawrence (nephew), 195

Lexington, Mass., *93*
    battle at, 92–93, *92,* 156, 214, 218

Liberty Hall Academy, 197

Lincoln, Benjamin, 142, 147, 213

Little Turtle, 182

Livingston, Robert R., 8, 9, 10, 112

Long Island, battle of, 115–16, 212, 214

Louisiana, 60

Louisiana Purchase, 217, 218

Louis XVI, King of France, xiii, 185, 186

McHenry, James, 219–20

Madison, James, 184, 218

Manhattan, N.Y., 115, 116

Marbury, William, 220

Marbury v. Madison, 220

Marion, Francis, 213

Marshall, John, 204–6, 208

Maryland, 2, 78, 179

Mason, George, 70–71, 81, *81*

Massachusetts, *87,* 90, 101, 172, 179

Middlebrook, N.J., 135

Mifflin, Thomas, 159

Mingos, 77–78

Mississippi Valley, 42, 77

Mohawks, 96

monarchy, xiii, 76, 156, 189

Monmouth, N.J., battle of, 131–34, *131, 132, 133,* 212, 213,
    214, 215

Monmouth Courthouse, 131

Monongahela, battle of, 52–56, *54*

Monroe, James, 120

Montgomery, Richard, 213

Montreal, Canada, 42

Morgan, Daniel, 144, *144,* 213–14

Morris, Gouverneur, 84–85, 136, *136*, 185–86

Morris, Robert, 75, 138–39

Morristown, N.J., 122–23, 139–40

Mount Vernon, 16, 29–30, *29, 30, 67*, 156, *164, 165*, 202, 206
  farming at, 67–68, 162–64, *162*, 184, 195
  George Washington at, xiv, *xiv*, 2, 3, 32, 40–41, 50, 59,
    66–72, 147, 154, 159–69, *161*, 192–93, 195–201

My Journey to the French (Washington), 45

Napoléon I, Emperor of France, 207

Navigation Act, 78

Nelson, Thomas, 148, *148*

Newburgh, N.Y., 155, *155*

New England, 128

New Hampshire, 179

New Haven, Conn., 137

New Jersey, 19, 118, 171

Newport, R.I., 135, 146

New York, 19, 77–78, *106*, 133, 136, 139, 143, 211
  battle losses suffered in, 115–18, *125*, 137
  Patriot and Tory disputes in, 110–11, 211

New York, N.Y., xiv, 2, 19, *19*, 61–62, 80, 81, 110, 112, *114*,
    116–17, 221
  battles in, *103*, 116
  George Washington's inauguration in, 7–12, *7, 9*, 221
  George Washington's march to, xiii–xiv, 2, 3–7, *4, 6*

New York Bay, 6

Nicola, Lewis, 155, 156, 189

Norfolk, Va., 20

North, Frederick, 82, *82*, 150

Northamptonshire, England, 13, *13*

North Bridge, battle at, 93–94, *93*

North Carolina, 179

Norwalk, Conn., 137

Nova Scotia, 110

Ohio River, 182, 187

Ohio territory, *21*, 182

Ohio Valley, 42, 46–50, 51, 52, 59, 60

Osgood, Samuel, 221

Otis, Samuel, 8

Ottawas, 77

Paine, Thomas, 107, *107*

Paris, Treaty of (1763), 76–77

Paris, Treaty of (1783), 151, 156, 216

Parliament, 13, 14, 77, 103, 106, 121
  Intolerable Acts passed by, 85, 87–88

taxes passed by, 78–82

Patriots, 71, 91, 95, 98, 99, *106*, 107, *114, 116*, 120, 121, 128,
    135, 142, *149*, 212, 213, 214
  burning of *Gaspee* by, 82–83, *83*
  Tories in disputes with, 110–11, 112
  see also American colonies; Continental army;
    Revolutionary War

Patterson, Colonel, 114

Pendleton, Edmund, 88, 96

Pennsylvania, 4, 19, 78, 118

Pennsylvania Gazette, 60, 93

Pennsylvania Society for the Promotion and Abolition of
    Slavery, 180

Petersburg, Va., 145

Philadelphia, Pa., 4, *4*, 80, 98, 100, 128, 136, 138, 145, 155,
    158, *181*, 189, 191
  Constitutional Convention in, 169–72, *170*, 217, 218,
    219
  First Continental Congress in, 89–90
  as nation's capital, 134, 180, 193, 221
  Second Continental Congress in, 94–97, 100
  State House of, 90
  U.S. loss of, 123–24

Philipse, Mary, 37–38, *37, 38*

Pickering, Timothy, 218

Pine Grove, 22–23, *22*, 26, 27

Pitt, William, 59, 81

Pittsburgh, 42, 51–52
  see also Fort Duquesne; Fort Le Boeuf; Fort Pitt

Pontiac, Chief, 77–78, *77*

"Pontiac's War," 77–78, 214

Pope, Nathaniel, 15

Popes Creek, 16, 21
  Congregation of, 17

Port Tobacco, 202, 203

Potomac River, xiv, 15, 16, 21, *21*, 26, 50, *161*, 180, 197, 207

Powell, Eliza, 192, *192*

Prescott, Edward, 15

Prescott, Samuel, 91

Princeton, N.J., battle at, 121–22, *121*, 177, 212, 214, 215

Proclamation of Neutrality (1793), 186, 217

Providence, R.I., 83

Pulaski, Casimir, 123, *123*

Puritans, 14, 19

Putnam, Israel, 99, 100, 106, *106*, 214

Quakers, Society of, 75

Quebec, battle for, 213, 214

Quincy, Josiah, 84

Raleigh Tavern, 71–72, 81–82, 86, *86*
Randolph, Edmund, 177, *177*, 217
Randolph, John, 217
Randolph, Peyton, 88, *88*, 217
Randolph Plan, 217
Rappahannock River, 22, *22*, 37
Rawlins (overseer), 199–200
Redcoats, 92–94, 98, *103*, 144
    at battle of Monmouth, N.J., 131–34
    in Boston, Mass., 105, 107–9, 212, 213
    see also Great Britain; Revolutionary War
Reed, Esther De Berdt, 139
Reed, Joseph, 114, 139
Relief of Free Negroes Unlawfully Held in Bondage, 180
Republican Party, 181–82, 189, 216, 217, 218
Revenue Act (1764), 78
Revere, Paul, 91
Revolution of 1800, 217
Revolutionary War, xiii, *1*, 9, 37, 40, 165, *165*, *177*, 179, *182*,
    183, 187, 212, 213–14, 216, 217, 219, 220, 221
    advantages of U.S. in, 99, 102, 120
    Britain's call for peace in, 114–15
    Britain's surrender in, *120*, 130, 149–52, *151*, 153, 154
    events leading to, 80, 82–88, 89–91, 216
    final battles of, 145–52, *151*, 211, 212, 214, 215, 219
    first battles of, 91–97, *92*, *93*, 156, 214, 218
    George Washington in, xiii, *1*, 5, 9, 27, 28, 37, 55, 97–99, *99*,
        103–9, *103*, 111, 112–41, *127*, *131*, 145–52, 153, 155,
        168, 174, 177, *177*, 179, 190, 211
    important battles of, 225–27
    New York battle losses suffered in, 115–18, *125*, 137
    peace declared in, 155–56, 160
    southern battles of, 142–52
    U.S. debts due to, 179–80, 187, 189, 218
    women's role in, 98
    see also Continental army; *names of specific battles*
Richmond, Va., 145
Rights of the British Colonies Asserted, The (Otis), 80
Ringwood, N.J., 156
Robbins, John, 92–93
Rochambeau, Jean-Baptiste-Donatien de Vimeur, Comte de,
    146, 147, 150
Rockbridge, Va., 197
Roosevelt, Franklin D., 189
Rules of Civility and Decent Behavior, 23–24, *23*
Rush, Benjamin, 116, *116*

St. Clair, Arthur, 182–83, *182*, 214
St. Pierre, Legardeur de, 43, *43*, 45
Salomon, Haym, 139
Sampson, Deborah, 98
Sandy Hook, N.J., 133
Saratoga, N.Y., battles of, 125–26, *125*, *126*, 141, 143, 211, 213,
    214
Savannah, Ga., battle of, *123*, 136–37, 213
Schuyler, Philip John, 214
Scotland, 14, 116
Sea Horse, 15
Second Continental Congress, 85, *89*, 94–97, 147, 168, 214, 216
Senate, U.S., 1, 8, 10, 11, 170, 187, 206, 214
Senecas, 47, 48, 212
Seven Years' War, *see* French and Indian War
Shawnee, 77–78
Sherman, Roger, 112
Shippen, Peggy, 140
Shirley, William, 61, *61*
slaves, slavery, 26, 30, 40, 63, 64, *68*, *69*, 82, 170, 184, 187,
    217, 218
    abolition of, 70, 180–81
    George Washington and, 67–70, 74-75, 147, 162, 181,
        188, 198
    laws on, 170, 188
    Martha Washington and, 63, 64, 70, 180–81, 198
    in Virginia, 20–21, 67, 68–70
smallpox, 40, 122
Sons of Liberty, 80, 220
South Carolina, 179
Spain, 135, 163, 179
Stamp Act (1765), 78–81, *78*, *79*, 113
Stamp Act Congress, 80
Stark, John, 214–15
Staten Island, N.Y., 114
Stony Point, N.Y., battles at, 137, *137*, 215
Stuart, Gilbert, 188, *188*
Sugar Act (1764), 78
Supreme Court, U.S., 176, *176*, 185, 204, 220

Tanacharison, Chief, 48
Tarleton, Banastre "Bloody Ban," 144, 213
Tennessee, 184
Thatcher, James, 149–50
Thomson, Charles, 2, *2*
tobacco, 15, 20–21, 67–68, 78
Tories, 140, 211
    Patriots in disputes with, 110–11, 112

Tories *(continued)*
  plot against George Washington by, 111–12
Townshend Acts (1767), 81–82
Travels in North America (Chastellux), 154
Trent, Jacob, 123–24
Trenton, N.J., 5–6, 118, 152
  battle of, 119–20, *120*, 121, 124, 177, 212, 214, 215
tuberculosis, 29, 39, 40

United States:
  American Indian battles with, 178, 182–84, 187, 211, 214
  Britain's postwar treaty with, 187
  Declaration of Independence by, 112-13, *113, 116*
  emergence of two-party system in, 181–82, 189, 216, 218
  formation of new government in, 168–72, 217
  French alliance with, 126, 130, 135, 138, 145–47, 148–49,
    150, 152
  George Washington elected president of, 1–7, *2, 4*, 172–73
  postwar debts of, 179–80, 187, 189, 218
  XYZ Affair and, 193–95, *194*, 216
  see also American colonies; Revolutionary War

Valley Forge, Pa., *127, 129*
  Continental army at, *123*, 127–30, *130*, 152, 214, 215, 219
Vermont, 184
Vernon, Edward, 29, *29*
Verplanck's Point, N.Y., 137
Villiers, Louis Coulon de, 49
Virginia, xiv, *20*, 32, *33, 51*, 55, 62, 78, 89, 145, 172, 179, 217
  agriculture and slavery in, 20–21, 67–70
  George Washington's childhood in, 20–31
  George Washington's protection of frontier in, 57–60, *58*
  see also House of Burgesses; Mount Vernon
Virginia Assembly, 27–28
Virginia militia, 41–45, *41*, 212
  in French and Indian War, 46–60
  George Washington as commander of, 46–60, 61, 96
  in Revolutionary War, 99, 212
Virginia Plan, 217
von Steuben, Frederick Wilhelm, 123, *123*, 129–30, *130*,
    132, 147, 215

Wakefield, 16, 21–22, *21*
Ward, Artemas, 96, 106, 110, 212, 215, 221
War of 1812, 218
War of Jenkins's Ear, 28–29, 51
Washington, Amphilis Twigden (great-great-
    grandmother), 13, 15

Washington, Anne Fairfax (sister-in-law), 32, 40
Washington, Anne Pope (great-grandmother), 15
Washington, Augustine (father), 16–17, 25–26, 27, 28, 199
Washington, Augustine (half brother), 16, 22, 26, 28
Washington, Bushrod (nephew), 163, 197
Washington, Butler (half brother), 16
Washington, Charles (brother), 22, 197–98
Washington, D.C., 180, 197
Washington, George, *ii, 96, 123, 136, 155, 158, 162, 163,*
    166, 173, 175, 181, 192, 196, 201, 205
  Adams and, xiii, 96, 177–78, 186, 206, 216
  and adoption of step-grandchildren, 153, 166–67, 193
  appointed leader of Continental army, 96–97, 100, 177
  aversion to monarchy by, xiii, 150, 156, 189
  Barbados trip of, 39–40, *39, 41*
  birth of, 17–18, *17, 19, 21*
  on call for independence, 90–91, 94
  Cherokee Nation talk of, 191
  cherry tree story of, *24, 25*, 28
  childhood of, xiii, 20–31, *21*
  as commander of Continental army, xiii, 28, 37, 61,
    96–99, *99*, 100, 103–9, *103*, 111, 112–41, 145–52,
    153, 155, 172, 177
  courtship of Martha Custis by, 62–64, *63*
  death of, 198–203, *200, 204-8*
  Delaware River crossing of, 5, 118–20, *119*
  education of, 23, 28, 31–32, 34, 63, 197
  election to presidency of, 1–7, *2, 4*, 172–73
  family background of, 13–17
  father's relationship with, 25–26
  Franklin and, xiii, 169, 171, 197
  in French and Indian War, 46–60, *49, 50, 55, 58*, 71, 90,
    163
  French Revolution and, 185–87
  as head of Constitutional Convention, 169–72
  health problems of, 40, 122, 168, 178–79, 199-201
  in House of Burgesses, 71–72, 79–80, 81–82, 86–87
  inauguration of, 1, 2, 6, 7–12, *7, 8, 9*, 221
  last will and testament of, 195–98
  Lord Fairfax and, 32–35, *33, 34*, 42
  in march to New York, xiii–xiv, 2, 3–7, *4, 6*
  marriage of, 38–39, 64–66, *64, 65*, 67, 72, 98, 147, 168,
    190, 192, 193, 197, 199, 201
  military strengths of, 28, 45, 54–56, 57–58, 59, 61–62, 71,
    151–52, 172
  in mission to Fort Le Boeuf, 41–45, *43, 44, 45*
  mother's relationship with, 2–3, *2*, 26, 27–28, 30–31, 33,
    38, 68, 154–55, *154*, 161

Washington, George *(continued)*
    at Mount Vernon, xiv, *xiv*, 2, 3, 32, 40–41, 50, 59,
        66–72, 147, 154, 159–69, *161*, 192–93, 195–201
    physical appearance of, 3, 62, 168, 188
    as president, xiii–xiv, 24, 70, 173–90, 207–8
    quotes of, 209–10
    resignation from Continental army of, 157, *157*, 158–60,
        159
    response to Intolerable Acts of, 86–88
    "retirement" from public life of, 159–69, 172, 192–93
    in Revolutionary War, xiii, *1*, 5, 9, 27, 28, 37, 55, 97–99,
        99, 103–9, *103*, 111, 112–41, *127*, *131*, 145–52, 153,
        155, 168, 174, 177, 179, 190, 211
    romantic interests of, 36–39, *38*
    slavery and, 67–70, 74–75, 147, 162, 181, 188, 198
    as soldier, xiii, 5, 7, 9, 27, 28, 29–31, *29*, *31*, 41–60, *41*,
        61, 63, 65, 66, 71
    Stamp Act and, 79–81
    as stepfather, 73, 98, 147, 153–54
    as surveyor, xiii, 32–35, *32*, *35*, 36, 37
    timeline of, 222–24
    Tories' plot against, 111–12
    at Valley Forge, *123*, 127–30, *127*, *129*, *130*, 152, 214,
        215, 219
    Virginia militia commanded by, 46–60, 61, 96
    Virginia's frontier protected by, 57–60, *58*
    XYZ Affair and, 193–95
Washington, George Augustine (nephew), 72
Washington, Jane (half sister), 16, 22
Washington, Jane Butler (father's first wife), 16
Washington, John (great-grandfather), 15
Washington, John (uncle), 16
Washington, John Augustine (brother), 22, 47, 55, 57, 91, 118
Washington, Lawrence (grandfather), 15–16
Washington, Lawrence (great-great-grandfather), 13–15
Washington, Lawrence (half brother), *xiv*, 16, 22, 26, *30*, 32, 41
    Barbados trip of, 39–40, *39*, 41
    military experience of, 28–30, *29*, 51
    tuberculosis of, 29, 39, 40
Washington, Martha Dandridge Custis (wife), 2, 28, 90, 97,
    106, 153, 154, 165, 166, 167, 183, *188*, 195, *201*
    as First Lady, 174, *175*
    George Washington's courtship of, 62–64, *63*
    George Washington's death and, 198–201, *200*, 207

marriages of, 38–39, 64–66, *64*, *65*, 67, 72, 98, 147, 168,
    190, 192, 193, 197, 199, 201
slavery and, 63, 64, 70, 180–81, 198
troops visited by, 129
Washington, Mary Ball (mother), 16–17, *17*, 34, 90
    death of, 2–3, 26, 179
    George Washington's relationship with, 2–3, *2*, 26,
        27–28, 30–31, 33, 38, 66, 154–55, *154*, 161
Washington, Mildred (aunt), 16
Washington, Mildred (sister), 22
Washington, Mildred Warner (grandmother), 16
Washington, Samuel (brother), 22
Washington, Sarah (niece), 40
Watson, Elkanah, 166
Wayne, Anthony "Mad Anthony," 124–25, *125*, 137, *137*,
    183–84, 215
Weems, Mason Locke, 24–26, *24*
Westchester County, N.Y., 135
West Indies, 104, 135, 145
Westmoreland County, Va., 16, 26
West Point, N.Y., 137–38, 140–41, 211, 215
Whipple, Abraham, 83, *83*
Whiskey Rebellion, 187, 220
White House, *64*, *65*, 66
Williamsburg, Va., 20, *20*, 45, 63, 67, 81, 88, 90
    Raleigh Tavern in, 71–72, 81–82, 86, *86*
    see also House of Burgesses
Wilson, Woodrow, 6–7
Winchester, Va., 57, 59
Wolcott, Oliver, 219
women, role in Revolutionary War of, 98
Wright, James, 221
Wright, Joseph, 167

XYZ Affair, 193–95, 216

Yonkers, N.Y., *37*
York River, 145, 149, *149*, 152
Yorktown, Va.:
    ball celebrating victory at, 154–55, *154*
    battle of, 145–49, *145*, *146*, *148*, 153, 211, 212, 213, 214,
        215, 219
    Britain's surrender at, *120*, 130, 149–52, *151*, 153, 154, 213
Young Man's Companion, The, 23, 36